Routledge Revivals

Thomas Cranmer and the English Reformation 1489-1556

Thomas Cranmer and the English Reformation 1489-1556

Albert Frederick Pollard

Routledge
Taylor & Francis Group
Routledge Revivals

First published in 1905 by Frank Cass and Company Limited

This edition first published in 2018 by Routledge
2 Park Square, Milton Park, Abingdon, Oxon, OX14 4RN
and by Routledge
52 Vanderbilt Avenue, New York, NY 10017, USA

Routledge is an imprint of the Taylor & Francis Group, an informa business

Publisher's Note
The publisher has gone to great lengths to ensure the quality of this reprint but points out that some imperfections in the original copies may be apparent.

Disclaimer
The publisher has made every effort to trace copyright holders and welcomes correspondence from those they have been unable to contact.
A Library of Congress record exists under ISBN:

ISBN 13: 978-0-367-15018-1 (hbk)
ISBN 13: 978-0-367-15021-1 (pbk)
ISBN 13: 978-0-429-05452-5 (ebk)

THOMAS CRANMER

Copyright Photo., Walker & Cockerell.

THOMAS CRANMER,

ARCHBISHOP OF CANTERBURY.

PAINTER, G. FLICCIUS.

THOMAS CRANMER

AND THE ENGLISH REFORMATION

1489 - 1556

BY

ALBERT FREDERICK POLLARD

FRANK CASS AND COMPANY, LTD.

1965

THIS EDITION PUBLISHED WITH PERMISSION BY
FRANK CASS & CO., LTD.
10 WOBURN WALK, W.C. 1

PRINTED IN THE UNITED STATES OF AMERICA

PREFACE

IF an author might frankly review his own book in his Preface, the following pages would take as their text the caution, "Beware of too much explaining lest we end by too much excusing." For the present volume seeks to explain as much as possible. To extenuate nothing is a golden rule, but the grossest injustice ensues upon a neglect of extenuating circumstances. All the proverbs notwithstanding, explanation is the first duty of the historian and the biographer; and Cranmer has been termed the most mysterious figure in the English Reformation. The obscurity is not in his character, but in the atmosphere which he breathed, and atmosphere is the most difficult of all things to re-create. As a rule there are no materials; for to people who live in it, a political or religious atmosphere is a familiar thing, which needs no explanation and therefore is not recorded in documents. Then the atmosphere changes, and can only be recalled to posterity by an observation and reflexion compared with which the mere ascertainment of facts is easy.

A failure to realise this unfamiliar atmosphere vitiates most of the estimates of Cranmer's career and character, and notably those of the Whig school represented by Hallam and Macaulay. Hallam indeed always recognises that Cranmer's "faults were the effect of circumstances and not of intention," but he blames the Archbishop for having "consented to place himself in a station where those circumstances occurred."[1] He might perhaps have made the great refusal; but unless some one had been willing to take up the burden with all its irksome conditions, there would have been no Reformation. And in one like Cranmer, who for years had been praying for the abolition of the Pope's power in England, it surely would have been a cowardly love of mental and physical ease to decline his share in the work because of the sacrifice it involved. He chose the better part, but it was one of labours and sorrows. To succeed Warham who had just surrendered the keys of ecclesiastical independence; to be Archbishop under Henry VIII. who had broken the powerful Wolsey without an effort; then, after two years' comparative peace with Somerset, to be flouted for four by Northumberland; and finally, under Mary, to hold views of the State which compelled non-resistance, and yet to have a conscience which said that submission was cowardice — such was Cranmer's lot. Compared with Henry VIII. he is weak, but none the less human for that. He is the storm-tossed plaything of forces which even Henry could not completely control; and his soul is expressed in the beautiful and plaintive strains of his Litany, which appealed to men's hearts in those troublous times with a directness now

[1] *Constitutional History*, ed. 1884, i., 98.

scarcely conceivable. His story is that of a conscience in the grip of a stronger power; but, unless I misread his mind, he surveyed his life's work in the hour of death and was satisfied.

It has been maintained by an eminent scholar recently dead[1] that the chief content of modern history is the emancipation of conscience from the control of authority. From that point of view the student of Tudor times will not be exclusive in his choice of heroes. He will find room in his calendar of saints for More as well as for Cranmer. Both had grave imperfections, and both took their share in enforcing the claims of authority over those of conscience. Nor perhaps is it true to say that they died in order that we might be free; but they died for conscience' sake, and unless they and others had died conscience would still be in chains. That was Cranmer's service in the cause of humanity; his Church owes him no less, for in the Book of Common Prayer he gave it the most effective of all its possessions.

The materials for sixteenth-century history are so vast that no one can hope to master them all in the allotted span of human life[2]; but the biographer's path has been greatly smoothed by the monumental series of *Letters and Papers, Foreign and Domestic, of the Reign of Henry VIII.*,[3] published

---

[1] Lord Acton.

[2] Dr. James Gairdner, C.B., has made the nearest approach after forty-five years' strenuous labour.

[3] Cited throughout the text as *L. and P.;* they are often inaccurately styled "State Papers," a description properly reserved for the

by the Record Office under the editorship of the late Mr. Brewer and Dr. James Gairdner, which so far as it goes (1544) completely supersedes all other sources for Cranmer's life. Another recently published authority of the highest value is the *Acts of the Privy Council*, extending from 1542 to 1599; but the domestic State Papers from 1547 onwards are poorly represented in Lemon's *Calendar* (1860); and although the correspondence of English agents abroad is more adequately summarised in Turnbull's *Foreign Calendar*, the more valuable despatches of foreign ambassadors in England are yet unpublished with the exception of two volumes issued by the French Government, Brown's *Venetian Calendar*, and the *Spanish Calendar*, which has not yet touched the reign of Edward VI. or Mary. The great collections in the British Museum are also for the most part unprinted.

Of contemporary chronicles, Hall's is the best for the reign of Henry VIII., and for that of Edward VI. the most useful authority is J. G. Nichols's *Literary Remains of Edward VI.* (Roxburghe Club, 1857, 2 vols.), which is perhaps more important for the numerous contemporary documents it prints than for the young King's *Journal*, which is its *pièce de resistance*. Of the many valuable chronicles published by the Camden Society may be mentioned *Wriothesley's Chronicle*, the *Greyfriars' Chronicle*,

eleven volumes of *State Papers of Henry VIII.*, published *in extenso* by the Record Commission, 1830–52. The *L. and P.* contain much besides State Papers.

the *Chronicle of Queen Jane and Queen Mary*, *Machyn's Diary*, and the *Narratives of the Reformation*.

With regard to church history, the primary source is the works of the Reformers themselves; they are here cited in the Parker Society's collected edition in fifty-four volumes (Cambridge, 1841–55). This includes the latest edition of Cranmer's own works (2 vols., 1844–46),[1] though that by Jenkyns (4 vols., Oxford, 1833) is hardly, if at all inferior. Next to these, Foxe's *Acts and Monuments* (ed. Townsend, 8 vols., 1843–49)[2] is the greatest quarry; his tone is, of course, biassed, but he prints a vast mass of documents with which he did not apparently tamper. The next most valuable collection is Strype, whose works on the Reformation in the best edition (Oxford, 1812–24) run to twenty-five volumes; of these the *Ecclesiastical Memorials* is the most important for the reigns of Henry VIII., Edward VI., and Mary. Strype's labours had been preceded by Fuller's *History* (1655; ed. Brewer, 6 vols., Oxford, 1845) and Heylyn's *Ecclesia Restaurata* (1661; ed. Robertson, London, 1849), which were partly based on the records of Convocation, destroyed soon after at the fire of London (1666). Bishop Burnet of Salisbury followed with what was long the most popular history of the Reformation (3 vols., 1679, 1715); its arrangement is atrocious, but the documents are valuable, espec-

[1] This is the edition cited in the text briefly as *Works*; the volumes are not numbered, but that containing Cranmer's works on the Lord's Supper was published first, and is here treated as volume i.; that containing his letters and miscellaneous pieces followed, and is here cited as vol. ii.

[2] This is the edition cited as "Foxe" in the text.

ially in the last greatly-augmented edition of Pocock (Oxford, 7 vols., 1865).[1] The latest history of the Reformation on an ambitious scale is that of Canon Dixon (6 vols., 1878–99), a work of great labour, but perhaps a criticism rather than a history of the Reformation. The best summary of the facts is given in Dr. Gairdner's volume (1902) in Stephens and Hunt's *History of the Church of England*, the point of view of which is somewhat like Dixon's. The general modern histories, such as Lingard's and Froude's are too well known to need further description; but it may be remarked that there is inadequate justification for the systematic detraction of Froude's *History* which has become the fashion. He held strong views, and he made some mistakes; but his mistakes were no greater than those of other historians, and there are not half a dozen histories in the English language which have been based on so exhaustive a survey of original materials.

Of the various Lives of Cranmer, Strype's (1694, folio, London) is the earliest, the fullest, and contains most original matter; but Strype was a most industrious compiler without any pretensions to style. The Life by H. J. Todd (2 vols., 1831) is more readable, but is too apologetic, and adds little to Strype; and Le Bas (2 vols., 1833) adds practically nothing to Todd. The memoir in Dean Hook's *Lives of the Archbishops of Canterbury* was written

[1] In the text the cumbrous method of reference adopted by Pocock in his index has been abandoned, and the references are simply to the volume and page of Pocock's edition.

under the influence of the Tractarian movement, and particularly of S. R. Maitland's attacks on the Reformers; the balance is redressed in Canon Mason's interesting sketch (1896) which, however, is stronger on the theological than on the historical side. Dr. Gairdner's article in the *Dictionary of National Biography* (vol. xiii., 1888) is, like all that author's work, a model of compressed accuracy.[1] Its chief defect is that Dr. Gairdner's eye had not lighted on the late Mr. R. E. Chester Waters's researches into Cranmer's family history, published in his *Chesters of Chicheley*, 1877. That monument of scientific genealogy is here for the first time used in a biography of Cranmer.

For a more exhaustive bibliography I must refer to the appendix to my *England under Protector Somerset* (1900, pp. 327–339) or to my contribution to the *Cambridge Modern History* (vol. ii., 1904, pp. 795–801). But I must acknowledge my debt of gratitude to the various owners of pictures who have generously permitted their reproduction in these pages, and to Messrs. Goupil for lending two negatives originally prepared for illustrating my volume on *Henry VIII.* The Rev. John Standish, Vicar of Scarrington, most kindly supplied me with information respecting Aslacton; and to the candid opin-

[1] There are various other Lives of Cranmer from different points of view, but they have no claim to be based on original research. For Cranmer's "Catechism" see Tite and Thomson's *Bibliography*, 1862; for his library see Mr. Edward Burbidge's two pamphlets, and for his handwriting see J. E. Bailey's *Autographs of Thomas Cranmer*, 1879.

ions of my wife and of my friend, Mr. Graham Wallas, I owe not merely the correction of many a slip, but the pruning of numerous passages.

A. F. POLLARD

PUTNEY, LONDON,
15 February, 1904.

CONTENTS

ILLUSTRATIONS

THOMAS CRANMER

CHAPTER I

PARENTAGE, BIRTH, AND EARLY YEARS

MIDWAY between the north-midland towns of Grantham and Nottingham, and just beyond the railway which joins them, lies the modest hamlet of Aslacton.[1] It is not of itself a parish; of old it belonged to Whatton on the south-east, and now it forms part of Scarrington on the north-west. Until recent years its spiritual needs were satisfied with a Primitive Methodist chapel and an Anglican mission room named, like some walks and mounds in the neighbourhood, after its one distinguished native. Its inhabitants do not number five hundred souls, and it covers less than thirteen hundred acres of land. The cross-roads, on which its cottages cluster, lead nowhere in particular, and the great Fosse Way passes it by in contempt four miles

[1] So it was generally spelt in Cranmer's time, and often is to-day, but it was in the sixteenth century, and is now also, spelt Aslocton, or Aslockton.

to the north-west. Beyond that lies Sherwood Forest, already in the days of Cranmer's youth celebrated as the scene of the legendary exploits of Robin Hood. To the south-east a stream, dignified by the name of the River Smite, meanders down to its junction with the Devon and then loses itself in the great river, the Trent, at Newark. Beyond this stream the ground rises to the heights whence, in Armada days,

> "Belvoir's lordly terraces the sign to Lincoln sent,
> And Lincoln sped the message on o'er the wide vale of Trent."[1]

Few inhabited spots have suffered less from modern civilisation; the nearest money office is three miles distant, and if a rustic of Aslacton requires the telegraph he has still farther to seek. Some six times a day, trains pass in either direction, but Aslacton owes its railway station less to its own than to the borrowed importance of neighbouring Whatton; and the proximity of a railroad at all is solely due to the fact that the pioneers who constructed the line from Grantham and Nottingham must needs pass near Aslacton.

Here on 2 July, 1489, was born "the first Protestant archbishop of this kingdom, and the greatest instrument, under God, of the happy Reformation of this Church of England: in whose piety, learning, wisdom, conduct, and blood the foundation of it was laid."[2] But Aslacton, although it was the place of

[1] Macaulay, *The Armada.*

[2] Strype, *Cranmer*, ed. 1820, p. 1.

Cranmer's birth, was not the original cradle of the race. The family took its name from Cranmer, a manor in the parish of Sutterton in Lincolnshire; and its arms, a *chevron between three cranes*, are an heraldic pun on the name, which signifies a lake abounding in cranes. It occurs as a place-name in the counties of Norfolk and Suffolk, and under the variant "Cranmore" is found in the west of England.[1] Imaginative county historians,[2] and fertile makers of pedigrees, have traced the genealogy of the Cranmers of Sutterton back to the reign of Edward I., when one Hugh de Cranmer is said to have wedded the daughter of William de Sutterton. But few genealogists of the sixteenth century were content with a line which began at so recent a date. It was an age of *parvenus*, and therefore of pedigree-makers, and the legislature has never weighted the imagination of genealogists with the penalties attaching to the forgery of other kinds of documents. The great Lord Burghley himself was a zealous hunter of pedigrees, and even Cranmer liked to believe that his forbears came over with William the Conqueror. When he discovered in the train of the French Ambassador a gentleman with a similar coat-of-arms to his own, he gave him a good dinner at Lambeth on the strength of the supposed relationship.

The truth is that the Cranmers' antecedents were obscure and their position humble enough. "I take it," said Cranmer, many years later, "that none of

[1] There were also "Cranmores" at Aslacton, a family of inferior social position to the Archbishop's.

[2] *E. g.*, R. Thoroton in his *Nottinghamshire*, ed. Throsby, 1797.

us all here, being gentlemen born, but had our beginnings that way from a low and base parentage."[1] No member of his family had been knighted or pricked as sheriff, none had been elected to serve in Parliament or summoned to fight his country's battles in the wars of the fourteenth century. It is, however, an exaggeration to say that there is no evidence for the existence of the various members of the family, whom the historian of Nottinghamshire has introduced into the fourteenth-century part of the pedigree; for we have it on the authority of the tax-collector that in 1338 one Hugh de Cranmer owned three acres and something more in the county of Lincoln.[2] It is no straining of probabilities to assume that this Hugh de Cranmer is he whose name was painted on the stained-glass windows of Sutterton Church,[3] and that both are identical with the Hugh who figures in the pedigrees as the grandfather of Edmund Cranmer, the first to connect the Cranmers with Aslacton.

This Edmund did not a little to promote the modest fortunes of the family. Early in the fifteenth century he married Isabella, daughter and heiress of William de Aslacton,[4] and her family was certainly of higher social standing than that of her husband. It may have been descended from Walkelin, presumably a Norman, who held Aslacton in the time of Domesday Book[5]; one of its

[1] *Narratives of the Reformation* (Camden Soc.), pp. 274–5.

[2] *Calendar of Close Rolls*, 1337–9, p. 493.

[3] Holles, *Church Notes in Lincolnshire*, *sub verbo* Sutterton.

[4] Thoroton, ed. Throsby, i., 262.

[5] *Testa de Nevill*, Notts, p. 3.

members had been sheriff of Nottingham and Derby shires in the reign of Henry III., and another had sat as knight for his native county in the parliament of Edward III.[1] Edmund Cranmer apparently sold his Lincolnshire inheritance, and with the proceeds purchased in 1425 lands adjoining his wife's in Aslacton. Their son John married Alice Marshall of South Carleton in North Muskham, Nottinghamshire, and by her had issue two sons, Thomas, the father of the future Archbishop, and John. The elder, of course, succeeded to the Aslacton lands, and the younger, in orthodox fashion, devoted himself to the Church.

Of the Archbishop's father we know more than of any earlier member of the family. He was probably born between 1450 and 1455, and some thirty years later he married Agnes, daughter of Lawrence Hatfield of Willoughby, in the Nottinghamshire hundred of Thurgarton. The suggestion[2] that these Hatfields were descended from the lords of Hatfield in Holderness is a conjecture unsupported by evidence; but they were a county family of some standing, and Agnes Hatfield's uncle married the daughter of Sir Thomas Molyneux of Hawton; his son, Henry Hatfield, was in later years surveyor of the Archbishop's lands.[3] By this marriage Thomas Cranmer had a large family; there were three boys and at least four girls. Of the daughters, Dorothy married Harold Rosell, of Ratcliffe-on-Trent,[4] and

[1] Lists of Sheriffs, *P. R. O.*, 1898; *Official Return of Members of Parl.*, i., 72.

[2] Poulson's *Holderness*, ii., 443.

[3] Cranmer, *Works* (Parker Soc.), ii., 265.

[4] Thoroton, i., 184.

Agnes wedded Edmund Cartwright[1] of Ossington, a family which produced more than one well-known name in English history. Two daughters, Margaret and Emmet, were unmarried at their father's death; one of them afterwards became the wife of that unknown brother-in-law of the Archbishop who perished in the fire at Lambeth Palace in December, 1543.[2] The other was scarcely more fortunate in her matrimonial relations; her first husband was "a milner," but during his lifetime she is said to have married a second, one Henry Bingham, and her daughter by one of these husbands (presumably the first) was wife of Dr. Christopher Nevinson, the Archbishop's commissary, facts which furnished material for an attack on Cranmer by his Prebendaries in 1543.[3]

With so large a family, the Cranmers' household can hardly have been luxurious. Despite the slow but steady improvement in the fortunes of the clan, the Archbishop's father possessed but moderate means, and the extent of his influence and estates can easily be exaggerated. Aslacton was a "lordship" as well as a hamlet, but it is not clear that Cranmer was lord of any of the various manors of which the "lordship" was composed. The "lord-

[1] Thoroton, iii., 173; Waters, *Chesters of Chicheley*, pp. 370–1.

[2] Stow's *Annals*, p. 988.

[3] For Nevinson, or Nevynson, see *Dict. Nat. Biog.*, xl., 308, where, however, no mention is made of his wife's relationship to the Archbishop; compare *L. and P.*, vol. xviii., *passim*. A fifth daughter is said to have been the wife of John Monins, Lieutenant of Dover Castle, and a sixth is reported to have married one Shepey, a knight, but the relationship of these ladies is highly problematical.

ship" itself belonged to the Crown, apparently as part and parcel of the duchy of Lancaster. Edward IV. gave it to the Marquis Montagu, brother of Warwick the King-Maker, but on the fall of the Nevilles it reverted to royal hands. Among the various persons appointed from time to time as "receivers" or other royal representatives in the "lordship" the name of Cranmer does not occur[1]; and from this fact, and from the smallness of the bequests in the elder Cranmer's will, it may be safely assumed that his rents hardly sufficed to keep him and his household in the moderate comfort to which the smaller English gentry of the time were accustomed.

These comparatively narrow circumstances determined the careers of Cranmer's sons. The eldest, John who was born in the spring of 1487, was expected to do as his father had done, keep his inheritance intact, extend it, or enhance his social position by marrying well, and beget sons to carry on the family line and traditions. To him education was a matter of little or no importance, and there is no evidence to show that his intelligence was one whit superior to that of his class. The inference is in the opposite direction, for had he possessed brains or ambition, the influence of the Archbishop could easily have secured for his brother an opportunity of distinguishing himself in some wider sphere of usefulness than the

[1] See *Calendar of Patent Rolls*, 1476–85, pp. 4, 19. The bailiwick of the Lordship of Aslacton was granted in 1476 to one Richard Holt, and the receivership of Aslacton to Gervase Clifton (cf. *Cal. Inquis. Post-Mortem*, Henry VII., i., 714. In 1780 Aslacton belonged to a Mr. Marriott (Thoroton, *Nottinghamshire*, i., 264).

local affairs of Aslacton. But in spite of his lands and his brother, John Cranmer never even rose to the dignity of a justice of the peace. He was perhaps successful in all to which his lowly ambition aspired. He won a wife who boasted among her remote ancestors a baron by writ, and his daughter actually married the youngest son of a living peer.[1]

It was beyond the means of the Cranmer estates to support two of the family in such a position, and both of John's younger brothers were quartered on the Church. There is no reason to suppose that either felt any special call to the spiritual state; the decision was made for them by their parents and their circumstances; younger sons, for whom the family property could not provide, as a matter of course took holy orders. And so Thomas Cranmer was, by no design of his own, launched on his fateful career. His younger brother, Edmund, born about 1491, was intimately associated with him throughout his life; he followed Thomas to Cambridge, assimilated his elder brother's views and like him, married a wife, received the Archdeaconry of Canterbury, escaped to the Continent on Mary's accession, and died abroad in 1571.[2]

The first step in a clerical career was a clerical education, and the Archbishop once told his secre-

---

[1] His first wife was Joan, daughter of John Fretcheville of Stavely, whose ancestor Ralph de Fretcheville was summoned to Parliament as a baron in 1298; his daughter Susanna (by a second wife) married Thomas Brooke, *alias* Cobham, the youngest son of the sixth Lord Cobham; he became steward of the Archbishop's household and died in 1547.

[2] Waters, *Chesters of Chicheley*, pp. 395–6.

tary that his father "did set him to school with a marvellous severe and cruel schoolmaster."[1] Another account,[2] written soon after Cranmer's death, states that he "learned his grammar of a rude parish clerk in that barbarous time." But as Morice goes on to speak of Cranmer's leaving his "grammar school" to go to Cambridge, it is probable that his instructor was not the local parish priest, but the master of some neighbouring school. Of these there were at least four within easy reach of Aslacton in Cranmer's boyhood, Grantham, Nottingham, Newark, and Southwell.[3] There is no evidence to determine at which of these schools he was educated; possibly it was at Southwell, for here in 1533 he recommended that his nephew and godson, Thomas Rosell, should be sent to school.[4] Wherever the pedagogue ruled his "tyranny towards youth" is said to have been

"such that, as he [Cranmer] thought, the said schoolmaster so appalled, dulled and daunted the tender and fine wits of his scholars, that they commonly more hated and abhorred good literature than favoured or embraced the same, whose memories were also thereby so mutilated and wounded that for his part he lost much of that benefit of memory and audacity in his youth that by nature was given to him, which he could never recover, as he divers times reported. And, albeit his father was very desirous to have him learned, yet would he not that he should be

[1] Morice, *Anecdotes* (Narratives of the Reformation) pp. 238–9.
[2] *Ibid.*, p. 218.
[3] See A. F. Leach, *English Schools at the Reformation*, pp. 322–3.
[4] Cranmer's *Letters* (Parker Soc. Ed.), pp. 256, 262.

ignorant in civil and gentlemanlike exercises, insomuch that he used him to shoot and many times permitted him to hunt and to hawk and to exercise and to ride rough horses. So that now being archbishop he feared not to ride the roughest horses that came into his stable. Which he would do very comely, as otherwise at all times there was none in his house that would become his horse better. And when time served for recreation after study he would both hawk and hunt, the game being prepared for him beforehand. And would sometimes shoot with the long bow, but many times kill his deer with the cross-bow, and yet his sight was not perfect, for he was purblind."[1]

The elder Cranmer was not, however, long to direct his son's training in outdoor sports or mental exercises. He died in the prime of life on 27 May, 1501, when his eldest son was fourteen, his second twelve, and his third ten years of age. He was buried in the church of St. John of Beverley at Whatton, at the east end of the north aisle, and a simple inscription on a plain slab of alabaster recorded the fact of his death.[2] His will was proved at York on the first of October following.[3] It was, like everything else we know of its author, entirely commonplace; and such bequests as he made to the Church were for the benefit of secular and not monastic establishments. That was a frequent sign of the decay of monastic influence; and Cranmer's benefactions did not amount to much. Ten shillings were

[1] Morice, pp. 239-40.

[2] *Ashmole MS.* 854, p. 155.

[3] *Testamenta Eboracensia* (Surtees Soc.), iv., 194.

left to Whatton to buy a new bell, and six shillings and eightpence went towards the maintenance of the Holy Trinity Chapel at Aslacton.[1] The paucity of these ecclesiastical bequests is a little surprising in view of the apparently clerical character of the elder Cranmer's friends. The overseer of his will was the Abbot of Welbeck, and among the witnesses to it were Thomas Wilkinson, vicar of Whatton, who became Abbot of Welbeck two years later, and Edward Collinson, a Canon of the same Premonstratensian Abbey. That Abbey was rector[2] of Whatton, and, considering the closeness of the relations between Cranmer and the Canons of Welbeck, it is somewhat strange that neither of his sons should have joined that religious house. The idea must almost have been suggested to the future Archbishop and rejected by him or by his parents.

To the members of his family Cranmer had little to leave except the lands entailed upon his eldest son. Five marks each were given to his two unmarried daughters, and twenty shillings a year each in land were left to Thomas and Edmund; if either of them died, the survivor was to have the shares of both. Perhaps there was more to leave than appears in the will; for the widow, who was appointed sole

---

[1] These sums should be multiplied by twenty to bring them to their modern equivalent; the chapel at Aslacton was apparently on the site of the present parish room named after Cranmer.

[2] Before the Reformation monasteries and other corporate bodies were often "rectors" (*i. e.*, owners of the tithe) of parishes; on the dissolution of Welbeck, the Archbishop bought the tithes of Aslacton and Whatton, and transferred them to his nephew, Thomas, the head of the family (*cf.* Massingberd, *Hist. Ref.* App.).

executrix and residuary legatee, was able to maintain two sons at Cambridge, and, it would seem, to endow the future Archbishop with something above his twenty shillings a year. Many years later, Cranmer wrote that he was better off as a scholar at Cambridge than he was as Archbishop,[1] and the earliest reference to him in the state papers of the time records that in 1528 "Master Doctor Cranmer" of Aslacton had, like Joseph, corn to sell in a time of scarcity.[2]

Meanwhile, their father's death made no change in the Cranmers' plans and position. Thomas remained under his severe and cruel schoolmaster for another two years, and then in 1503 or 1504 he went up to Cambridge, whither, some five years later, he was followed by his brother Edmund. He is assumed to have entered at Jesus College, of which he was elected fellow a few years later. The college had been founded only some six or seven years before on the site of the nunnery of St. Rhadegunde, which had been dissolved on account of the gross immorality prevailing among the inmates.[3] There was little in the intellectual atmosphere of Cambridge to stimulate the mental activity of even the most inquisitive undergraduate. The Roman hierarchy still discouraged the study of Greek as the language of the schismatic and rival Church of the East; it had been taught more or less spasmodically for nearly a gen-

---

[1] *Works*, ii., 437.

[2] *L. and P.*, iv., 3819.

[3] J. Bass Mullinger, *Univ. of Cambridge*, i., 320; A. Gray, *History of Jesus College*, 1902, *passim*.

eration at Oxford, but had not penetrated to the recesses of the sister university. Nor does the classical Latin of Virgil and Cicero, Horace and Tacitus appear to have been in greater favour. The University Library at the end of the fifteenth century seems to have consisted of between five and six hundred volumes, and in this somewhat meagre collection there was not a Greek nor a classical Latin author; even patristic theology was poorly represented, and the library only possessed part of the works of the four great Fathers of the Latin Church, Ambrose, Gregory, Jerome, and Augustine. The books were almost exclusively concerned with mediæval scholastic philosophy, the dry bones of which had as yet scarcely been stirred by the breath of the New Learning.

So Cranmer's education proceeded uneventfully along the dusty, well-worn paths of the *trivium* and *quadrivium*. "He was nozzled," writes his contemporary biographer,[1] "in the grossest kind of sophistry, logic, philosophy, moral and natural (not in the text of the old philosophers, but chiefly in the dark riddles of Duns and other subtle questionists) to his age of twenty-two years." The Archbishop himself declares that his tutor was "such an one who, when he came to any hard chapter, which he well understood not, would find some pretty toy to shift it off, and to skip over to another chapter, of which he could better skill."[2] The name of this learned don has not been preserved, but the fellows of Jesus

[1] *Narratives of the Reformation*, p. 219.

[2] Jenkyns, iii., 472.

College, at the time of Cranmer's entrance, were none of them men of remarkable intellect. The Master was William Chubbes,[1] who had held that post since the foundation of the college in 1497; he was, it is true, the author of two books, but one was an introduction to logic, and the other was a commentary on Duns Scotus; and it is not unfair to assume that they typified a scholastic learning then in the last stage of senile decay. Chubbes died in the second or third year of Cranmer's residence at Jesus, and his successor was Dr. John Eccleston, of whom little is known except that he became chancellor of Ely Cathedral, and vice-chancellor of the University of Cambridge. He presided over the college for two years; and then, after the six months' reign of Thomas Alcock, who probably owed his election to his relationship to Bishop John Alcock, the founder of the college, the choice of the fellows fell upon William Capon, who remained Master for thirty years. His chief claims to distinction are the facts that he was chaplain to Wolsey, by whom he was selected to be Dean of his short-lived college at Ipswich, and was brother of the more celebrated John Capon, Bishop of Bangor and Salisbury. Of the fellows scarcely one calls for notice; Sir Thomas Elyot,[2] the translator of Isocrates and Plutarch, the friend of Ascham and More, and the author of one

[1] *Dict. Nat. Biogr.*, x., 298. See also Cooper's *Athenæ Cantabrigienses* for Chubbes and the other fellows of Jesus; a list of those noticed is given in the house-lists at the end of the volume. Further information is in A. Gray's *History of Jesus College*, 1902.

[2] *Dict. Nat. Biogr.*, xvii., 347, which also contains lives of Goodrich and Bale.

of the earliest Latin-English dictionaries, has been claimed as an *alumnus* of Jesus College, but on disputable grounds. The star of the college was, however, in the ascendant. Besides Cranmer himself, a distinguished fellow was elected in 1510 in the person of Thomas Goodrich, afterwards Bishop of Ely, and Lord Chancellor of England; and not long afterwards the college was joined by John Bale, the father of English biographers.

In the wider sphere of the university light was also beginning to shine. In 1497 the illustrious John Fisher, afterwards Bishop of Rochester, and Cardinal, was made confessor to Margaret Beaufort,[1] the mother of Henry VII. He was at the time Master of Michaelhouse, Cambridge; four years later he became Vice-chancellor of the university, and 1502 saw the first fruits of his influence over the greatest benefactress of Oxford and Cambridge in the establishment of the Lady Margaret chairs of divinity and of the Lady Margaret Preachership. The divinity professor was to lecture on most days in the year, and the preacher was to preach in the neglected vernacular tongue. These endowments were followed by the foundation of Christ's College in 1505, and then by that of St. John's College.[2] In 1506, probably at Fisher's suggestion, the King himself and his mother visited Cambridge, and in the same year the newly-awakened interest in learning is indicated by the offer of a degree in divinity

[1] See Halsted, *Life of Margaret Beaufort*, 1839.

[2] Baker, *Hist. of St. John's College*, ed. Mayor; Bass Mullinger, *Univ. of Cambridge*.

to the greatest scholar of his age, Erasmus of Rotterdam.[1]

That these public events of his undergraduate career had some influence in broadening Cranmer's outlook scarcely admits of doubt; but for the present he was bound by the limits of the conventional studies requisite for his degree; and it was not until after he had graduated B.A. in 1510 or 1511 that he began to emancipate himself from their trammels. Even then his line of inquiry was strictly prescribed, for soon afterwards he was elected one of the twelve fellows of Jesus College, eleven of whom were compelled by the statutes to study theology. These statutes were the work of three successive bishops of Ely, Alcock, the founder of Jesus, James Stanley, the step-son of Margaret Beaufort and an early friend of Erasmus, and Nicholas West; and their prohibition of the study of canon law is a curious illustration of the unpopularity in which its abuse had involved it. Cranmer accordingly had no option but to pursue his theological course, but there was ample scope for reform in its methods, and he now began to turn from the mediæval schoolmen to "Faber, Erasmus, and good Latin authors," including probably the great Fathers of the Latin Church. It may be no more than a coincidence that in the same year (1511), Erasmus took up his residence in Cambridge as Lady Margaret Lecturer in Divinity, and it would be rash to assume any personal intercourse between the Dutch humanist and the retiring young graduate,

[1] See Nichols, *Letters of Erasmus*, 1901, p. 402; Lewis, *Life of Fisher*, App. viii.

twenty-one years his junior.[1] That Cranmer attended Erasmus's lectures is possible; but it is by no means clear to what extent Erasmus lectured either on divinity, as he was bound by the terms of his office to do, or on Greek, in which he was naturally more interested. Cranmer made no mark at this time as a Greek scholar, and Erasmus's subsequent encomium[2] of him as "a most upright man of spotless life" was evoked, not by personal friendship, but by the fact that Cranmer had promised him the same liberality as he had enjoyed from the Archbishop's predecessor, Warham.

The tenure of his fellowship and the course of his studies were soon interrupted by Cranmer's marriage. Jesus College was situated in a somewhat remote part of Cambridge, and apparently the nearest spot at which Jesus men could foregather with members of other colleges was the Dolphin Inn at the Bridge Street end of All Saints' Lane, a site now occupied by part of Trinity College.[3] Inns had not then degenerated into mere drinking-shops; they were rather hotels and clubs, and the hosts were in better social estimation than the publican of to-day. With the mistress of the Dolphin lived a young relative named Joan, who is described as "a gentleman's daughter."[4] Cranmer fell in love with her

[1] The fact that Erasmus does not mention Cranmer has been adduced to prove that the latter's university career was undistinguished (Jane M. Stone, *Queen Mary*, p. 380); but the argument would be fatal to many other reputations.

[2] Erasmus, *Epistolæ*, mcclxi.

[3] Bass Mullinger, i., 612; Mason, *Cranmer*, p. 7.

[4] Foxe, *Acts and Monuments*, ed. Townsend, viii., 4.

and eventually married her. She continued to reside at the Dolphin, and Cranmer's frequent resort to the house gave rise to the subsequent fable that he himself was an ostler at the inn.[1] This was one of many calumnies, but in reality there was nothing disgraceful about the marriage except from the point of view of perverted class prejudice, which regards it as more honourable to seduce than to marry girls of humble rank. Cranmer was not in holy orders, and it is entirely due to theological hatred that his marriage was singled out for objurgation by those who passed over in silence the illicit connexions then commonly formed by churchmen from the highest to the lowest degrees.

This marriage necessarily deprived Cranmer of his fellowship, but he was immediately appointed "common reader" in Buckingham College, a recent foundation, now known as Magdalen College.[2] This post he held for less than twelve months, for about a year after his marriage his wife died in childbed, and his old college paid Cranmer the compliment of re-electing him to his fellowship. The honour was the more marked because this extension of the term "unmarried" to a widower was an interpretation of college statutes which remained unique for centuries.[3] It should dissipate any idea that Cranmer had lost caste by his marriage, and it is at the same time indisputable testimony to the esteem in which

[1] *Narratives of the Reformation*, p. 269; the northern rebels in 1536 called him a tavernkeeper.—*L. and P.*, xi., 714.

[2] *Dict. Nat. Biogr.*, liii., 447.

[3] Bass Mullinger, i., 612; Le Bas, *Cranmer*, i., 29.

his character and intellectual attainments were held by those in a position to judge them.

Meanwhile, under the influence of his bereavement, Cranmer pursued his studies with increased vigour. In 1516 Erasmus speaks of the change which had come over the intellectual atmosphere of Cambridge in the last few years[1]; scholasticism was gradually giving way to the study of literature and of the Bible. Cranmer threw himself into the movement, and the publication of Erasmus's New Testament in 1516 and of Luther's Ninety-Five Theses in 1517 marks the approximate date at which the future English reformer began a systematic examination of the Scriptures.

"Then he" [says his biographer],[2] "considering what great controversy was in matters of religion (not only in trifles but in the chiefest articles of our salvation), bent himself to try out the truth herein: and, forasmuch as he perceived that he could not judge indifferently in so weighty matters without the knowledge of the Holy Scriptures (before he were infected with any man's opinions or errors), he applied his whole study three years to the said Scriptures. After this he gave his mind to good writers both new and old, not rashly running over them, for he was a slow reader, but a diligent marker of whatsoever he read; for he seldom read without pen in hand, and whatsoever made either for one part or the other of things being in controversy, he wrote it out if it were short, or at the least, noted the author and the place, that he might find it and write it out by leisure; which was a great help to him in debating

[1] Erasmus, *Epistolæ*, cxlviii. [2] *Narr. Ref.*, p. 219.

of matters ever after. This kind of study he used till he was made Doctor of Divinity which was about the thirty-fourth of his age."

Even his bitterest enemies bore witness to Cranmer's immense industry and personal attractions. "He had in his favour," writes one of them,[1] "a dignified presence, adorned with a semblance of goodness, considerable reputation for learning, and manners so courteous, kindly, and pleasant, that he seemed like an old friend to those whom he encountered for the first time. He gave signs of modesty, seriousness, and application," qualities which earned him steady promotion in his college and university. Soon after his re-election to a fellowship he was appointed Lecturer in Divinity in Jesus College; before 1520 he was ordained, and in that year he was selected to be one of the university preachers. He was also entrusted with the task of examining candidates for degrees in divinity, and in this capacity he endeavoured to raise the standard of Biblical knowledge by requiring from them some evidence of their having studied the Scriptures.[2] Finally, in 1524, he was offered by Wolsey a canonry in the newly-founded Cardinal College at Oxford—an offer which, fortunately perhaps for himself, he declined.

It is a significant fact that most of these Canons, selected for their eminence in learning or character, soon fell under suspicion of attachment to Lutheran

[1] *Bishop Cranmer's Recantacyons*, ed. Gairdner, p. 3.

[2] Foxe, viii., 5.

doctrines. As early as 1521 a number of Cambridge men had begun to meet at the White Horse tavern to examine and discuss the novel views put forward by the Wittenberg monk. The inn became known as "Germany," its frequenters as "Germans," and if Oxford's reception of the Renaissance was more ready than that of Cambridge, the latter university has at least the honour of having afforded an earlier welcome to the Reformation. Among these Cambridge Reformers were some of the greatest names in the movement: Tyndale and Coverdale, the translators of the Bible; Latimer, the prophet of the Reformation; and Bilney and Barnes, Crome and Lambert, some of its earliest martyrs. The rapid spread of the new doctrines excited alarm in high orthodox circles, and the King himself descended into the arena with his royal fulminations against Lutheran heresies. Sir Thomas More was vexed that any one should so far carry into practice the principles laid down in the *Utopia*, where all religions were tolerated, as to dissent from the orthodox faith; and soon after his appointment as High Steward of Cambridge in 1525 commissions were issued to check these vagaries. Severer measures were taken by Wolsey in 1528, and some of the Reformers were induced to renounce their opinions.

Cranmer himself was affected by his industrious examination of the Scriptures and of the new doctrines, and about 1525 he began in private to pray for the abolition of papal power in England.[1] But he avoided any open expression of his views, for he

[1] *Works*, ii., 327; *L. and P.*, 1543, ii., 303.

does not appear to have incurred any suspicion with regard to his orthodoxy. Naturally of a reticent and unaggressive disposition, he was the very reverse of an enthusiast; his slowness in reading was characteristic. New ideas won their way to his mind with painful, hesitant steps; and they were only adopted after years of mature reflexion. His caution bordered on timidity, not so much from moral cowardice, as from an intellectual perception of both sides to the question. He never possessed the burning zeal which blinds men to all aspects of truth except one, and enables them to go forward in the sublime confidence that they are themselves entirely right and their opponents entirely wrong. His career was that of a conservative reformer, reluctantly abandoning ground which he felt to be untenable, but somewhat doubtful of the security of his next foothold.

He was still, however, occupied almost solely with academic work, and besides his college and university duties he appears occasionally to have taken charge of private pupils. At any rate, two youths of the name of Cressy[1] were in his care in 1529;

[1] The exact relation between Cranmer and the Cressys is difficult to trace. There was an "ancient and genteel" family of that name settled at Holme near Hodsack, Nottinghamshire, to which the famous Benedictine, Hugh Paulinus Cressy (see *Dict. Nat. Biog.*, xii., 114), belonged; and later in the sixteenth century Cranmer's grandnephew, Thomas, and one William Cressy married sisters. The Cressy family had held lands in Nottinghamshire since the reign of Edward II., and more than one had attained to knightly rank; there were branches of it in other counties (see *Cal. Inquisitionum post mortem*, iv., 125, 224, 262, 272, 431, 462; *Cal. of Ancient Deeds*, i., 403, ii., 520, and iii., *passim;* Clutterbuck's *Hertfordshire*, i., 407

their mother was in some way related to Cranmer, and their father owned a house at Waltham in Essex. Here in the summer Cranmer took refuge with his two pupils when that terror of the sixteenth century, the plague, made Cambridge an undesirable habitation; and here occurred the incident which changed the whole course of Cranmer's life and helped to alter the course of English history.

---

and other references in Marshall's *Genealogist's Guide*). The Cressy here referred to was possibly Robert Cressy, a notary sometimes employed by Wolsey (see *L. and P.*, i., 4332, ii., 3925, iv., 6); but the only Cressy connected with Waltham appears to be the John Cressy who, with Joan his wife, was buried in Waltham Church. Fuller says that the name had died out in Waltham before his day (*circa* 1650.) None of the inquisitions in the Record Office throw any light on the matter.

CHAPTER II

CRANMER AND THE DIVORCE OF CATHERINE OF ARAGON

OF all the incidents affecting Cranmer's life the most important is the divorce of Catherine of Aragon.[1] That divorce and its ramifications were the web into which the threads of Cranmer's life were woven. Through it he first attracted the notice of Henry VIII.; to his services in that cause he owed his elevation to the See of Canterbury, the part he played in the history of the English Reformation, and, finally, his martyrdom. It therefore becomes

[1] It is impossible to avoid the use of the term "divorce" in spite of its obvious inaccuracy. From neither of the two conflicting points of view was there any divorce at all. The Anglican view was that Henry VIII. and Catherine had never been legally married, and the so-called divorce was really a declaration of nullity. Roman Catholics, on the other hand, declared that they were legally married and as the Pope gave sentence to that effect, there was no legal "divorce." Hence Harpsfield's treatise on the subject is entitled "The Pretended Divorce." Nor, indeed, does the canon law recognise such a thing as divorce at all; there may be separation *a mensa et toro*, but that does not destroy the marriage-bond at all; or there may be a declaration that a marriage has been null and void from the beginning. These declarations were common in the early sixteenth century, the complexities of the canon law affording considerable facilities for obtaining them.

imperative to indicate as briefly as may be the origin of that episode and its influence on the Reformation in which Cranmer lived and moved and had his being. Without some such introduction it is impossible to weigh Cranmer's character in the balance, or to estimate the effect of his career on English history.

Important, however, though the divorce was as the occasion of the Reformation, no theory could be more shallow than that which seeks to represent Henry's desire to put away an unattractive wife as its one and only cause. Before the faintest whisper of any such project as the divorce could have reached him, an Imperial officer, writing from Rome to Charles V. on 8 June, 1527, alluded to the possibility of the King of England's turning the English Church into a separate patriarchate and denying obedience to the Papal See.[1] He thought such a development probable, if the Imperialists who had just sacked Rome retained the Pope in their custody; and, indeed, nothing could be more natural than that England should repudiate a spiritual jurisdiction which moved at the will of a secular foe. The papal claims were tolerable only so long as the mediæval ideal of the unity of the civilised world under one spiritual and one temporal head remained intact; but they could not survive the growth of the spirit of nationality and the effect of the impression that papal powers could be made to serve particular interests. This abuse first attained flagrant proportions when Charles VIII. crossed the Alps in 1494 and made Italy the cockpit of Europe. The Vicar of Christ might have looked on with

[1] *L. and P.*, vol. iv., Pref., p. clxx.

comparative unconcern, had he been content with spiritual pre-eminence; but his efforts to grasp the shadow of temporal power involved him in the fray, and forced him to side now with one and now with another secular prince in order to extend the bounds of his petty Italian domains. In this struggle his lack of material resources compelled resort to spiritual arms; and the weapons, wielded of yore in the cause of the faith, became pawns in a game which was played with Italian acres for stakes. Temporal princes were branded as "sons of perdition and children of iniquity," not because their morals were bad or their creeds unsound, but because they stood in the way of papal greed. The Catholic Emperor, Charles V., told Clement VII. that the sack of Rome was the just judgment of God[1]; and one of his envoys proposed that the Pope should forfeit his fiefs as the root of all the evil.[2] The Pope's spiritual influence contracted as his worldly possessions expanded; and his estimation and credit have never increased so fast as in the generation which followed the loss of his temporal power.

England, however, was not particularly moved by papal subservience to secular interests so long as it was merely a question of the increase or decrease of the extent of the Papal States, or even of the relative preponderance of French and Spanish influence in Italy. But as soon as a matter of decisive importance to England arose, she discovered a striking grievance. Spain and France might put up with

[1] *Calendar of Spanish State Papers*, 1527–29, p. 309.

[2] *Ibid.*, pp. 209–210.

the prostitution of papal prerogatives in the interests of temporal princes, because the kings of Spain and of France were precisely those who benefited by the process. If the Pope was a Spaniard to-day, he might be a Frenchman to-morrow; but it was safe to say that in no case would the Pope be English. Even Wolsey and Pole were unable to break down the hostile barrier. It was, indeed, admitted that there should as a rule be one English Cardinal, but what was one in a body of forty? and it is little wonder that the nation repudiated the jurisdiction of a court in which its influence was measured on such a contemptible scale.

Such were the conditions that were first brought home to Englishmen's minds by the question of the divorce of Catherine of Aragon. That question was not the cause, but only the occasion of the permanent breach with Rome. Had it been the only ground of difference there would have been no obstacle to reconciliation after the death of Catherine of Aragon and Anne Boleyn in 1536. Henry VIII. had no love for heresy; he had been brought up in strict adherence to the Catholic faith, and for nearly twenty years he had distinguished himself by his defence of the Papal See. He had launched into war against Louis XII. because that king attacked the Pope's temporal States; he had written a book to confute Luther's denial of papal prerogatives; and papal blessings had followed him all his life.[1] The

[1] Sir Thomas More in 1521 urged Henry not to maintain so strongly in his book that the primacy of the Pope was of divine institution. More then doubted that dogma, but later on was converted to it.

importance of the divorce lies in the fact that it changed this friendship into enmity, and alienated the only power which might have kept in check the anti-papal and anti-sacerdotal tendencies then growing up in England.

But great as Henry's power was, its exercise was attended by such potent effects only because it decided a balance of other forces: alone it would have been powerless against the Pope and the priests. No ruler can effect anything except by utilising forces which exist independently of his own individual will, and it is idle to deny that such anti-ecclesiastical forces existed in the reign of Henry VIII. In 1512, when Englishmen wished to insult the Scots, they called them "Pope's men,"[1] and at the same time the people of London were said to be so hostile to the Church that any jury would condemn a cleric though he were as innocent as Abel.[2] In 1515 petitions were presented to Parliament against clerical exactions, and they gave rise to stormy debates[3]; prelates wrote in alarm of a party which was bent on the subversion of the Church, and bitterly complained that that party found favour at Court.[4] Wolsey sought to save his order by urging the speedy dissolution of Parliament[5] and by refusing, with one exception[6], to call another for the remaining fourteen years of his rule. Henry VIII.

---

while Henry's mind moved in the opposite direction. (More, *English Works*, p. 1424; *L. and P.*, vii., 289.)

[1] *L. and P.*, I., ii., 3320. [2] *Ibid.*, II., i., 2.

[3] *Ibid.*, II., i., 1312, 1315. *Cf.* I., ii., 5725.

[4] *Ibid.*, II., ii., 4074, 4083. [5] *Ibid.*, II., i., 1223. [6] Viz., in 1523.

knew perfectly well that if he chose to quarrel with Rome he would find abundant lay support.

While his divorce was not the sole cause of the breach with Rome, it is equally clear that Henry's passion for Anne Boleyn was not the sole cause for the divorce or the origin of the doubts respecting the legality of his marriage with Catherine of Aragon. When Julius II. was first asked in 1503 to grant a dispensation for Henry's marriage with his brother Arthur's widow, the Pope replied[1] that it was a great matter, and that he did not know whether it were competent for him to grant a dispensation in such a case. His dispensing power had, indeed, been denied by a General Council, and it was by no means universally admitted that the Pope was superior to General Councils. There was no doubt that such a marriage was canonically forbidden as sin; Catherine's father, Ferdinand of Aragon, felt it necessary to remove scruples which Henry might entertain on the subject[2]; her confessor was deprived of his post for venturing to suggest doubts in her mind,[3] and Archbishop Warham held similar views.[4] These objections were overridden by Henry's faith in the Pope and desire for Catherine's dower. The marriage was consummated, and in all probability nothing more would have been heard of its doubtful validity but for the extraordinary fatality which attended its issue. Four children came to the pair before the

[1] Adrian de Castello to Henry VII. in Pocock's *Records of the Reformation*, i., 1; *L. and P.*, iv., 3773.

[2] *Cal. Spanish State Papers*, ii., 8.

[3] *Ibid.* Preface, pp. xiii., etc.

[4] *L. and P.*, iv., 2579.

autumn of 1514; but every one was still-born or died soon after birth, and in that year it was reported in Rome that the lack of heirs was leading Henry to contemplate the divorce of his Spanish wife.[1] His relations with Spain were strained at the time; but presently they mended, and the birth of the Princess Mary in 1516 revived the King's hopes of a son and successor. They were doomed to disappointment; Catherine had more miscarriages and still-born children, but not one that survived, and by 1525 it was perfectly certain that if Henry remained married to Catherine he must relinquish all hopes of a male heir to the throne.

It is difficult to realise what that meant to Englishmen of the early part of the sixteenth century, for three glorious reigns have long ago banished any prejudices that may have been entertained against female sovereigns. But in 1531 a well-informed foreign ambassador could solemnly declare to his govern-

[1] *Calendar of Venetian State Papers*, 1509-19, p. 479; this interesting and important fact was only revealed by the publication of the Venetian State papers in 1866. Before that date, the earliest suggestion of the divorce was believed to have been made by Henry's confessor, Longland, afterwards Bishop of Lincoln. The anonymous author of the "Life and Death of Cranmer," (*Nar. Ref.*, p. 219) states that Henry was persuaded of the invalidity of his marriage by Longland, and his assertion is supported by a letter written in 1532, in which the date of Longland's suggestion is assigned to 1522, or 1523 (*L. and P.*, v., 1114). So, too, in 1536 the northern rebels thought that Longland was the beginning of all the trouble (*ibid.*, xi., 705) and compare Shakespeare, *Henry VIII.*, Act II., sc. iv., where Henry says: "First I began in private with you, my Lord of Lincoln." Other persons credited with the original proposal are the Bishop of Tarbes, Wolsey, and Stafileo, Dean of the Rota.

Copyright Photo., Walker & Cockerell.

QUEEN CATHERINE OF ARAGON.

ment that the laws of England did not permit a woman to mount the English throne.[1] There was, of course, no such law; nevertheless, that seemed to be the theory on which the succession had been regulated. The Empress Matilda, the only woman who had tried to grasp the English sceptre, had been driven from the land after a bloody civil war. John of Gaunt had maintained in Parliament that the crown descended only through males, and the Lancastrian kings had in practice made good the claim that Henry IV., the son of Edward III.'s younger son, had a better title than Philippa, the daughter of an elder. In 1485 Margaret Beaufort was the Lancastrian heir to the throne, yet she was passed over in favour of her son Henry VII., who had no jot of hereditary right which he did not derive from her. Why should the Princess Mary's title be any better than that of Margaret Beaufort? and if the attempt of one Queen to mount the throne had kindled the flames of civil strife, would not the attempt of another fan the barely extinguished embers of the Wars of the Roses? Other fears reinforced this theory of the succession. Englishmen throughout the century had a dread of being brought by marriage under a foreign yoke; by that means Brittany had lost its independence, the Netherlands had been fettered to Spain, and Bohemia and Hungary to Austria. If a Queen ascended the throne she ran the risk either of rousing internal strife by marrying a subject, or of promoting external dominion by giving herself and her realm to an alien prince.

[1] *Cal. Venetian State Papers*, 1527–33, p. 300.

The divorce of Catherine of Aragon was only one of the means suggested for avoiding the difficulty. Campeggio, who came to try the case in England, at one time entertained the idea that the Princess Mary might be married to her half-brother, the Duke of Richmond, Henry VIII.'s illegitimate son.[1] He appeared to see nothing unnatural in such a union, nor did he anticipate that the Pope would make any difficulty about granting the dispensation. Clement VII. himself proposed more than once that Henry should take a second wife without troubling about the divorce of his first[2]; and, indeed, there were precedents for such a course not merely in Scripture, but in more recent times. It was not so very long since a pope had allowed a king of Castile to take a second wife on account of the sterility of his first, under the condition that, if he had no children by the second within a specified time, he should return again to the first.[3] After all, it was not the Reformation which first introduced curiosities into the law of marriage.

The expedient, however, which found most favour with Henry VIII. and his advisers was that of setting up the claim of the Duke of Richmond. The patent of his creation in 1525 gave him, much to Queen Catherine's disgust, precedence over the Princess Mary; he was endowed with titles and offices which

[1] *L. and P.*, iv., 4881; it was claimed that the Pope could legalise marriages between brothers and sisters of the full blood (*ibid.*, v., 468), and of course popes have often permitted marriages between aunts and nephews, uncles and nieces (*cf.* Canon Mason, *Cranmer*, p. 10).

[2] *L. and P.*, iv., 6627.

[3] *Cal. of Spanish State Papers*, ii., 379.

QUEEN ANNE BOLEYN.

AFTER THE PICTURE BY LUCAS CORNELEY, NOW IN THE POSSESSION OF THE EARL OF ROMNEY.

BY PERMISSION OF THE EARL OF ROMNEY.

legitimate children of Henry VII. had enjoyed, and in 1527 the Spanish ambassador reported a scheme for making him King of Ireland.[1] In various negotiations for his marriage it was broadly hinted that he might safely be regarded as the heir presumptive of England,[2] and Charles V. believed that the betrothal of Mary to a French prince in 1527 was mainly designed to remove her from England and from the Duke of Richmond's path to the throne.[3] Some years later it was thought that the provision in the Act of Succession empowering Henry to leave the crown by will was intended to facilitate its devolution upon the Duke; and before expressing disgust at so violent an expedient, it is well to remember that a century and a half later a considerable party in England preferred the claim of an illegitimate but Protestant son of a king to that of his legitimate but Catholic brother.[4]

This solution of the difficulty had, however, two defects in Henry's eyes. It did not satisfy his conscience in the matter of his marriage with Catherine, and it brought him no nearer a union with Anne Boleyn. Now, there is no need to assume that Henry's scruples were entirely fictitious. He is not the only figure in history who has possessed the useful faculty of really convincing his conscience that what is personally desirable and politically expedient must therefore be morally right. He was,

[1] *Cal. of Spanish State Papers*, III., ii., 109.

[2] *L. and P.*, iv., 3051.

[3] *Cal. Spanish State Papers*, III., ii., 482.

[4] Namely, Monmouth and James II.

moreover, in some respects a superstitious man, and he could hardly fail to be impressed by the unique coincidence of which he was the victim. Never before had there been such a mortality among the children of an English king; never before had an English king married his brother's widow. In that theological age men less superstitious than Henry might easily have seen some connexion between these circumstances and the Scriptural prohibition against marriages such as his[1]; and it is one of the ironies of history that writers who maintain most sincerely that Henry's marriage was null in the sight of God and man have sometimes been his severest judges for having dissolved it. The basis of such a position lies, of course, in equitable considerations. *Quod fieri non debuit factum valet* was the common-sense view of the Lutheran divines on the point, and no court of equity would have granted a divorce, for its injustice to Catherine was flagrant and unredeemed. But, unfortunately, Catherine's case, like all great political issues, was judged, not by equity, but by law and expedience. The political advantages of a divorce were patent, and if the Pope's dispensing power was denied, it was also clear that the marriage was null in point of law.

At first Henry VIII. was by no means inclined to deny the papal dispensing power. He was, on the contrary, relying on it to remove an impediment to his marriage with Anne Boleyn arising from his illicit

[1] The French Ambassador, Du Bellay, afterwards a Cardinal, declared that "God had long ago passed sentence upon the marriage" (*L. and P.*, iv., 4899; Du Bellay to Montmorency, Nov. 1st, 1528).

relations with her sister Mary.[1] He experienced no difficulty in obtaining a dispensation to that effect, and he had some grounds for expecting an equally favourable reply to his demand for a divorce. Within his own family circle he saw ample precedents for such a course. His younger sister, Mary Tudor, had been twice married, first to Louis XII. of France, and secondly to the Duke of Suffolk; both husbands obtained divorces from previous wives without the least difficulty. Louis's first wife had been sent to a nunnery solely because he wanted to marry the Duchess of Brittany and offered the Pope his support in return for the boon. The Duke of Suffolk's case was still more to the point, for he obtained a divorce on the identical ground on which his brother-in-law was seeking one, namely, the invalidity of a previous dispensation.[2] Then, too, at the same moment that Henry's envoys were pressing his divorce, representatives of his sister Margaret, Queen of Scotland, were urging the Pope to annul her marriage with Angus for reasons much more flimsy than those which Henry VIII. put forward.[3] Yet her demand was granted without much trouble, and surely, Henry might think, a powerful king like himself was

[1] These relations were long believed in England (*cf.* Le Bas, *Life of Cranmer*, i., 18) to be a Roman Catholic libel similar to the assertion that Henry VIII. was father of Anne Boleyn. The latter, indeed, is a fiction, but there is no doubt about the relations between Henry VIII. and Mary Boleyn. See Stephan Ehses, *Römische Dokumente zur Geschichte der Ehescheidung Heinrich VIII. von England, 1527–1534*, 1893, and *English Historical Review*, vols. xi. and xii.

[2] *L. and P.*, iv., 5859.

[3] *Ibid.*, iv., 4130, 4131.

entitled to as much consideration as his sister and brothers-in-law.

His petition then did not seem altogether unreasonable, nor did Clement VII. treat it as such; but the Pope was still in the grip of the Imperialists who had pillaged his capital and kept him in ignominious confinement in the castle of S. Angelo. He could hardly be expected to court ruin by divorcing his gaoler's aunt; but if the French, now in alliance with Henry, would only advance and deliver him from the hands of his enemies, he would see what he could do.[1] Meanwhile he endeavoured to gain time by granting commissions which turned out to be worthless. They succeeded, however, in their object, for in 1528 the French commander, Lautrec, marched down through Italy, captured Melfi, and shut up the Spaniards in Naples. Spanish dominion in Italy seemed doomed to perish. Clement felt himself something more than the Emperor's chaplain, and an ample commission was granted to Wolsey and Campeggio to try the case.[2] Even if one were unwilling, the other might proceed and pronounce sentence by himself, and all appeals from the jurisdiction of the legatine court were forbidden. The Pope also gave a written promise that he would not revoke nor do anything to invalidate the commission, but would confirm the Cardinals' sentence.[3] This was tantamount to a verdict in Henry's favour, and he might well think that his case was won.

But no sooner had Campeggio started than the

---

[1] *L. and P.*, iv., 3682. [2] *Ibid.*, iv., 4345.

[3] *Eng. Hist. Rev.*, xii., 7; Ehses, *Römische Dokumente*, No. 23.

fortune of war was reversed. The French were defeated, and the Pope's secretary wrote off in hot haste to Campeggio that as the Emperor was victorious the Cardinal must not on any pretext pronounce a decision without a fresh commission from Rome. He must protract the matter as long as possible, for, in view of Charles's predominance, the granting of Henry's divorce would mean the utter ruin of the Church "as it is entirely within the power of the Emperor's servants."[1] Clement himself assured Charles that nothing would be done to the prejudice of his aunt. Campeggio's proceedings in England were therefore merely a farce intended to divert the English until the final event of the war in Italy should make up Clement's mind. On 21 June, 1529, hostilities were brought to an end by the crushing defeat of Landriano. The Pope, with an intelligent anticipation of coming events, had declared a few days before that he meant to become an Imperialist and to live and die as such,[2] and early in July he concluded a family compact with Charles at Barcelona.[3] Clement's nephew was to marry Charles's illegitimate daughter; the tyranny of his family was to be reimposed on Florence, and all towns wrested from the Papal States were to be restored. The Pope in return was to quash the proceedings against Catherine of Aragon. Campeggio was informed beforehand of the Pope's intentions; the case, had, however, made considerable progress, and on 23 July Henry, ignorant of the understanding between Clement and

[1] *L. and P.*, iv., 4721, 4736–37.
[2] *Spanish Cal.*, IV., i., 72.
[3] *Ibid.*, 117.

Charles, expected Campeggio to pronounce his sentence. The court was crowded, Campeggio stood up and began to speak, but instead of delivering judgment he adjourned the case.[1] "By the Mass," burst out Suffolk, giving the table a great blow with his hand, "now I see that the old saw is true, that there was never a legate or cardinal that did good in England!"

The effect of this blow on a man of Henry's choleric temper and boundless self-will may well be imagined, but with all his passionate egotism the King combined a notable power of self-control. No furious outburst on his part seems to have followed the legate's decision, and friends of the Queen vainly flattered themselves that the affair would blow over. But early in August the King made arrangements for summoning Parliament,[2] and then started on a progress in the country. On the 4th he was at Waltham, on the 6th he was hunting all day at Hunsdon. Thence he moved to Tyttenhanger, and three days later returned to Waltham; he was accompanied by Dr. Edward Fox, his almoner, and by Stephen Gardiner, his secretary. The harbingers quartered Fox and Gardiner in Cressy's house,

[1] His procedure is said to have been quite normal, because he only claimed the holidays usually taken by the Rota; but this was little more than a pretext. At any rate, when Charles V. was pressing for a decision in Catherine's favour in the following year, his ambassador declared that it was usual for cases of such importance to be carried on in spite of the holidays. *L. and P.*, iv., 6452.

[2] The writs were actually dated 9 Aug., but the determination to summon Parliament must have been reached before Henry left London; it was his reply to Clement's revocation of the divorce case.

where Cranmer was staying with Cressy's sons. Both were old acquaintances of Cranmer's, for Fox was educated at King's College, of which he was now Provost, and Gardiner was Master of Trinity Hall. Nor was this the first occasion on which Cranmer had been in the precincts of the Court. Nearly a year before, he had been sent to London by the Master of Jesus, apparently to negotiate some business with regard to the property held by the college in Southwark, and he returned, bringing letters from Cromwell, even then well known as Wolsey's factotum.[1]

Naturally the three friends, meeting at dinner in Cressy's house, fell to discussing the great question of the divorce. Cranmer was asked his opinion; he professed that he had not studied the matter, but being a theologian and not a lawyer (the statutes of his college forbade the study of canon law), he had little patience with the law's delays, and suggested the more speedy method of taking the question out of the hands of the lawyers and submitting it to the divines of the universities.[2] No one to-day would think of appealing to such an arbitrament, but, as Ranke says, "we must recollect that the universities were then regarded not only as establishments for education, but as supreme tribunals for the decision of scientific questions"[3]; and when the Elector Frederick of Saxony founded Wittenberg in 1502 he declared that he and all the neighbourhood would

[1] *L. and P.*, iv., 4872.

[2] Morice in *Narratives of the Reformation*, p. 241.

[3] *Hist. of the Reformation*, trs. by Austin, i., 314.

resort to it "as to an oracle." To these oracles Cranmer now proposed an appeal. They were indeed the only tribunals apart from the Papacy to whose verdict any respect would be paid. The Popes of a previous generation had practically destroyed the authority of General Councils, and the Papacy was now the handmaid of Charles V. The anarchy in Christendom inevitably encouraged separatist tendencies, but it would at least give an appearance of moral justification to individual action on the part of the English Church if the universities of Europe approved of the grounds on which it acted.

So Fox and Gardiner eagerly welcomed Cranmer's suggestion,[1] and a day or two later, after the Court had removed from Waltham, they mentioned the matter to Henry. The King was no less pleased with the idea. He thereupon, says Morice, "commanded them to send for Dr. Cranmer. And so by and by being sent for, he came to the King's presence at Greenwich." If Morice is correct as to the place, Henry certainly acted with no undue precipitation, for he did not return to Greenwich until November,[2] when the meeting of Parliament ren-

[1] According to a more doubtful version of Cranmer's advice, he declared that "if the King rightly understood his own office, neither Pope nor any other potentate whatsoever, neither in causes civil nor ecclesiastical, hath anything to do with him or any of his actions, within his own realm and dominion; but he himself, under God, hath the supreme government of this land in all causes whatsoever"; whereupon "The King swore, by his wonted oath, Mother of God, that man hath the right sow by the ear" (Bailey, *Life of Fisher*, pp. 89–90; *cf.* Foxe, viii., 8). There is an *ex post facto* flavour about this story and it rests on no contemporary authority.

[2] See the itinerary of Henry VIII. in *L. and P.*, iv., 5965, and other

dered his presence in London necessary. He had other matters to occupy him, and the interval saw the fall of Wolsey and the preparation of those parliamentary measures which began the subjection of the Church in England to the royal supremacy and its consequent separation from Rome. "And," continues Morice, "after some special communication with the said Dr. Cranmer, the King retained him to write his mind in that his cause of divorcement, and committed him unto the Earl of Wiltshire, Queen Anne's father, to be entertained of him at Durham Place, where the Earl did lie, until he had penned his mind and opinion concerning the said cause."

With this task Cranmer was busy during December and January, and he is no doubt the "wonderfully virtuous and wise man," by whose counsels the King then described himself as being encouraged. Other steps were promptly taken to carry out his advice, and in November Dr. Richard Croke, the great Greek scholar, was sent to Italy to ransack libraries for writings which would tell in Henry's favour, and to secure the adhesion of noted doctors in the universities. As soon as Cranmer's book was completed, it was circulated, apparently in manuscript, among the leading dons of Cambridge, and he was himself sent down to reinforce by word of mouth the argu-

---

references to his progress during August–November. It is interesting to compare Foxe's account (*Acts and Monuments*, viii., 7) with his authority (*Narr. Ref.*, p. 242). Thus, Morice's "by and by" becomes, in Foxe "the next day, when the King removed to Greenwich," although in reality there intervened a month's residence at Windsor.

ments of his pen.[1] Both methods met with success; in one day he is said to have converted six or seven learned men who had hitherto been opposed to the divorce; and when, in February, Gardiner and Fox were urging the nomination of a committee of university scholars to determine the question, objection was raised to many of their nominees on the ground that they had already expressed approval of Cranmer's book.[2]

It does not appear that Cranmer had any part or lot in the manœuvres of the King's agents to obtain a favourable vote in Senate-house at Cambridge. He had been selected to accompany the Earl of Wiltshire,[3] Stokesley, afterwards Bishop of London, and Lee, afterwards Archbishop of York, on their embassy to the Pope and to the Emperor; and, though the ambassadors did not start, as has often been

[1] I find no mention of the book having been printed; Strype suggests that the treatise on the divorce in Cotton MS. Vespasian B. v., (Brit. Mus.), which is signed by Cranmer, is his original work (see Burnet, *Ref.*, ed. Pocock, i., 166; iv., 146–7; vii., 239). Pocock agrees with Strype, but the signature, Thomas *Cantuariensis*, could not have been written before 1533.

[2] *L. and P.*, iv., 6247.

[3] There is no evidence that Cranmer was ever chaplain to Anne Boleyn or her father; or that he was acquainted with the family before Henry VIII. quartered him on the Earl at Durham Place. Dr. Gairdner, who makes the assertion in his edition of Brewer (ii., 223), does not repeat it in his life of Cranmer in the *Dict. Nat. Biog.* (1888), though he does, without citing any authority, in his *History of the English Church* (1902), p. 137; he has himself pointed out Brewer's error in supposing that Cranmer was the Earl's chaplain who was employed in the divorce question in 1527–28 (cf. *L. and P.*, iv., 3638); the chaplain in question was John Barlow, possibly brother of the Bishop of St. Davids.

asserted,[1] in December, they left England late in January or early in February, 1530, before the matter came to a decision in the University. Soon after their departure the verdicts of Cambridge and Oxford in Henry's favour were sent after them to be laid before the Pope in the hope that some impression might be made upon his mind. The envoys utilised their presence in France to urge the French King to obtain similar decisions from the Sorbonne and other learned bodies in his dominions. Eventually, Paris and Orleans, Angers, Bourges, and Toulouse adopted Henry's view against the papal power to dispense; these votes were not obtained without some manipulation, but to represent them all as due to bribery is to accuse the pre-Reformation universities of a degree of corruption which the most zealous Protestant would scarcely believe to be possible. The truth is that the power of the Pope to dispense in such cases was, as Julius II. admitted, really a matter of doubt; and while individuals may have been bribed by Henry's agents on the one hand or by Charles's on the other, there is no more reason to question the honesty of the mass of the opinions given in Henry's favour than of those given against him.

Meanwhile the ambassadors proceeded by slow stages through France—it was beneath their dignity to travel "in post,"—and they were too late to witness

---

[1] *E. g.*, by Canon Mason, *Cranmer*, p. 16; nor was Cranmer, as his biographers have often assumed, formally accredited as one of the ambassadors; he was only attached to the embassy with special reference to the university business

the occasion on which for the last time in history a Holy Roman Emperor received his crown from the hands of a Pope. That ceremony took place at Bologna on 24 February, but it was the middle of March before Cranmer and his colleagues reached the city.[1] The Emperor was still there negotiating with Clement, and, appalled by the din of the Imperial arms, the Pope had no ears for requests from a distant king. Even when Charles was gone, his power remained: and though Clement repeatedly declared that he wished Henry would marry Anne Boleyn without further ado, and so relieve him of the responsibility for what might happen,[2] he would take no step which might expose him to the Emperor's wrath. So Wiltshire and Lee returned in the early summer to France, while Stokesley was left at Bologna to deal with the university there, and Cranmer joined Croke with a similar object at Venice. In view of the fact that the Emperor and the Pope had just rearranged the political map of Italy after their fancy, and that Clement had drawn up a bull prohibiting all doctors, notaries, and others, from maintaining the invalidity of Henry's marriage,[3] it is surprising that the English agents should have met with any success. Yet Ferrara, Bologna, and Padua determined in their favour, and in June Cranmer is said to have offered to debate the question with any doctor in Rome. Thence he wrote on 12

[1] Canon Mason thinks that they witnessed this ceremony, but on 12 March, Casale writes from Bologna, "The English ambassadors will be here to-morrow or the next day."—*L. and P.*, iv., 6268.

[2] *Ibid.*, iv., 6290; Le Grand, *Hist. du Divorce*, iii., 394.

[3] *L. and P.*, iv., 6279.

July, admitting that their success was small; they dared not attempt, he says, to know any man's mind, because of the Pope.[1] He did not escape the effects of the July climate at Rome, and lay there ill for a fortnight. On his recovery he returned to the charge with no better success than before. He wanted a papal brief in Henry's favour, but whenever the Pope made the slightest concession in the way of postponing an adverse decision, the Emperor's envoys made such an outcry, and so terrified him that the concession was quickly withdrawn.[2] Cranmer declared that he had never known such inconstancy; but this, we must recollect, was his first experience of Clement's diplomacy. Personally he seems to have made a favourable impression on the Pope, who paid him the compliment of appointing him Penitentiary for England. Finally Cranmer left Rome in September, bringing with him to England little result of his mission, except the votes of the Italian universities, the credit for which was disputed by Stokesley and Croke. The latter had been an old Cambridge friend of Cranmer's, and it is worth noting how highly Croke thought of Cranmer's influence with the King. He hopes that Henry will believe only Cranmer's version, and even sends his reports open to Cranmer, that he may determine whether or no they should be delivered to the King; he left "everything to Cranmer's discretion and friendship."[3]

[1] *L. and P.*, iv., 6531; Cranmer's letter is not extant; but it is quoted in one of Croke's to Henry VIII.

[2] *Ib.*, iv., 6543; Pocock, *Records*, i., 409. [3] *L. and P.*, iv., 6701.

There was now an apparent lull in the matter of the divorce. Parliament did not sit at all in the year 1530, and at Rome Henry contented himself with placing obstacles in the way of a decision which now could only be adverse; two years were consumed in discussing whether his agent should be admitted to plead that Henry could not be legally cited before the court. The time was not wasted in England; "nothing else," wrote a Florentine in London, "is thought of every day, except arranging affairs in such a way that they do no longer be in want of the Pope, neither for filling vacancies in the Church, nor for any other purpose." [1] While the Curia was debating technicalities, Henry VIII. was undermining the foundations of the papal power in England, and taking measures which would render the Pope's sentence a *brutum fulmen* whenever it might be given. Cranmer, however, had no share in the proceedings which ended in the King's being acknowledged by Convocation in 1531 as Supreme Head of the Church in England; he was not a member of that body, but seems to have been quietly employed in further probing the intricacies of the divorce case. Reginald Pole's treatise on the subject was submitted to him for examination in that year, and Cranmer reported that Pole's arguments were so skilfully marshalled and plausibly put that if the book were published, the minds of the people would be incontrovertibly fixed in hostility to the King's cause.[2] For his services he appears to have been rewarded with the

[1] *L. and P.*, iv., 6774.

[2] Strype, *Memorials of Cranmer*, App. I.

Archdeaconry of Taunton,[1] a town which by a curious coincidence was represented in Parliament by his friend and ally, Thomas Cromwell.[2] How far either of these two heroes of the English Reformation influenced the King at this time by private advice it is not possible to ascertain. Both were in frequent communication with their sovereign; but on the other hand, Henry VIII.'s policy after Wolsey's fall was mainly his own, and the general course of the Reformation was a perfectly natural development from existing circumstances, which it is idle to attribute to the influence of any one man.

Cranmer's quiet studies were soon interrupted. His colleagues in Italy had spoken very highly of his diplomatic abilities, and early in 1532, Henry, who was a shrewd judge of men, selected him for the post of ambassador to the Emperor Charles V.[3] He was expected to do his best to present the Divorce in as favourable a light as possible to the Emperor and his ministers, but more especially to

[1] Morice says "Deanery of Taunton in Devon," which is a singular mistake. Le Neve (*Fasti Eccl. Angl.*, i., 168,) makes Cranmer Archdeacon of Taunton from 1525 to 1533, but Gardiner held that office in 1529. Possibly Gardiner resigned it in 1531 when he was made Bishop of Winchester, and Cranmer succeeded him. The registers of Bath and Wells are silent on the matter.

[2] *Official Return of Members of Parliament*, i., 370.

[3] His instructions are dated 24 January, 1531 [-2], in them he is styled "consiliarius regis," which shows that he had been admitted a member of the King's ordinary council, a body to be carefully distinguished from the much smaller and more important Privy Council. The Privy Council was evolved out of the ordinary council much as the Cabinet has been evolved out of the now bulky and unmanageable Privy Council.

the Princes of Germany, whom he was secretly to sound with respect to a possible alliance between them and England; and he was to endeavour to obtain the repeal of some restrictions on trade between Englishmen and Charles V.'s subjects in the Netherlands. He joined the Imperial Court at Ratisbon, and soon found himself helpless as regards the last part of his instructions, because Charles left the determination of commercial affairs in the Low Countries in the hands of his prudent sister, Mary the Regent. In July he quietly repaired to the Court of Saxony, where the Elector, John Frederick, had recently succeeded his father; he was commissioned to assure the Elector and the Dukes of Lüneburg and Anhalt of assistance from Henry VIII. and Francis I. in their opposition to Charles V. Suggestions had also been made in the previous year that the two kings should extend similar protection to the Landgrave Philip of Hesse, the ablest of the German Protestant princes.[1] When these projects were formed the prospect of civil war in Germany seemed imminent; the Protestants had been condemned at the Diet of Augsburg in 1530, and Charles V. was threatening to reduce them by force of arms to obedience to himself and the Catholic Church, while they, in self-defence, had formed the Schmalkaldic League. But before Cranmer arrived at Ratisbon the situation had altered completely. The Turk was on the point of overrunning not only Hungary, but Germany; and the pressure of this peril forced the two parties together. To pur-

[1] *L. and P.*, v., 584.

chase the aid of the Protestant princes Charles made them such concessions at Nürnberg as to ensure, at any rate for the time, the peaceable exercise of their religion; and they were now more eager to show their zeal in defence of the fatherland than to turn their arms against their sovereign.[1] There were other obstacles to an understanding between Henry VIII. and the German Protestants: Henry disliked their view of the mass, and they disapproved of Henry's matrimonial conduct.

But if Cranmer brought away from Germany no advantageous alliance for England, he formed there a bond which, however much it may have increased his domestic felicity, proved a serious embarrassment at more than one stage in his public career. During the discussions with dukes and divines at Nürnberg, he was naturally thrown into contact with the eminent pastor of that Lutheran city, Osiander,[2] who, although he may be roughly described as a Lutheran, differed in several respects from the great Reformer, and favoured a definition of the doctrines of the Eucharist and Justification by Faith which would tend to reconcile them to some extent with Catholic views. His arguments were probably not without effect upon Cranmer's theological development; and

[1] Ranke, *Deutsche Geschichte im Zeitalter der Reformation*, iii., 413, etc.

[2] *Ibid.*, v., 449; *Allgemeine Deutsche Biographie*, xxiv., 473–483; Döllinger, *Reformation*, ii., 81–111; iii., 397–437. The humanists and continental reformers had a perfect passion for giving their names a classical form; thus Gerard became Erasmus, and Schwarzerd was translated into Melanchthon. Osiander's real name was Hosmer.

in his turn the English divine was able to convince Osiander of the invalidity of Henry's first marriage; he also persuaded the German to prosecute the labours on which he had long been engaged for the harmony of the four Gospels, and the volume was published in 1537 with a dedication to Cranmer.[1] In the course of his visits to Osiander's house Cranmer became attached to his host's niece, Margaret,[2] and he had apparently married her before he left the city. The step was a strong one, for Cranmer was now in priest's orders, and the canons of the Western Church strictly imposed upon priests the obligation of celibacy.[3] The authority of those canons was at the time being rudely shaken in England, but there was no indication that they would be so far overthrown as to permit the marriage of priests. On the other hand, neither Popes nor Kings had been in the habit of inquiring too closely into the private affairs of high-placed ecclesiastics. Wolsey had formed far less defensible unions, and Clement VII. himself was said at the time to have taken "two wives" with him to his interview with Francis I. at Marseilles.[4] The worst that Cranmer had to fear was that his morality might be likened to that of the Pope and the Cardinal.

Another of Cranmer's ambassadorial duties was to arrange with the Emperor the form which Henry's assistance against the Turks should take. Both the

---

[1] Strype, *Memorials of Cranmer*, i., 15.

[2] She is often erroneously called Anne, even by the lawyers at Cranmer's trial, and in the Parker Society's *Works*.

[3] Canon Mason, *Cranmer*, p. 25.

[4] *L. and P.*, vi., 1147.

English and French kings were bound by treaty to join in the defence of Christendom, but there was usually an easy method of escape from such obligations. Henry and Francis would only offer men, and Charles would only take money; and before the difference was adjusted the retreat of the Turks and the disbanding of the Emperor's army relieved the immediate necessity. Cranmer followed the Imperial forces from Ratisbon to Vienna in September, and from Vienna to Villach in October. On the way he visited the scene of the battle between the Turks and the Imperial forces, and he noted in his letters[1] many things which might enlighten his master on the condition of the Emperor's power in Germany and the prospect of his becoming a dangerous foe. His Italian and Spanish troops did more damage, says Cranmer, than the Turks themselves; they spread desolation far and wide along their march; and so disgusted were the "boors" that they gathered in the mountains and fell upon the troops and killed them whenever opportunity offered.[2] Neither Charles nor his brother Ferdinand[3] was beloved in the country, and the Emperor had lost the esteem of military men by his failure to prosecute his advantage over the Turks and free his brother's kingdoms from their ravages.

[1] Cranmer, *Works* (Parker Soc.), ii., 231–236.

[2] *Ibid.*, ii., 234; for the ravages committed by troops in Germany compare Sastrow, *Social Germany in Luther's Time*, tr. Vandam, 1902.

[3] Ferdinand, already King of Bohemia and Hungary, had recently been elected King of the Romans, and his elevation was disliked by other German princes.

Cranmer dated the last of these letters on 20 October from Villach in Carinthia, whence the Emperor was to cross the Alps and again interview Clement VII. on his way to Spain. He got as far as Mantua, but before that second meeting at Bologna took place he had received his recall to England. Warham, Archbishop of Canterbury, had died in August, and Cranmer was destined to be his successor. Gardiner, perhaps, might have had the office but for his opposition to Henry in the parliamentary session of the previous spring; and the knowledge embittered the relations between the two men for the rest of their lives.

Much has been made of this sudden promotion to the archbishopric of Canterbury of one who had at best only held an archdeaconry; but the fact has been overlooked that the preferment of many of the greatest primates of England has been equally rapid.[1] Of Cranmer's predecessors, Becket, Winchelsey, and Islip were only archdeacons; Langton and Meopham were only canons; Kilwardby and Peckham were only priors; Bradwardine was chancellor of St. Paul's, and Wethershed of Lincoln, when they were raised to the Metropolitan See. It had been the exception rather than the rule for a bishop to be translated to Canterbury; and so far as his previous preferment was concerned, Cranmer's promotion could be justified by numerous precedents. Nor does it appear that a better choice could have been made with regard to personal qualities; the only living churchman with whom Cranmer could be compared in intellect was Pole, and Pole, who had already refused the

[1] See Le Neve, *Fasti Eccl. Angl.*, ed. Hardy.

archbishopric of York, was out of the question. The real objection was not to Cranmer's person, but to the policy which he pursued.

Warham is said to have foretold that Cranmer would step into his shoes,[1] but to the new archbishop himself the nomination came as a somewhat unpleasant surprise. A man of strong domestic affections, he feared separation from the wife he had recently married; and there is no reason to doubt his assertion that he protracted his return journey to England in the vain hope that Henry would in the meantime change his mind.[2] Henry, however, soon had private reasons for hastening on Cranmer's election, confirmation by the Pope, and consecration. As Queen Elizabeth was born on 7 September, 1533, Anne Boleyn's pregnancy was no doubt known to the King in January of that year. It was important to save her character as far as was possible, and still more important that her issue should be legitimate according to England's laws, which by hook or by crook must be made to suit the circumstances. On or about St. Paul's Day, 25 January, Henry and Anne were privately married; but that was not enough without an authoritative declaration of the nullity of the King's previous union with Catherine of Aragon. It was hopeless to expect such a favour from Clement VII., but it might be obtained from an Archbishop of Canterbury.

[1] Nicholas Harpsfield, *A Treatise on the Pretended Divorce* (Camden Soc., 1878), p. 178.

[2] He took seven weeks over it, when it might easily have been accomplished in three; see report of his trial in Foxe, viii., 55.

Even that was not sufficient without a legal recognition of the Archbishop's Court as the supreme and final court of English ecclesiastical jurisdiction.

These were the objects which Henry VIII. pursued in the spring of 1532 with consummate skill and audacity. Cranmer reached England in January, 1533; the usual practice of leaving rich bishoprics vacant for at least a year in order that their revenues might in the interval accrue to the Crown was abandoned, and Cranmer became Archbishop-elect of Canterbury. To meet his expenses Henry lent him a thousand pounds, and intimated pretty forcibly to the Pope that he must grant Cranmer his bulls at once and without the usual fees. Clement must have known the purpose for which the bulls were wanted, and it seems amazing that Henry should have made such demands, and still more so that they should have been granted. But the English King knew his business; in the previous year he had with some difficulty induced Parliament to leave it to him whether the Act of Annates should be put in force or not [1];

[1] This astute provision was embodied in the Act at Henry's personal instance; Chapuys (*L. and P.*, v., 879) relates how the King went down to Parliament three times to pass "the article about the Annates," and Giles de la Pomeroy, the French envoy, speaks of his cunning in persuading Parliament to leave the execution of the Act to him; his letter, although printed under the right date in Froude, ed., 1893, i., 354, has been erroneously placed in Dr. Gairdner's *Letters and Papers*, under the year 1531, instead of 1532 (*Ibid.*, v., 150). It is pretended that the royal pressure was needed to get the general principle of the Act through Parliament; but it is much more probable that it was needed to ensure the enactment of this particular clause, which constituted a remarkable extension of the royal authority.

and the persuasive he now applied to the Pope was the hint that refusal would cost him the First-fruits of all English benefices. The Pope and the Cardinals sighed, but after all it was better that they should go without some of their perquisites for Cranmer's bulls; it was better that sentence should be given by him against Catherine of Aragon than that the Roman curia should forfeit all the wealth it drew from England. So on 21 February, in spite of the efforts of Chapuys, who sent an envoy to the Pope to warn him against Cranmer, the bulls were sped with unwonted celerity.

The lever placed in Henry's hands by the Act of Annates was used for other purposes. It served to make the Pope and his ministers adopt an attitude of apparent friendliness to England, and it was actually under this appearance of concord that the Act forbidding appeals to Rome was passed in 1533. Henry was pleasing the Pope, not only by withholding his consent to the Act of Annates, but by opposing a General Council which Clement feared above everything else,[1] and which Charles V. was demanding as part of his compact with the German Protestants. Clement, moreover, was bribed by the French offer of marriage between his niece, Catherine de Medici, and the future Henry II., and he seemed about to desert the Emperor's cause.[2] Catherine of Aragon's friends in England were furious; they cursed Charles for being so slack in her defence, and

[1] A proposal was threatened for the restoration of the Papal States to the Emperor. *L. and P.*, vi., 212.

[2] *Ibid.*, vi., 296.

they cursed especially the Pope for expediting Cranmer's bulls and delaying the sentence in Catherine's favour. Henry took the papal nuncio down to Parliament to advertise the excellent terms upon which he stood with the Holy See[1]; and he even told the unsuspicious priest that, although his studies on the subject of papal authority had caused him to retract his early defence of the Pope, yet Clement might perhaps give him occasion to probe the matter further still and reconfirm what he had originally written![2] Of course this was all a piece of clever and not very scrupulous bluff, but political morality has always been a tender plant, and it was frail indeed in the sixteenth century. The means were none the less successful; the appearance of concord between Henry and the Pope disheartened the opponents of the Act of Appeals and its passage left the King master of the situation in England. Clement had confirmed an Archbishop who would assuredly decide the divorce case in Henry's favour, and Parliament had made it illegal to appeal from his decision.

On 30 March Cranmer was consecrated. Four days before, he had drawn up a formal protest to the effect that he considered the oath of obedience to the Pope, which he would take at his consecration, a form and not a reality, and that he did not intend to bind himself to do anything contrary to the King and commonwealth of England, or to restrain his

[1] *L. and P.*, vi., 89: "Many think there is a secret agreement between the King and the Pope," cf. vi., 142.

[2] *Ibid.*, vi., 296

liberty in things pertaining to the reformation of the Christian religion and the government of the Church of England.[1] At his trial this protest was represented as a scandalous act, amounting to perjury.[2] It was due rather to an excess of scruple on Cranmer's part. Most men would have taken the oath without question, thinking that any future Act of Parliament repudiating the papal jurisdiction would be a sufficient release from its obligations.[3] Cranmer was not satisfied with this; he foresaw that England would throw off its allegiance to Rome, and he determined that there should be no misconception as to his own action. It was, however, necessary that he should take the oath, because it had been the law, or at least the custom, so to do, and it was doubtful whether he could be regarded as a properly constituted Archbishop unless he fulfilled all the prescribed formalities. The contention that all who had sworn obedience to the Holy See should always and in all circumstances be bound by their oath was a convenient weapon in the hands of

[1] Jenkyns, *Cranmer*, iv., 247 etc.; *L. and P.*, vi., 291; Dixon, *Hist. Church of England*, i., 158.

[2] Foxe, viii., 55; "He made a protestation one day, to keep never a whit of that he would swear the next day."

[3] If he had quietly said nothing, his action would, according to the arguments of his enemies at his trial, have been justifiable. In defending their own conduct in swearing the oath of royal Supremacy and then repudiating it, they declared that a bad oath should not be kept. So that Cranmer might have sworn the oath to the Pope which he believed bad, and then broken it without guilt. The guilt apparently consisted in declaring intentions which should have been kept secret (*cf.* Jenkyns, iv., 87-89).

Popes,[1] but no one had done more to weaken the force of oaths by their frequent grants of absolution. Such a contention would indeed tend to stereotype political and ecclesiastical conditions, and the state of the world would present a curious aspect to-day if at any period in its history oaths of allegiance had become perpetually binding. They are, in fact, feeble expedients which in public affairs are considered binding only so long as convenient; they never alter the course of events, and under the circumstances the counsel of perfection is undoubtedly "Swear not at all." Cranmer, however, had no alternative, and while his conduct afforded his prosecutors too good a forensic opportunity to be lost, it need not materially affect his judgment at the bar of history.

Twelve days after his consecration Cranmer wrote to the King, humbly begging for licence to proceed with the trial of the question between him and Catherine.[2] He gave as a reason for haste the murmurs of the people, but the real reason was the condition of Anne Boleyn. The way had been already prepared by Convocation, which had assented to

[1] The more enlightened of the Fathers who assembled at the Council of Trent insisted that no reformation of the Papacy was possible unless members of the council were released from their oaths to the Pope, and their assertion was justified by the event. Rigid observance of these oaths would have made the Reformation impossible in every country that recognised the Pope's authority. *La petite morale est l'ennemi de la grande.* If the oath had been sworn to an enemy of the Pope he could have dispensed with Cranmer's obligation to keep it, as he did in the case of Francis I. in 1526; but the morality of an action does not really depend upon the question whether it is licensed or not by the Pope.

[2] Cranmer, *Works* (Parker Soc.), ii., 237.

two propositions: first, that as a matter of law the Pope had no authority to permit marriages between a man and his deceased brother's wife when the previous union had been consummated; and, secondly, that as a matter of fact the marriage between Prince Arthur and Catherine of Aragon had been so consummated.[1] All Cranmer had to do was to act upon the decision of the Church in England, and Convocation must share with him the responsibility. He opened his court in May at Dunstable, some four miles from Ampthill, in Bedfordshire, where Catherine was then residing. She was duly summoned to appear,[2] but she refused to recognise Cranmer's jurisdiction, and was declared contumacious. That suited the court very well; the case was quietly hurried on, and sentence was given on the 23rd.[3] It was a mere repetition of the decree of Convocation; the marriage of Henry and Catherine was declared to have been void from the beginning, because the Pope did not possess the dispensing powers he claimed.

Five days later Cranmer pronounced, at Lambeth, that the King's marriage with Anne Boleyn was valid. Assuming the correctness of the previous decision, that Henry had never been married to Catherine, there was no reason for this second declaration except to quiet the popular mind. But the vagueness of the Archbishop's sentence spoilt its effect; it afforded no information as to the date or manner of the marriage, and to this day it remains

[1] *L. and P.*, vi., 311, 317, 491.

[2] Cranmer, *Works*, ii., 241, 244.

[3] *L. and P.*, vi., 469, 470, 525; *cf.* Burnet, i., 220–221.

a matter of mystery.[1] Almost immediately afterwards, on Whitsunday, the first of June, Cranmer crowned Anne Boleyn as Queen in Westminster Abbey.[2] The coronation feast was celebrated with no little splendour, but Anne's enjoyment of it was sadly marred by the state of her health.[3] Three months later she gave birth, at Greenwich Palace, to the future Queen Elizabeth, and it accorded well with the fitness of things that the first Metropolitan of the Reformed Church of England stood as godfather[4] to the infant under whose guidance the cause of the Reformation finally triumphed.

[1] The only original authority for the date of the marriage is Cranmer's statement in a letter of 17 June, 1533, to the effect that it took place "about S. Paul's day last" *i. e.*, 25 January (Cranmer, *Works*, ed. Parker Society, ii., 246; Ellis, *Original Letters*, 1st Ser., ii., 33-34; *Harleian MS*, 6148, f. 33; *Archæologia*, xviii., 78; Todd, *Life of Cranmer*, i., 80). Stow, in his *Annals*, p. 533, gives this date, but Hall, who is followed by Holinshed, gives 14 November, 1532. This antedating of the marriage was probably intended to shield Anne's character; Burnet (*Hist. Reformation*, ed. Pocock, i., 218) argues from the date of Elizabeth's birth, that Anne must have been married by the beginning of December, "for," he says, "all the writers of both sides agree that she was married before she conceived with child." This is a particularly reckless statement on Burnet's part. Nor is it known who performed the ceremony Chapuys, the imperial ambassador, reported as early as 23 February (*L. and P.*, vii., 180) that Cranmer was the priest, but the Archbishop himself (*Works*, ii., 246) denounces the rumour as false, and says he did not know of the marriage until a fortnight after the ceremony.

[2] See the description in *Tudor Tracts*, ed. A. F. Pollard, 1903, pp. 10-28.

[3] *L. and P.*, vii., 584, 601.

[4] Elizabeth was born on Sunday, 7 September, and baptised by Stokesley, Bishop of London, on the following Wednesday. Shakespeare (*Henry VIII.*, Act V., sc. i.) represents the birth as taking place in the night, but it was between 3 and 4 P M. (*Ib.*, vii., 1111.)

QUEEN ELIZABETH.

FROM THE PICTURE AT ST. JAMES PALACE.

CHAPTER III

CRANMER AND THE ROYAL SUPREMACY

"I PROTEST before you all," affirmed Cranmer at his trial, "there was never a man came more unwillingly to a bishopric than I."[1] "For the Passion of God," wrote another famous prelate[2] to a friend at Court when about to be offered an episcopal See, "if it be possible yet, assay as far as you may to convey this bishopric from me"; and he signed his letter "Yours to his little power. Add whatsoever you will more to it, so you add not bishop." Twenty years later this same divine was suggested for the Archbishopric of Canterbury, but even this splendid temptation failed to move him from his attitude of *nolo episcopari*. Parker was as loath to accept the primacy from Queen Elizabeth as Cranmer had been from her father[3]; and when Latimer

[1] Foxe, viii., 55.

[2] *L. and P.*, XIV., ii., 501. Todd, *Deans of Canterbury*, p. 4. The writer was Nicholas Wotton, Dean of both the primatial cathedrals, doctor of both laws (canon and civil), and reputed professor of both creeds, Catholic and Protestant, He kept his preferment in the reigns of Henry VIII., Edward VI., Mary, and Elizabeth (see art. by the present writer in *Dict. Nat. Biog.*, lxiii., 57–60).

[3] *Parker's Correspondence* (Parker Soc.), p. 70.

discarded his rochet in 1539 he danced for joy at the thought of his freedom[1]; not all the pressure of the Court nor even a petition from the House of Commons could induce him to resume his episcopal garb in the reign of Edward VI.

Seldom, indeed, has an episcopal career offered fewer attractions than during the sixteenth century. The possession of place without power is purgatory to all but ignoble minds, and lack of power was only one of the hardships which fell to the lot of Henry's bishops; others were provided by the prison and the stake. But men of spirit could face fetters and flames with greater dignity than they could sit on a throne, erstwhile that of Augustine, but now the footstool of him who wielded the sceptre of England. The Church had fallen from her high estate; the mighty institution which had humbled emperors in the dust was become the handmaid of princes. The successor of him, who had stood as a suppliant three days in the snow at Canossa, had with impunity sacked the Holy City and held the Vicar of Christ as his prisoner; and the Archbishop of Canterbury had sunk into the position of a minister of a spiritual jurisdiction which belonged to the King.

This revolution was already effected before Cranmer was elected to the Metropolitan See; it only needed some legal formalities to give it complete recognition. No one can really be satisfied with the theory that this *peripeteia* was solely due to the violence, avarice, and lust of a single man. The phen-

[1] Foxe, vii., 463.

omenon was not peculiar to one, but common to almost all the nations of Europe; priests were not more hated in England than they were in Germany, and the secularisation of church property proceeded apace even in Catholic countries. The Church of England was painfully servile to Henry VIII., but it never licensed bigamy, as Clement VII. proposed to do at Rome, and as Luther and Melanchthon did in Germany. The subordination of Church to State was in the sixteenth century a common characteristic rather than a distinguishing feature, and it is therefore idle to seek its explanation in purely local circumstances like the temper of Henry VIII.

There had for many hundreds of years been an unceasing struggle in every country between the civil and the ecclesiastical power. In England the Church reached the zenith of its influence during the thirteenth century; and from the legislation of Edward I. it had gradually declined until the Wycliffite movement, with its appeal to the State to purify a corrupt Church, seemed likely to anticipate some of the most striking effects of the Reformation. But the alliance between the Lancastrian monarchs and the Church, the emancipation of the Popes from their Babylonish captivity at Avignon, and their victory over the Conciliar movement delayed the decisive hour; and then the Wars of the Roses interposed another obstacle in the path of reform. The main result of that struggle was an enormous increase of royal power. Feudal aristocracy committed political suicide, and even the House of Commons maimed itself for generations. Henry VII. completed the process. His most effective method of strengthening his position was the elimination of all alternative governments, and pretenders were removed by force or by fraud, while the remaining feudal lords were converted into Tudor officials or relegated to obscurity.

But his astute policy would have been vain without the co-operation of powerful secular tendencies. The amazing geographical discoveries extending throughout the fifteenth century, and the consequent impetus given to commerce diverted men's minds from the pursuit of political ends to the prosecution of personal gain, and a community bent on trade is more interested in strong government than in self-government. The simultaneous revival of learning, and particularly the study of Roman civil law, added fresh dignity to the name of Prince; common law and feudal custom, both of them checks on royal despotism, became barbarous in the eyes of men who were fascinated with the symmetry of the Code and its scientific maxims of despotism. To promote the study of the Roman civil law was an object dear to all the Tudors; their officials were mostly civilians, and the Roman law, which was adopted far and wide on the Continent, and even in Scotland, was almost received into England.[1] It was a weapon which kings could use against canon and common law, against papal and popular claims. To Roman emperors divine honours were paid after death, and to Tudor sovereigns honours

[1] Professor F. W. Maitland, *English Law and the Renaissance*, 1901; *Eng. Hist. Rev.*, xv., 168–169.

too near the divine were rendered while they lived. No poet before the age of the Tudors would have thought of the "divinity" which "doth hedge a king," and a great French historian has described the sixteenth-century sovereign as a kind of new Messiah.[1] He was the embodiment of the fresh national aspirations which had ousted the universal and cosmopolitan ideals of the Middle Ages, and intense loyalty to the King left little room for the old allegiance to the Church.

The last reinforcement the King received was from the Reformation itself. The voice of the Church, which exalted the Pope but slighted the King, gave way to the Scriptures, which knew nothing of Popes or Archbishops, but were emphatic about the claims of secular princes. In the Old Testament kings rather than priests were the Lord's Anointed. In the New, resistance to authority was pronounced a heinous offence, and the powers that be were derived from divine ordination. Cranmer's political theory resembled that of St. Paul. Luther long regarded Charles V. as the lineal successor of the Cæsar whose authority Christ had recognised; and when he gave up his faith in Charles he transferred it to his territorial sovereign, the Elector of Saxony, and preached an unlimited passive obedience. The divine right of kings was a Reformation theory.

Parallel with this extraordinary growth of the royal prestige and power there went a corresponding

[1] Michelet, *Histoire de France*, ed. 1879, ix., 301. (Chap. xii.), *Le Nouveau Messie est le roi.*

decline in clerical influence. Externally the Church stood erect, robed in its old magnificence; papal pretensions were never louder nor clerical privileges more exorbitant than at the dawn of the sixteenth century; and it was a novel extension of ecclesiastical abuses which precipitated the conflict at Wittenberg. But it was then with the Church as it was with the French monarchy on the eve of the Revolution; both had monopolised power only to be crushed by its weight; and while the imposing edifice seemed to grow in height, its foundations in the hearts and understandings of men were slowly rotting away. The debasement of clerical morals, the corruption of papal courts, the immunity of clerical criminals, the wealth of the clergy, their exactions from the laity, and the oppressiveness of their jurisdiction had made the Church more unpopular than it had been before or has been since.[1] One of the first uses to which the printing-press was put was to satirise and denounce the clergy; and whether the accusations contained in this popular literature were substantially true or not, they prove that the Church had lost its hold upon the affections of men. These grievances found their first and freest utterance in Germany. They were equally felt in England, but in England there was a strong central government, which, for the moment, was guided by clerical hands.

During the first few years of Henry VIII.'s reign his chief advisers were Bishops Fox and Ruthal, and

[1] See *Cambridge Modern History*, vol. i., chap. xix., by H. C. Lea, for a brief but admirable statement of these grievances.

Archbishop Warham ; presently they were eclipsed by Wolsey's rising star, which ruled the ascendant for fifteen years. By keeping Parliament at a distance and by playing upon the vain young King's Continental ambitions, Wolsey staved off the attack on the Church. But his power was built on a vanishing base. The Treaty of Cambrai in 1529 closed the avenues to England's influence abroad, and made Henry's gaze introspective. It was as great a blow to Wolsey as his failure to obtain a divorce for his master,[1] and he was too great a statesman not to perceive what would be the effect. His failure in foreign policy would mean his fall, and his fall, as he repeatedly told Campeggio, Du Bellay, and Clement VII., would mean the irretrievable ruin of the Church in England.[2] It was owing, wrote Campeggio, to Wolsey's vigilance and solicitude that the Holy See retained its authority[3]; and Du Bellay declared on the eve of Wolsey's fall that the intention was, as soon as he was gone, to attack the Church and to confiscate its riches ; he wrote the information in cipher, but said that such a precaution was really superfluous, because the policy was openly proclaimed. He thought no ecclesiastic would again be made Chancellor, and predicted "terrible alarms" for the Church in the coming Parliament.[4]

It is, therefore, perfectly obvious that the anti-

[1] *L. and P.*, iv., 5231, 5581, 5679, 5701; and compare the present writer's *Henry VIII.*, chapter iv.

[2] *Ibid.*, iv., 4897, 5210, 5572, 5803, 5945.

[3] *Ibid.*, iv., 4898.

[4] *Ibid.*, iv., 6011, *cf.* iv., 5862, 5953, 5983, 5995, 6017–18.

ecclesiastical legislation of the Reformation Parliament was no mere whim on the part of Henry VIII., or chance suggestion on the part of any adviser[1]; it was so far dictated by circumstances that intelligent observers could predict its general tenor before that Parliament met. Wolsey fell, as he himself and others had foretold, and with him clerical influence was eliminated from the Government. The Chancellorship, which from time immemorial had been held by prelates,[2] was, as Du Bellay anticipated, entrusted to a layman, Sir Thomas More. The keepership of the Privy Seal, which had been occupied in Henry VIII.'s reign by three successive bishops, was now transferred to Anne Boleyn's father; the clerkship of Parliament, hitherto considered as peculiarly a clerical office, was given to Sir Edward North; and, though Gardiner remained Secretary, Du Bellay thought that his influence would have been much enhanced had he abandoned his spiritual

[1] In Mr. R. B. Merriman's *Life and Letters of Cromwell* (1902, chap. vi.) the credit or discredit of the whole business is attributed to Cromwell, mainly on the strength of Pole's assertion that Henry VIII. was despairing of success when this "emissary of Satan" came and suggested to him the repudiation of the Pope's authority. But Pole was writing nine or ten years after the event; he admits that he did not hear Cromwell's alleged advice to the King, and before the interview is supposed to have taken place we are told in a contemporary letter that "nothing else was thought of every day in England except to arrange how to do without the Pope." (*L. and P.*, iv., 6774.) A biographer is often tempted to attribute great movements to the influence of one subordinate agent.

[2] The only lay chancellor in the previous two centuries appears to have been Thomas Beaufort, chancellor 1410–12, and afterwards Duke of Exeter.

calling.[1] The Government thus assumed an unwonted lay complexion; at the same time it was brought into harmony with the spirit which animated the House of Commons, while the simultaneous creation of half a dozen peers tended to equalise the temporal and spiritual vote in the House of Lords.[2]

Parliament began its work in November, 1529, with bills to limit clerical fees for probate, to check the abuse of pluralities and non-residence, and to forbid the acquisition of breweries and tanneries by the clergy. These modest proposals at once provoked the cry of "The Church in danger!", as it had been provoked in 1512 by a proposal to exempt spiritual persons below the rank of subdeacon from the "benefit of clergy" if they had committed murder or felony.[3] "My Lords," cried Bishop Fisher, "you see daily what bills come hither from the Commons' House, and all is to the destruction of the Church. For God's sake, see what a realm the kingdom of Bohemia was; and when the Church went down, then fell the glory of that kingdom. Now with the Commons is nothing but 'Down with the Church!' And all this, meseemeth, is for lack of faith only."[4] The bills were rejected by means of the spiritual votes in the House of Lords; and as a

[1] *L. and P.*, iv., 6019.

[2] *Cf.*, J. H. Round, *Peerage Studies*, 1901, pp. 330–366. Mr. Round, in contending that the lay peers had a majority as early as 1534, neglects the fact that several of the lay peers were minors, and so could not vote, while a spiritual peer was never a minor.

[3] *L. and P.*, II., i., 1313.

[4] Hall, *Chronicle*, p. 766.

way out of the deadlock between the two Houses, Henry suggested a conference, in which the temporal peers, united with the Commons, outvoted the bishops and abbots and passed the bills.[1] In 1531, Convocation was compelled, under the threat of *Præmunire*, to pay a large fine to the King and to give him the title "Supreme Head of the Church." Even in those degenerate days the proposal excited resistance, and the papal nuncio went down to stiffen the backs of the clergy. But it was all of no avail; Archbishop Warham declared that *ira principis mors est*,[2] and Convocation had to content itself with the qualifying clause, "as far as the law of Christ allows." It was, thought Chapuys, the Imperial ambassador, an empty phrase, for no one would venture to dispute with the King the question where his supremacy ended and that of Christ began.[3]

In 1532 the Act forbidding the payment of Annates to Rome was passed, and the famous petition of the Commons against the clergy was presented.[4] On the assumption that there were no real abuses in the Church at that time, and that all the evidence of their existence is necessarily a false and malicious

[1] Stubbs, *Seventeen Lectures*, ed. 1887, p. 317.

[2] *L. and P.*, vol. v., p. 137.

[3] *Ibid.*, v., No. 105.

[4] There are four drafts of this petition in the Record Office (see *L. and P.*, v., 1016); one of them is printed in full by Mr. Merriman (*Life of Cromwell*, i., 104–111). Two of the drafts are in a strange handwriting, probably that of some independent member of Parliament; these are filled with interlineations in Cromwell's hand, and it is probably from them that he prepared a copy to be submitted to the King.

libel, this petition has been represented as a Court concoction prepared to facilitate the evil designs of the King; and the Commons are supposed to have been hypnotised into the belief that they suffered from grievances which were entirely fictitious. However that may be, two sets of demands were laid before Convocation; one came from the King, the other was the petition of the Commons. Henry wished the Church to abdicate its right of independent legislation, to consent to a reform of ecclesiastical laws, and to recognise the necessity of the King's approval of existing canons. On the other hand the Commons complained of the citation of laymen out of their dioceses, the delays in obtaining probate and in the institution of parsons, the conferment of benefices on minors, the devotion of the clergy to worldly affairs, the exaction of heavy fees, and the harsh procedure of the spiritual courts in cases of heresy. These reforms were granted by Convocation; most of them passed the House of Commons; but in the House of Lords, the bishops and abbots, aided by Sir Thomas More, rejected the demands of the King, while accepting those of the Commons. Before the end of the year Audley succeeded More as Chancellor, Cromwell stepped into Gardiner's shoes as Henry's chief adviser, and the lay element had become supreme in the Government, in both Houses of Parliament, and in the country at large. The Church in England had been forced into that dependence on the State from which she has never since been able or willing to shake herself free.

Such were the conditions under which Cranmer accepted the archiepiscopal See, and they must be taken into careful consideration in judging his action and in estimating his character. Apart from his adoption of the principles of the Reformation, which can only be a defect in the eyes of Roman Catholics, the worst suspicion under which he labours is that of having been in some sort a traitor to his order, of having handed over to secular hands the keys of ecclesiastical independence. The surrender of a position to the enemy is always an unpopular act, but it may in certain circumstances be necessary and patriotic. If the city is beleaguered without hope of succour, if the refusal to yield only means that it will be stormed and left to the uncovenanted mercies of the foe, the commander who takes upon himself the responsibility of capitulation is braver than he who declines. There can be no doubt that the Church in England, however distasteful the process may have been, was consulting both its own interests and those of the nation at large in seeking to come to terms with the secular power, and in endeavouring, by the surrender of its least tenable rights and privileges, to retain as much as might be of its catholicity and its connection with the past. It may be asserted that, had Warham been a Becket, had the whole Church been animated with a spirit of firm resistance, it might have withstood the assault. But it is far more probable that its ruin would have been more irretrievable, its break with the past more complete. The course of the Reformation in England might then have followed more closely its course in Germany or even in Switzerland; and so far from seeking only to remove abuses, men might have set themselves to raise a new edifice upon other foundations. The result would have probably been to kindle the flames of civil wars of religion.

Further, it must be observed that it was not Cranmer who handed over the keys at all, but the prelate whom Roman Catholic writers describe as the "saintly and venerable Warham."[1] It was he who persuaded Convocation to acknowledge the royal supremacy, and he did so with less justification than Cranmer might have urged. For Warham believed the royal supremacy to be an evil; Cranmer thought it a good. Just before his death the aged Archbishop drew up a protest against the recent infractions of ecclesiastical immunities[2]; he recalled the case of Henry II. and hinted that Henry VIII. might go the way of other kings who had violated the liberties of the Church. Cranmer's view was different; he was profoundly impressed with the abuses in the Church, which for years he had ascribed to the papal jurisdiction. The only means of reform was the royal supremacy. He thought, as the vast majority of English churchmen have thought after him, that the Church gained more than it lost through its connection with the State, and he was not so foolish as to quarrel with the conditions upon which alone that connection was possible. These conditions had been laid down by others, and for them he

---

[1] Gasquet, *Henry VIII. and the Monasteries*, 1893, i., 67

[2] *L. and P.*, v., 1247.

was not responsible. He entered upon his archiepiscopal career knowing perfectly well that his mission was to be, as Henry expressed it, "the principal minister of *our* spiritual jurisdiction."[1] With that condition, he would, even if he disliked it, be forced to comply; the King who had broken Wolsey without an effort, and afterwards sent a Cardinal to the block, would not be deterred by Cranmer.

For the present, however, the abolition of the papal jurisdiction added dignity to the Archbishopric of Canterbury. When, in 1544, the Archbishop of York died, Cranmer assumed a function hitherto exercised by Popes, and sent his successor a pall.[2] This was a solitary instance of the adoption by an English Archbishop of an expedient employed by the Popes to enhance their authority and fill their coffers[3]; but primates of England retained for a longer period the right of issuing dispensations and licences which previously belonged to the Roman pontiff; they were found useful in releasing Henry VIII. from inconvenient matrimonial bonds. For a year, too, the Archbishop's court remained the supreme tribunal in England for ecclesiastical causes, but its authority was soon limited by the legalisation of appeals from it to Chancery, and by the transference to secular courts of matters which had before been regarded as subject

[1] *L. and P.*, vi., 332.

[2] Bishop Stubbs in *Gentleman's Magazine*, 1860, ii., 522; Mason, *Cranmer*, p. 53.

[3] Pole was the last Archbishop of Canterbury to wear the pall (*cf.* Burnet, ii., 545); it was an object of frequent denunciation (*cf.* Pilkington, *Works*, p. 582, and Gough, *Index to Parker Soc. Publ.* s. v. "Pall").

to ecclesiastical jurisdiction. Henry VIII. even meditated placing the marriage laws under the cognisance of civil tribunals,[1] but many generations passed away before this very modern idea was put into execution.

Meanwhile the King's presumption in cutting the Gordian knot of the divorce question by having it decided in England roused Clement VII. to action; and on 11 July, 1533, the sentence of excommunication was drawn up at Rome,[2] though its publication was deferred. Henry thereupon withdrew his ambassadors from the papal court, confirmed the Act of Annates, and prepared an appeal from the Pope to a General Council. Clement, at last, was alarmed; he began to fear that he really would lose his spiritual jurisdiction in England; and he probably derived little comfort from the assurances of his Imperialist friends that, after all, England was but "an unprofitable island," and that its loss would be more than compensated by the increased devotion of Spain and of the other dominions of the Emperor.[3] The appeal to a General Council was served on the Pope by Bonner[4] on 7 November, while Clement was visiting Francis I. at Marseilles[5]; and Cranmer was advised to intimate a similar appeal in case the Pope should "make some manner of prejudicial process against me and my Church."[6] He accord-

[1] *L. and P.*, v., 805; vii., 232.

[2] *Ibid.*, vi., 654–655, 807, 953.

[3] *Ibid.*, vi., 997.

[4] The future Bishop of London and champion of the Pope.

[5] *L. and P.*, vi., 721, 998.

[6] Strype, *Memorials of Cranmer*, i., 31–32; Cranmer, *Works*, ii., 268.

ingly wrote to Bonner to ask him to do this service: but as the letter was not dated till 27 November, Cranmer's appeal was too late.[1] His apprehensions were well founded, for he was doubtless one of the bishops whom the Pope "cursed" in the summer for their share in the divorce,[2] and in September a brief was drawn up for his deprivation and excommunication.[3]

Henry's action in appealing to a General Council dashed the hopes which Francis I. entertained of effecting an accommodation between his old ally, England, and his new friend, the Pope.[4] He made, however, another effort by sending Du Bellay, Bishop of Paris, to London in the winter to induce Henry to resume negotiations with the papal court. Henry would only promise that if Clement would declare his first marriage null and his second valid, he would refrain from further measures against the Pope's authority. With these assurances the Bishop set out for Rome, and Burnet has a story,[5] told on the authority of Du Bellay's brother, of how a reconciliation between England and Rome was only frustrated by the precipitation of the Imperialist cardinals, who refused to wait a few extra days for

---

[1] *L. and P.*, vi., 1425; Burnet, *Reformation*, ed. Pocock, vol. vi., pp. 56–67. The Pope left Marseilles for Rome on 12 November.

[2] *L. and P.*, vi., 1055.

[3] *Ibid.*, vi., 1104.

[4] "Ye have clearly marred all," he complained to the English ambassadors; "as fast as I study to win the Pope, you study to lose him" (*ibid.*, vi., 1427).

[5] Burnet, *Reformation*, ed. Pocock, iii., 182–83; Du Bellay, *Mémoires*; cf. *L. and P.*, vol. vii., App. Nos. 8, 12, 13.

the return of a courier. Burnet discerns the hand of Providence in this narrow escape from peace with Rome; but in reality the promise of peace was quite illusory, and Parliament was at the moment engaged in severing the last of the bonds between the English Church and the Roman See. Henry had, in fact, thrown off all disguise as soon as his specious appearance of conciliation had done its work, and his confirmation of the Act forbidding the payment of Annates to Rome[1] was ratified by a fresh Act, passed in the session of Parliament which lasted from January to March, 1534. This second Act of Annates defined the method henceforth to be observed for the appointment of English bishops. Chapters were to elect the candidate named in the King's letters missive, and if they failed to do so within twelve days the King might appoint by letters patent.[2] A second Act of Appeals, besides repeating and confirming the abolition of appeals to Rome, embodied those concessions to the King which had been made by Convocation in 1532, but rejected in the House of Lords. Convocation was not to meet or legislate without the King's assent; a commission, nominated by the King, might reform the Canon Law; there was to be an appeal from the Archbishop's court to Chancery; and religious houses which were exempt from episcopal authority were subjected to that of the King. Another Act forbade the payment of Peter's pence; and a check upon prosecutions for heresy was provided by an Act

[1] *L. and P.*, vi., 793.

[2] 25 Hen. VIII, c. 20; this was made the usual method in 1547,

which required the evidence of two lay witnesses for every charge.[1]

The final Act of that session was a constitutional innovation of great importance. The succession to the crown, which had hitherto been regulated by vague right, was now determined by a definite law to be vested in Henry's heirs by Anne Boleyn. This Act was to be enforced by an oath which might be tendered to any one, and at the head of the commission appointed to administer it was the Archbishop of Canterbury.[2] Among the first who were required to take the oath were Fisher and More; both had been implicated in the previous year in the extraordinary affair of Elizabeth Barton,[3] the Nun of Kent, in whose alleged visions it is impossible to distinguish the imposture from the genuine delusions. Some eight years before, she had earned a reputation for sanctity by denouncing the sensual lives of the clergy, and this reputation was afterwards used to put obstacles in the way of Henry's divorce. She drew, it is stated in the *Confutation of Unwritten Verities* doubtfully attributed to Cranmer, "into her confederacy, both of heresy and treason, holy monks of the Charter House, obstinate (they would be called Observant) friars of Greenwich, nice nuns of Sion, black monks (both of cowls and conditions) of

[1] Cf. *L. and P.*, vii., 393.

[2] His colleagues are given in *L. and P.* (vii., 391) as Audley, Norfolk, and Suffolk; Strype (*Mem. of Cranmer*, i., 36) names Audley, Cromwell, and the Abbot of Westminster.

[3] For Elizabeth Barton see *L. and P.* and *Spanish Calendar* for 1533-34; Wright's *Suppression of the Monasteries* (Camden Soc.), pp. 13-34.

Christ Church and St. Austin's of Canterbury, knights, squires, learned men, priests, and many other."[1] She predicted that Henry would lose his kingdom within seven months if he married Anne Boleyn, and declared that in her visions she had seen the very place in hell that was prepared for him.[2] This kind of prophesying would nowadays be safely left to confute itself, but in that superstitious age it was a source of public danger. The nun could scarcely be treated as innocuous when men like Warham and Fisher fell under her influence. Warham is said, in a contemporary account, to have been diverted by her warnings from an intention to pronounce sentence in favour of Henry's divorce. Many others disaffected to the Government had held communications with her, including Queen Catherine's chaplains. More sought an interview with her, but was not deceived, and his name was struck out of the bill passed against her and her adherents. But Fisher believed in her holiness, and there is some point in Cromwell's remonstrance to him that he would have made a more careful inquiry before accepting her visions if she had approved instead of denouncing the King's proceedings.[3] It was Cranmer who took the first steps to expose the imposture; he saw the Nun of Kent in the summer of 1533,[4] and induced her to confess. In accordance with his invariable practice of making Parlia-

[1] Cranmer, *Works*, ii., 65.

[2] Gairdner, *Church History*, 1902, p. 144.

[3] Burnet, ed. Pocock, iv., 195–201.

[4] Cranmer, *Works*, ii., 252, 271–274.

ment his accomplice in all acts of severity, Henry had her condemned by Act of Attainder, and she was executed in April, 1534. Cranmer, however, interceded earnestly and successfully on behalf of the monks of Christ Church, who had been among her dupes or accomplices.[1]

Their connection with the Nun of Kent naturally suggested the administration to Fisher and More of the oath imposed by the Act of Succession; a further reason may possibly be found in the sentence pronounced by the Pope on 23 March, 1534, in favour of the validity of Henry's marriage with Catherine of Aragon. The oath would serve as a useful touchstone of allegiance to the verdict of the Pope or to that of the English Church. So, on 13 April, Fisher and More were called before Cranmer and his colleagues at Lambeth.[2] The form of the oath had not been prescribed by Parliament, but drawn up by the commissioners; and More, while willing to swear to the succession itself on the ground that that was a matter within the competence of Parliament, objected to the oath[3] and to the preamble of the Act because it contained a denial of Papal authority, which he maintained was incompatible with his conscience. Fisher also refused, and Cranmer, who was generally on the side

[1] Cranmer, *Works*, ii., 271.

[2] More, *Works*, p. 1528; Burnet, i., 256; Strype, *Cranmer*, i., 36–38.

[3] More's objections to the legality of the oath prompted an Act of Parliament, passed the next session, declaring the form of oath proposed by the commissioners to be the one intended by Parliament.

SIR THOMAS MORE.

AFTER THE PAINTING BY HOLBEIN

of mercy, urged the King to accept the oath in the form in which they were willing to take it.[1] He thought this would be a sufficient recognition of Henry's authority, but the King discovered an implied assertion of that of the Pope. Cranmer's mediation proved vain, and Fisher and More were condemned to loss of goods and imprisonment for life. With their subsequent execution on the charge of maliciously trying to deprive the King of his title of Supreme Head of the Church Cranmer had, fortunately for his reputation, nothing to do.[2]

In the meantime Convocation, universities, and monasteries were occupied in debating the question whether the Bishop of Rome had any more authority in England than any other foreign bishop. In the previous year preachers had been required to proclaim the superiority of General Councils to Popes, and it had been ordered that the Pope should be officially styled plain Bishop of Rome. His authority in England was now repudiated with something like unanimity. Fear, no doubt, had something to do with it, but the decision would hardly have become permanent had it been based on nothing but fear. In November, 1534, Parliament met once more to give legal effect to this repudiation of the Papal authority and to the recognition of Henry's

---

[1] *L. and P.*, vii., 499, 500.

[2] It is often said inaccurately that More was executed for refusing to take the Oath of Supremacy, though no oath was imposed by that Act and no penalty attached to its infraction. But the Treason Act, passed in the same session, made it high treason to attempt to deprive the King of any of his titles, and it was on this Act that More was tried and condemned.

ecclesiastical supremacy, conceded three years before by Convocation. It went farther than Convocation had gone, and omitted the clause qualifying the supremacy. It professed only to corroborate and confirm a pre-existing right. The King's Majesty, it declared, "justly and rightfully is and ought to be the Supreme Head of the Church of England," and it proceeded to annex and unite to the Imperial Crown "all honours, dignities, pre-eminences, jurisdictions, privileges, authorities, immunities, profits, and commodities to the said Dignity of Supreme Head of the same Church belonging and appertaining."[1] The title was incorporated with the King's style by an order in council dated 15 January, 1535.[2]

This Act of Supremacy is one of the shortest in the statute-book; it remained in force for less than twenty years, and Henry VIII. was the only monarch who personally exercised for any length of time the powers it conferred.[3] He was also better qualified than any other English sovereign for the position. His morals, it is true, left much to be desired, but they were not worse than those of some Popes. His mind and conscience had been nourished on mediæval scholastic philosophy and on mediæval canon law, and throughout his reign his theological views were in general harmony with those of the

[1] 26 Henry VIII. c. i.

[2] *L. and P.*, viii., 52.

[3] In Edward VI.'s reign the Supremacy was exercised by the Council; Mary was, of course, Supreme Head for the first year of her reign, but she soon abolished the title and it has never been restored. Elizabeth and her successors have only been styled "supreme governors."

majority of his clergy. He always believed in rites and ceremonies; he might dally with Lutheranism, or rather permit his ministers to dally with it for political purposes, but he always remained a Catholic at heart. His convictions were not due to ignorance, for few men were so well read in heretical theology; he kept a private cabinet full of Lutheran books and read them with eagerness and intelligence. He loved nothing better than a theological argument with his bishops, and most of them regarded his supremacy not without reason as the most effectual bulwark against the storms of heresy which had submerged the Church in Germany.

Nor did his extensive powers trench quite so much upon the Church's prerogative as has sometimes been supposed. The King's authority was only a *potestas jurisdictionis* and not at all a *potestas ordinis*.[1] The title "Supreme Head" was an offensive phrase, which implied to most men more than even Henry thought of claiming. It seemed to indicate a pretension to spiritual powers which were entirely outside the lay province. But Henry himself declared that the title conferred on him no new powers; he never asserted[2] that he could ordain a

[1] See Makower, *Constit. Hist. Church of England*, Eng. transl., p. 255.

[2] Yet this question was debated among his bishops and others; and Cranmer maintained that princes and governors might make bishops and so might the people by their election; see Burnet, ed. Pocock, iv., 481–487; Strype, *Cranmer*, ii., 749–751; Jenkyns, ii., 98, *et sqq.*, and Dixon, ii., 303–308. Some of the answers given in these documents indicate the high-water marks of what has been called "Byzantinism" in England.

sub-deacon, baptise, marry, impose penance, pronounce absolution, let alone say mass. The whole sacramental system was left in the hands of the Church. The King was empowered in certain circumstances to nominate bishops, but it was never assumed that such nomination conferred any spiritual powers; they were the result of confirmation and consecration at the hands of the Church. Henry claimed to control the machine, but he did not pretend to supply the motive power; he might select the channels through which spiritual privileges flowed, but he was not the channel through which, nor the fountain from which, they flowed. He was willing, to use his own words, to leave the clergy control of men's souls, provided the State had control of their bodies.[1]

Again, it is necessary to guard against the idea that Henry forced a Church that was previously free under a galling Erastian yoke. Such a view errs as much in one direction as the view that Henry freed the Church does in the other. The freedom of the Church had long before shrunk to a shadow. Bishops and Abbots, who had once been freely elected by their chapters, had for centuries been joint nominees of Pope and King. A prelate depended exclusively upon the King for his temporalities and upon the Pope for his spiritualities.[2] The representative idea

[1] *L. and P.*, v., 1013.

[2] Archbishop Warham, shortly before his death, explained his view of the Pope's authority, which, as Warham was no extreme Papalist, may be accepted as correct (*L. and P.*, v., 1247). His acts in consecrating bishops were done, he says, in his capacity as commissary

embodied in elections had gone out of them and left them a meaningless form; while the supposed right of the English provinces to legislate independently of King and of Pope has been conclusively proved to be mainly a myth.[1] Had the jurisdiction of the Pope been only abolished, the English Church would undoubtedly have acquired that right; but before the Papal jurisdiction was abolished Henry took care that Convocation should transfer to himself those legislative powers which the Pope had exercised. The Church in England was not freed from the yoke of an extraneous jurisdiction or from the burden of first-fruits and tenths; they were merely transferred from the Pope to the King. Henry, in fact, neither liberated nor enslaved the Church; he simply substituted a sole for a dual control. The change was no doubt acceptable to most, and it might appear like a liberation, because the despotism was a native and not an alien one. But it became at once more effective and more severe. Dual controls are usually inefficient, and between Kings

of the Pope, and they were really the Pope's acts. Moreover, a bishop received his jurisdiction, not by election or consecration, but by being declared bishop in Consistory at Rome. The dependence of the English Church on Rome was therefore a reality, and no mere form. When it was abolished by the second Act of Annates, the confirmation of the bishop by other English bishops was obviously intended to take the place of the previous declaration in Consistory, which, according to Warham, really made a man a bishop. This confirmation was certainly not in intention the formality to which it has been reduced by practice and by a recent decision of the English courts.

[1] Professor F. W. Maitland, *The Roman Canon Law*, 1898.

and Popes the Church had lapsed into impotent anarchy. The rigour of the new supremacy may best be justified on the plea that not otherwise could the Church have been reformed.

It was, however, an expedient repugnant to modern ideas. In the latter years of Henry's reign "the King's doctrine" became the usual phrase for orthodoxy. Such a condition could not be permanent, for it was opposed to the foundations of Protestantism as well as to those of Catholicism, and occasioned the simultaneous execution of martyrs to both faiths, the one class on the scaffold as traitors, the other at the stake as heretics.[1] It was only possible in days when a powerful sovereign could stand between the two opposing forces, balancing one against the other, and when regard for the State as represented in the King's person outweighed every other consideration. Henry's supremacy was personal, not parliamentary; he and his daughter Elizabeth denied to their Parliaments any share in their ecclesiastical prerogative. Parliament and Convocation were co-ordinate legislative bodies, independent of one another, but subject to the sovereign. Such was the Tudor system, but it barely outlived the Tudor dynasty. No other monarch has been able to wield their double sceptre; and as the power of the Crown declined, its secular authority was seized by Parliament, which also attempted to grasp its ecclesiastical supremacy. Con-

[1] The most notorious case occurred on 30 July, 1540, when Barnes, Jerome, and Gerrard were burnt for heresy, and Featherstone, Powell, and Abel were hanged for treason, all at Smithfield. (See Wriothesley, *Chronicle*, Camden Soc., i., 120–121.)

vocation disputed the claim, but was unable to vindicate its own, and the royal supremacy as exercised by Henry VIII. has died a natural death, leaving as yet no recognised successor, and a state of affairs not far removed from ecclesiastical anarchy.

CHAPTER IV

CRANMER AND REFORM

"THAT our said Sovereign Lord shall have full power and authority from time to time to visit, repress, redress, reform, order, correct, restrain, and amend all such errors, heresies, abuses, offences, contempts, and enormities, whatsoever they be, which by any manner spiritual authority or jurisdiction are or may lawfully be reformed, repressed . . . most to the pleasure of Almighty God, the increase of virtue in Christ's religion, and for the conservation of the peace, unity, and tranquillity of this realm." Such were the objects, as defined in the Act of Supremacy, which the King, armed with his two-edged sword of temporal and spiritual authority, now set out to accomplish. They were as vague as they were ample; the Supreme Head might think that he had been girt with these weapons to reform abuses which heretics cast in the teeth of the Church, or he might imagine that he had been called to extirpate heresies which feebler Popes had failed to crush. Cranmer looked for the one consummation, and Gardiner hoped for the other; and the parties which followed their lead fought a twelve-years' fight for the control of the royal supremacy and the direction of England's ecclesiastical policy. Henry held the balance, inclining now to this side, now to that, as his political or personal ends made it desirable to cultivate friendship with Protestant or Catholic powers. When, in 1539, the King threw his whole weight into the scale against the New Learning, he did so partly because, as Bishop Stubbs has said,[1] he "symbolised consistently with Gardiner and not with Cranmer," but partly, perhaps, because he saw that unless he redressed the balance the Protestants would predominate, and the equilibrium, on which his power was based, would be destroyed; and, as a matter of fact, the balance did turn decisively in their favour as soon as Henry VIII. was removed from the scene.

The growth of the Protestant party and the development of its religious principles in England during the reign of Henry VIII. have been somewhat obscured by modern attempts[2] to minimise the influence of Protestantism in England, and to emphasise both the continuity of Catholic doctrine in the Church, and the identity of the mediæval Church *in* England with the modern Church *of* England.[3] The

---

[1] Stubbs, *Lectures on Mediæval and Modern History*, ed. 1887, p. 299.

[2] *E. g.*, Canon Dixon's great work, *The History of the Church of England, 1530–1570*, 6 vols.

[3] The excess to which the practice of exaggerating the independence of the English Church during the Middle Ages, and of laying stress on its modern Catholicism has gone, has led one critic to affirm that some writers believe the Church to have been Protestant before the Reformation and Catholic after it.

Church is of course the same Church before and after the Reformation, but then Saul and Paul were the same man before and after conversion, and proof of the identity does not refute the change. Men do not change their bodies when they change their minds, and an institution may preserve its outward form while its spirit is altered. Except for the substitution of the royal for the papal supremacy, the Church retained its organisation almost intact, but the intention which underlay its forms and its formularies was profoundly modified by Cranmer himself, and by the influence of the new doctrines which are conveniently if not quite accurately described as Protestant.[1]

The origin of these new doctrines or heresies in England is not correctly ascribed to Luther; the spread of Lutheranism on the Continent undoubtedly gave impetus to the movement in England, but the views of the English Reformers approach so much more nearly to those of Wycliffe than to those of Luther, that the Englishman rather than the German must be regarded as the morning star of the Anglican Reformation. Even as Wycliffe had done, so Cranmer, Ridley, Latimer, and Hooper looked to the State to reform a corrupt Church; like him they

[1] The term properly applies only to those who adopted the Protest drawn up by some of the German princes against the decrees of the Diet of Spires in 1529, but the need of some common designation for the religious opponents of Rome led to its use outside Germany, and it began to be applied to English Reformers in the reign of Edward VI. (See the present writer's *Tudor Tracts*, p. xxiii., *note*). It was of course never admitted into the formularies of the English Church.

regarded the wealth of the clergy as an impediment to the exercise of spiritual influence, and, like him, they gradually receded from the Catholic doctrine of the mass. Most of the English Reformers were acquainted with Wycliffe's works; Cranmer declares that he set forth the truth of the Gospel,[1] Hooper recalls how he resisted "the popish doctrine of the mass,"[2] Ridley how he denied transubstantiation,[3] and Bale how he denounced the friars[4]; and it is not perhaps without significance that Henry VIII. himself in 1530 sent to Oxford for a copy of the articles on which Wycliffe had been condemned.[5] The control of the press exercised by the authorities prevented his works being printed, but numbers of them circulated in manuscript, and Bale records[6] with triumph that, in spite of the efforts to suppress them, not one had utterly perished.

"It is certain," says Dr. Rashdall, "that the Reformation had virtually broken out in the secret bible-readings of the Cambridge reformers before either the trumpet-call of Luther or the exigencies of Henry VIII.'s personal and political position set men free once more to talk openly against the pope and the monks, and to teach a simpler and more spiritual gospel than the system against which Wycliffe had striven."[7]

It is not probable that all the cases of heresy which occurred in the early years of Henry VIII.'s

[1] Cranmer, *Works*, i., 14.
[2] Hooper, *Works*, i., 527.
[3] Ridley, *Works*, p. 158.
[4] Bale, *Select Works*, p. 171.
[5] *L. and P.*, iv., 6546.
[6] Bale, *Works*, p. 140.
[7] *Dict. of Nat. Biog.*, art. "Wycliffe," lxiii., 218.

reign were due to the lingering subterranean influence of Wycliffe, and the popular tract, *Wycliffe's Wicket*, the possession of which was frequently made a charge against their victims by the clerical courts, was not from the Reformer's pen. But of the prevalence of heretical opinions in England before Luther's revolt against Indulgences there is ample evidence. Foxe recounts the martyrdom of ten men and women between 1509 and 1518; many suffered a less extreme form of persecution, and in the year 1517 alone thirty-five persons in the diocese of London were forced to abjure their opinions.[1] Nor does Foxe's witness stand alone; occasionally instances of heresy are mentioned in the State papers,[2] and on 8 November, 1511, Ammonius, Henry VIII.'s Latin secretary, writing to his friend Erasmus, attributes the scarcity and dearness of wood to the holocaust caused by the heretics.[3] It was a grim and heartless joke, no doubt; but there would have been no point in it unless there had been a notable number of heretics burnt. And the secretary's letter proceeds to state that his servant's brother, "lout as he is, has founded a sect and has his followers." Three months later the movement had become so pronounced that Warham summoned a convocation of his province for the express purpose of extirpat-

[1] Foxe, *Acts and Monuments*, iv., 206.

[2] E. g., *L. and P.*, i., 1381; *cf.* H. E. Jacobs, *The Lutheran Movement in England*, p. 3; "as late as 1521, the Bishop of London arrested nearly five hundred Lollards, who probably had no connection with the movement then beginning in Germany."

[3] *Ibid.*, i., 1948.

ing heresy.[1] In October, 1516, More declared that the *Epistolæ Obscurorum Virorum*, that scathing attack on the clergy, was popular everywhere.[2] Two months later one Humphrey Bonner was accused of ridiculing the Holy See in his sermons,[3] and Henry's famous book against Luther appears to have been begun in the spring of 1518,[4] before Luther had attracted any attention outside Germany, and to have been originally directed against heretics among his own subjects.

Under these circumstances Luther's books and doctrines fell upon fruitful soil in England. In 1521 Oxford was said to be infected with Lutheranism,[5] and at Cambridge it was even more prevalent. Henry VIII.'s book and the solemn committal to the flames of Luther's writings in St. Paul's Churchyard on 12th May in that year, before Wolsey, the Papal nuncio, and other high dignitaries, did little to stop the infection; and during the next ten years the German Reformer's views gained ever wider acceptance in England. Anne Boleyn and her father were once described by Chapuys as being more Lutheran than Luther himself[6]; and even Henry VIII. was beginning to look with lenient eyes on men who might be useful pawns in the struggle with Rome.[7]

[1] *L. and P.*, i., 4312. [2] *Ibid.*, ii., 2492. [3] *Ibid.*, ii., 2692.

[4] *Ibid.*, ii., 4257. Henry was certainly engaged in writing a book at that time, and its arguments were submitted to Wolsey and to other "great learned men." Nothing more is heard of it until 1521.

[5] *Ibid.*, iii., 1193. [6] *Ibid.*, v., 148.

[7] In 1529 he ordered Wolsey to discharge the Abbot of Reading, who was accused of Lutheranism, "unless the matter be very heinous."—(*Ibid.*, iv., 5925; cf. *Ibid.*, iv., 6325, 6385; v., App. 7.)

But not every one who was called Lutheran in England adopted the doctrines of Wittenberg; the phrase was a generic term used to express any sort of hostility to Rome or the clergy, and even the possession of the Bible in English was sometimes sufficient to make its owner a Lutheran suspect. The number of Englishmen who were really Lutherans was probably small, and Cranmer at the time of his appointment as Archbishop was certainly not one of them. He may have been affected to some extent by Osiander's views during his stay in Germany, but it is doubtful whether Osiander himself could properly be called a Lutheran.

The pressing need in Cranmer's eyes and in those of most reforming churchmen was not a change of doctrine so much as a change of conduct, and the revival of Scriptural knowledge among both clergy and laity. As soon as he had been enthroned at Canterbury (3 December, 1533), he commenced a visitation of his diocese. In 1534 he directed his commissary to visit Norwich, where the Bishop had distinguished himself by the persecution of Bilney[1] and other reformers. Next followed a metropolitical visitation of the southern province. It involved Cranmer, as it had generally involved his predecessors, in disputes with his suffragan bishops. Personal jealousy embittered the quarrel; probably both Gardiner of Winchester and Stokesley of London considered that they had better claims than Cranmer to sit in Augustine's chair; and they were

[1] See *Dict. Nat. Biogr.*, v., 40.

naturally disposed to resent his visitation, because their own sympathies were conservative and the Archbishop's were in favour of change. Gardiner objected that his See had been visited not long before by Warham, and in his zeal for the royal supremacy he made the not very scrupulous protest that Cranmer's assumption of the title "primate" was an infraction of the King's ecclesiastical prerogative. He seems to have thought that all bishops should be equal under the Crown—at least so long as Cranmer was Archbishop; and indeed a proposal was put forward in Parliament in 1532 for the transference to the King of the primate's powers over his bishops.[1] Stokesley cavilled at the use of the style *legatus natus* of the Apostolic See, which had belonged to Archbishops of Canterbury for centuries, and had not yet been legally abolished. The King, however, upheld Cranmer in both cases, and his visitation duly proceeded. Another attempt, instigated, probably, by personal enmity to Cranmer, was made against his primatial dignity. The Archbishop of Canterbury was head of two ecclesiastical courts, the Court of Arches and the Court of Audience, in the latter of which he heard appeals from other dioceses besides his own. It was now asserted that former Archbishops held this court only in virtue of their legatine authority from the Pope, and that, the Papal jurisdiction having been repudiated, the Court of Audience had no legal basis.[2] Cranmer contested

[1] *L. and P.*, v., 850.

[2] See the reply to the Archbishop printed by Strype (*Cranmer*, ii., 714-716); the "order concerning the Proctors of the Court of Arches,"

this idea and appears again to have been upheld by Henry; but eventually the other view prevailed, and when, in very recent times, an Archbishop once more held a Court of Audience at Lambeth, the "court" was admitted to be no real court at all, and its decisions to have no legal binding power.[1]

Meanwhile, in 1534, Cranmer issued a pastoral in which he enjoined silence respecting masses for the dead, prayers to saints, pilgrimages, and the celibacy of the clergy. These practices were the subject of much denunciation, and Cranmer hoped that within a year an authoritative decision on these points would be adopted. He also persuaded Convocation to petition for an authorised version of the Bible in English. Four years before, there had been a persistent rumour that Henry was in favour of this measure[2]; but the tendencies encouraged by Tyndale's translations alarmed the King, and his promise of the boon was made conditional upon the abandonment of unorthodox views.[3] So now the petition of Convocation was accompanied by a demand for the suppression of heretical books. Cranmer also, in conjunction with Cromwell and Anne Boleyn, used his influence to procure the promotion of Reformers to the bench of Bishops. He had long befriended

which Strype attributes to Cranmer, seems to have been really due to Warham, and the protest against it which he prints (*Ibid.*, ii., 717–728) to belong to 1532 or some earlier date.

[1] *Cf.* Canon MacColl, *The Reformation Settlement*, 10th ed., p. 567.

[2] *L. and P.*, iv., 6385.

[3] *Ibid.*, iv., 6487.

Latimer,[1] who in 1535 was appointed to the See of Worcester; Shaxton was made Bishop of Salisbury, Foxe of Hereford, Hilsey of Rochester, and Barlow of S. David's, with the result that for a few years the episcopal bench was more inclined to reform than the lower house of Convocation. Nevertheless the conservative element on the bench frustrated for the time Cranmer's projected Bible in English. He divided the task of revision among various prelates, and Gardiner performed his portion, but Stokesley did nothing, declaring that it was "abusing the people to give them liberty to read the Scriptures."[2]

The year 1535 was, however, notable mainly for the visitation of the monasteries under the authority of Thomas Cromwell, who, to the derogation of the Church, had been appointed Henry's Vicar-General in ecclesiastical matters. To facilitate his operations all episcopal jurisdictions, including Cranmer's, were for the time suspended, and so the Archbishop of Canterbury was relieved of all responsibility for the methods employed to destroy the monasteries. That the monasteries needed drastic reformation Cranmer was no doubt convinced, and he probably had little sympathy with the principle of monasticism; but he can have had no enthusiasm for the way in which their vast estates were used to bribe the laity into supporting Henry's government. Without denying that the county families and noble houses,

[1] In 1533 all the prelates except Cranmer were said to be demanding Latimer's suppression. (*L. and P.*, vi., 1249.)

[2] Strype, *Cranmer*, i., 48.

founded on the spoils of the Church, have thereby been enabled in the past to do their country some service, it may be doubted whether the permanent results have been beneficial; and it may be admitted that from the point of view of education and of provision for the sick and poor, the dissipation of monastic property was a waste of one of the most splendid opportunities in English history.

Another tragedy, with which Cranmer was more nearly concerned, was enacted in 1536. Whether Anne Boleyn was guilty or innocent of the charges on which she was beheaded is a question with which Cranmer's biographer is not called upon to deal,[1] for the Archbishop's part in the matter related not to the Queen's death, but to her divorce. He was inexpressibly shocked at her fall, and, so far as we know, he was the only man of the time who had the courage to plead with Henry on her behalf. He had never had better opinion in woman, he wrote, than he had in her; and next to the King he was most bound unto her of all creatures living; he ventured to express a hope that she would be found innocent, and even reminded Henry that he, too, had offended God.[2] Anne was, however, condemned by a court of twenty-six temporal peers, over which her uncle presided, and Cranmer was then called in to pronounce her divorce. The reasons for this extraordinary step are still obscure, and the grounds on which the divorce was declared

[1] I have discussed the point in my *Henry VIII.*, chap. v.

[2] *Works.*, ii., 324; *see also* Paul Friedmann, *Anne Boleyn*, 1884, vol. ii., chap. xvii.

were kept profoundly secret. Why, if Henry merely wanted to get rid of his Queen, was he not satisfied with her execution? What object could possibly be served by proclaiming the marriage to have been null from the beginning, and by bastardising the Princess Elizabeth as well as the Princess Mary? It may be that Henry had become sensitive to the force of public opinion against the marriage, for his envoys had just failed to persuade the Lutherans of its validity. Anne, moreover, had had at least two miscarriages; similar misfortunes had convinced Henry of the nullity of his marriage with Catherine, and conscientious scruples grow by what they feed on.

However this may be, Cranmer had to decide the question by canon law; and the hopeless confusion into which canon law had fallen now that the Papal jurisdiction, the keystone of the arch, had been abolished, gave rise to the strangest anomalies. Two canonical objections to the marriage were raised. The first was an alleged precontract between Anne and the Earl of Northumberland, which was supported by some circumstantial evidence, although the Earl himself solemnly denied its existence. There was a more valid objection. Henry's previous relations with Mary Boleyn had created an affinity between him and her sister Anne, which, by canon law, was a bar to their marriage. For this reason Henry had obtained a dispensation from Clement VII. in 1528; but since that date the Pope's dispensing power had been repudiated, and the old canonical objection was therefore revived.[1] The King in his anxiety to divorce Catherine had denied the power of the Pope to dispense; by so doing he had, probably without realising it at first, invalidated his marriage with Anne, which rested upon the same dispensing power. The realisation of this fact, stimulated no doubt by his failure to obtain recognition for her in any quarter outside England, was probably responsible for her divorce, though not for her death; and, monstrous as it seems from the point of view of justice and equity, the divorce of Anne Boleyn was probably legal. A less opportunist government than that of Henry VIII. would have endeavoured to put the existing canon laws on a firmer and more reasonable basis, but the King had already enough on his hands, and the position of the canon law in England has to this day remained somewhat anomalous.

On the day (19 May) that Anne Boleyn was beheaded, Cranmer granted Henry a special licence to

[1] There are some objections to this view. Firstly, the affinity created by Henry's relations with Mary Boleyn was different from the affinity created by Prince Arthur's marriage with Catherine; the former was only held to be an obstacle by canon law, the latter by Divine law; and many would have admitted the Pope's power to dispense with canon law, who denied his power to dispense with Divine laws. Secondly, in the tract on the divorce attributed to Cranmer (Burnet, ed. Pocock, iv., 146), it is asserted that an affinity fatal to marriage is only created *nuptiali fœdere*. On the other hand, the Pope's dispensing power had been denied altogether, and it is by no means clear that Cranmer's views (if they were Cranmer's) on affinity had been recognised as canon law in England in 1536. Chapuys definitely states (*L. and P.*, xi., 41) that the ground of Cranmer's sentence was Henry's relations with Mary Boleyn, and not Anne's precontract with Northumberland.

LADY JANE SEYMOUR.

AFTER THE PAINTING BY HANS HOLBEIN THE YOUNGER, NOW AT VIENNA.

marry a third wife.[1] Jane Seymour was descended on her mother's side from Edward III., and the stringency of the canon law was still so great that the Archbishop had to grant at the same time a dispensation relieving the parties from the impediment to their marriage arising from consanguinity. They were betrothed on the 20th and were privately married at York Place ten days later.[2] After sixteen months Queen Jane gave birth on 12 October, 1537, to the future Edward VI., over whose birth, wrote Latimer, there was as much joy as over that of S. John the Baptist. Cranmer was godfather to the infant at his christening on the 15th.[3] Nine days afterwards the Queen died. Had she lived she would have saved Henry and the English Church from the serio-comic episode of Anne of Cleves and from the tragedy of Catherine Howard.

From these unsavoury matters of royal matrimony the Archbishop turned with relief to more congenial work. In February, 1536, he had preached a notable sermon in S. Paul's Churchyard, "and," writes Chapuys, "of the two hours that he preached one and a half were occupied with blasphemies against His Holiness and his predecessors.[4] The special

---

[1] The expression is not strictly correct; according to Henry's view, which was endorsed by the Church, Catherine of Aragon and Anne Boleyn had never been his wives, so Jane Seymour was the first.

[2] They are often incorrectly said to have been married on the day after Anne's execution. It does not appear who officiated.

[3] Strype, *Eccl. Memorials*, I., ii., 1–10; Cranmer did not perform the ceremony.

[4] *L. and P.*, x., 282, 283.

object of his discourse appears to have been not, as Chapuys implies, to deny the existence of purgatory, that dim realm in which were laid the unseen foundations of the Roman Church, but to denounce the idea that Popes could release men's souls from durance. He also sought, according to Chapuys, to prove that all the Scriptural passages about Antichrist referred to the Italian pontiff; and if so, he entered upon a sort of controversy of which the annals of the Reformed churches are too full.

Other doctrines besides that of purgatory occupied the bishops' attention. "The prelates here," writes Chapuys on 1 April, "are daily in communication in the house of the Archbishop of Canterbury for the determination of certain articles and for the reform of ecclesiastical ceremonies."[1] They were, in fact, engaged in debates which resulted in the Ten Articles, the first definition of the faith put forward under the royal supremacy. It was a compromise between the old faith and the new; but it was a victory for the latter, in so far as "no compromise" had hitherto been the Catholic attitude. The matter was, indeed, started in Convocation in June in the form of a complaint preferred by the lower house of sixty-seven Lutheran errors then current in England which the clergy thought should be repressed.[2] Fuller says these errors contained "the Protestant religion in ore"; and it was not likely that Cranmer and the newly appointed prelates of the upper house would

[1] *L. and P.*, x., 601.

[2] These are printed in Fuller's *Church History*, 1656, bk. v., 209–212, or ed. Brewer, 1845, iii., 128–136.

consent to their indiscriminate condemnation. The result seems to have been a deadlock between the two parties, and Henry VIII. took the matter into his own hands,[1] and himself penned a set of articles. These were revised by Cranmer and laid before Convocation by Bishop Foxe on 11 July; and the clergy who in the same session admitted Dr. Petre to the highest seat in their assembly on the ground that he was Cromwell's proctor, and Cromwell was the Supreme Head's Vicegerent,[2] did not venture to reject the royal theology.

The articles were passed, subscribed, and printed.[3] Five were devoted to points of faith and five to ceremonies. Three sacraments, baptism, penance, and the Eucharist, were strongly upheld; works of charity were declared to be necessary to salvation, auricular confession was not to be contemned, and justification could only be attained "by contrition and faith, joined with charity." Images were to stand in the churches, saints to be invoked as intercessors, the usual Catholic ceremonies to be observed, and prayers to be offered for the departed. On the other hand, the Bible and the three Creeds were to be regarded as the standard of orthodoxy, a position

[1] *L. and P.*, xi., 1110; the King says "he was constrained to put his own pen to the book and conceive certain articles which were agreed upon by Convocation." Cf. *ibid.*, Nos. 59, 123, 377, 954.

[2] See Wilkins, *Concilia*, iii., 803.

[3] They are printed in full from the Convocation records (soon afterwards burnt) in Fuller's *Church History*, 1656, bk. v., 213–225 (or in 1845 ed., vol. iii., 145–159), and from *Cotton MS.*, Cleopatra, E. v., p. 59, in Pocock's *Burnet*, iv., 272–290; an epitome is given in Strype's *Cranmer*, i., 58–62.

from which the Reformed Church of England has never varied; amendment of life was pronounced a necessary part of penance, faith was joined with charity as necessary to justification, and the article on the Eucharist did not go beyond an assertion of the Real Presence; there was to be no censing, kneeling, or offering to images; the invocation of the saints was "to be done without any vain superstition, as to think that any saint is more merciful, or will hear us sooner than Christ"; ceremonies were declared to have no "power to remit sin" nor masses to deliver souls from purgatory. The mention of only three sacraments does not perhaps imply a repudiation of the other four, though the attempt then made to introduce a fourth, the sacrament of holy orders, failed. On the whole, the Ten Articles were a notable advance towards the purification of the Church, and Cranmer and his reforming colleagues had reason to feel satisfied that they had brought the King thus far. Many of the worst abuses had been removed at least from the seat of authority; the whole system of Indulgences, which had provoked Luther's revolt, was repudiated; the polytheism, into which popular worship of saints and images tended to degenerate, was checked[1]; and amendment of life rather than performance of useless penances was held up as the true symbol of repentance. The Articles were, in fact, an excellent embodiment of the practical, as distinguished from the doctrinal Reformation, which was the first and foremost object of the movement.

[1] *Cf.* Hallam, *Hist. of England*, 1884, i., p. 87.

The same practical object is apparent in the Injunctions[1] issued by Cromwell in August to enforce the Ten Articles. Attention was called to the fact that the Articles distinguished the "real doctrine of Salvation" from the "rites and ceremonies of the Church," that the people might know "what was necessary in religion, and what was instituted for the decent and politic order of the Church." Superstition, holy-days, images, relics, miracles, and pilgrimages were to be discouraged, and men were exhorted to keep God's commandments, to provide for their families, and to bestow what they could afford on the poor rather than spend it in offerings to relics and images or in making pilgrimages to shrines. The clergy were to urge fathers to teach their children the *Paternoster*, the Articles of Faith, and the commandments in their mother-tongue, and to bring them up in learning or in some honest occupation or trade. A Bible in Latin and English[2] was to be provided in the choir of every church for every man to read. The clergy were to eschew taverns and alehouses, cards or other unlawful games, and to set an example to others by devoting their leisure to the study of the Scriptures and by the purity of their lives; they were to expend a fortieth of their incomes on the poor, and if they had a hundred pounds[3] or more a year they were to provide exhibitions for poor scholars at some school or

---

[1] Printed in Pocock's *Burnet*, iv., 308–313.

[2] See below, pp. 112–114.

[3] It is necessary to multiply sums of money by ten, twelve, or even fifteen to bring them up to their present value.

university. The ecclesiastical government of Henry VIII. has been bitterly, and in some respects, justly, denounced, but at least it set before the Church some ideals which have not yet been attained.

Nor were the reforms which Henry did accomplish allowed to pass without protest. Reaction was gathering its forces, and while Cromwell was denouncing pilgrimages to the shrines of the saints, another sort of pilgrimage was organising from which he and his colleagues had more to fear. It is not, however, quite accurate to represent the rising in northern England in the autumn of 1536, known as the Pilgrimage of Grace, as exclusively a religious movement; the first acts of rebellion broke out not against the visitors of monasteries, but against the collectors of taxes; and while the people in the north undoubtedly suffered from the break-up of monastic establishments, they had other grievances and feared other ills. The second article of the Lincolnshire rebels was a demand for the repeal of the recent Statute of Uses. The enclosure movement was responsible for at least as many homeless vagrants as the ejection of the monks from their cells, and evicted tenants had no pensions like the monks to alleviate their sufferings. More prosperous people, too, were alarmed by reports that taxes were to be levied on every baptism, marriage, and burial, and fines on the beasts of the field; that churches within five miles of another were to be destroyed as superfluous, and their jewels and plate confiscated; and that there was to be a rigid inquisition into every man's property. These seditious rumours did their work, and in the autumn of 1536 Lincolnshire first and Yorkshire next flamed out in revolt. It was a great opportunity for the Pope's adherents in England, but even the most reactionary of the English Catholics seemed to have little enthusiasm for the Papal cause. His claims to spiritual supremacy were mentioned during the conference at Pontefract, but it was suggested that he should delegate his functions to the Archbishops of Canterbury and York, "so that the said Bishop of Rome have no further meddling."[1] The popular demand in the north, so far as religion was concerned, seems to have been for the restoration of Catholicism minus the Pope, and one of the rebels' articles went to the root of the whole conflict between mediæval and modern ideas. It denied the power of any nation to repudiate received canon laws without the consent of a General Council[2]; that was the old ideal against which England protested by asserting her right to reform her national Church herself. Cranmer was naturally singled out for attack, both as a patron of heretics and because of his sentence against Catherine of Aragon.[3] The rebels demanded that he should be handed over to them, or banished the realm, and one of their popular songs ran :

[1] *L. and P.*, xi., 1182, 1244, 1246.

[2] *Ibid*, xi., 1182 ; this denial does not support a modern theory that canon laws were not valid in England unless confirmed by the English Church.

[3] *Ibid*, xi., 1182.

[4] *Ibid*, xi., 786.

Crim,[1] Cran,[2] and Riche,[3]
With three L[4] and their liche.
As some men teach,
God them amend.
And that Aske[5] may,
Without delay,
Here make a stay,
And well to end.

South of the Trent, however, the old faith had no such staunch friends as Aske and his followers, and early in 1537 the revolt was quenched, or rather burnt itself out. It may have taught Henry to be cautious in religious innovations, and possibly to its influence may be traced the fact that the four sacraments which had been omitted from the Ten Articles of 1536 were included in the *Institution of a Christian Man*, published in 1537. This was an exposition of the orthodox faith, as understood in England, on which the Bishops were engaged from February until June; but all their prolonged debates produced no better definition of the Faith than that contained in the King's Ten Articles. The insistence on the

---

[1] *I. e.*, Cromwell.

[2] Cranmer.

[3] Richard, first baron Rich, Solicitor-General and afterwards Lord Chancellor; see *Dict. Nat. Biog.*, xlviii., 123–127; the name was no doubt pronounced as it is in German, *Reich*, and would rhyme with "liche," which is simply "like."

[4] Possibly Leigh and Layton, the two royal visitors of monasteries, and Latimer; Lee, Archbishop of York, is probably not intended, but Longland of Lincoln might be one, and even Dr. London might have a claim.

[5] The leader of the Pilgrimage of Grace.

seven sacraments was the only concession made to the reactionary party, and the doctrine of Purgatory was repudiated as emphatically as before. Nevertheless Henry VIII. took no responsibility for the book; he had not had time, he wrote in August,[1] to examine it properly, but he trusted to the wisdom of his prelates and gave his consent to its publication. It was accordingly known as *The Bishops' Book*, and the preface written by Bishop Foxe of Hereford declares that it represented the final and unanimous agreement of the assembled Bishops and divines.[2]

The same year saw the publication of the first authorised version of the Bible in English, a project on which Cranmer had long set his heart. Versions of the Scriptures in vernacular tongues had existed for some time both in England and on the Continent, and with a view to belittling the work of the Reformers, their importance has lately been much exaggerated. For they were made from the Vulgate, which was itself a bad translation of inferior versions of the orginal documents. Tyndale's was the first English translation from the original Hebrew and Greek, and Tyndale's has been condemned and burnt not so much because of the errors which it undoubtedly contained, as because of the approaches it

[1] Subsequently, however, he made a considerable number of annotations upon it which Cranmer took the liberty to criticise. Henry's notes and Cranmer's criticisms are printed in Jenkyns' *Cranmer*, ii., 21 *et sqq.*, and in the Parker Society's edition of Cranmer's *Works*, ii., 83 *et sqq.*; *cf.* also *ibid.*, ii., 359-360.

[2] It was issued in Sept., 1537; the revision of it published in 1543 was known as *The King's Book*.

made to truth. It was shocking to a generation which believed that Jesus Christ had endowed the Church with the institutions, rites, and ceremonies it possessed in the sixteenth century, to find πρεσβύτερος translated "elder" instead of "priest," ἐκκλησία as "congregation" instead of "church," μετανοεῖν as "repent" instead of "do penance," and ἀγάπη as "love" instead of "charity." Sir Thomas More had no objection to the truth being made known to the select few, but an attempt like Tyndale's to bring it home to "the boy that driveth his plough" he regarded as "a design to depreciate the authority of an ordained priesthood and of an organised Church."[1] More's views in this matter were shared by Henry VIII. and by most of his Bishops; but in 1534 Cranmer had induced Convocation to petition for another English version, and

---

[1] Gairdner, *The English Church in the Sixteenth Century*, 1902, pp. 190–1. Dr. Gairdner appears to agree with More in considering Tyndale's translation of the Scriptures as "a mischievous perversion of those writings intended to advance heretical opinions." Tyndale's object was to spread the knowledge of the Scriptures irrespective of the question whether that knowledge made men heretics or confirmed their Catholicism. If a knowledge of the Scriptures tended to make men heretics, that was the fault of the Church. And as for the "mischievous perversion," that surely consisted in enforcing a translation which implied a whole world of ideas not contained in the original. "Priest," "do penance," "charity," and "church" all denoted to the men of the sixteenth century ideas which are not to be found in the New Testament; and no Greek scholar would dispute the fact that Tyndale's expressions were less of a perversion of the truth than those they displaced. If Tyndale's translation is a "mischievous perversion," what is the Revised Version, which for the most part adopts Tyndale's phrases?

Cromwell encouraged Coverdale to make his translation in 1535. It was much inferior to Tyndale's, making no pretence to original scholarship, and being derived mainly from the Vulgate, and from Luther's German translation ; but its sale, which had hitherto gone on unauthorised, was licensed by the King in 1537, probably to enable the clergy to comply with the Injunctions of 1536, ordering the provision of an English Bible in every church before August, 1537. This, however, was not the version which Cranmer sent to Cromwell on the 4th of that month, declaring that he liked it "better than any other translation heretofore made," and urging that it might be licensed for sale "until such time that we Bishops shall set forth a better translation, which I think will not be till a day after doomsday."[1] This latter version had been prepared by John Rogers, the martyr, who, according to Bradford, "broke the ice valiantly" in Queen Mary's reign. Rogers had been entrusted by Tyndale with the manuscript of his incomplete translation of the Bible, including the whole of the New Testament and the Old as far as Jonah; he incorporated all the former, and the latter as far as the second book of Chronicles; the rest he borrowed from Coverdale.[2] The book was originally printed at Antwerp, but Grafton, the English printer, purchased the sheets and sent a copy to Cranmer,

[1] Cranmer, *Works*, ii., 344.

[2] See *Dict. Nat. Biog.*, s. v. Rogers, John (1500?–1555). The dedication was signed Thomas Matthew, and the Bible was known as "Matthew's Bible," but there is no reason to doubt the identity of Rogers and Matthew.

who was so pleased with it that he wrote the above letter to Cromwell. The result exceeded his expectations and nine days later he again wrote to Cromwell.[1]

"My very singular good lord, in my most hearty wise I commend me unto your lordship. And whereas I understand that your lordship, at my request, hath not only exhibited the bible which I sent unto you, to the king's majesty, but also hath obtained of his grace that the same shall be allowed by his authority to be bought and read within this realm; my lord, for this your pain taken in this behalf, I give unto you my most hearty thanks, assuring your lordship for the contentation of my mind, you have shewed me more pleasure herein than if you had given me a thousand pound; and I doubt not but that hereby such fruit of good knowledge shall ensue that it shall well appear hereafter what high and acceptable service you have done unto God and the king; which shall so much redound to your honour that, besides God's reward, you shall obtain perpetual memory for the same within this realm. And as for me, you may reckon me your bondman for the same. And I dare be bold to say, so may ye do my lord of Worcester."[2]

A fortnight later he once more wrote to thank the Vicegerent for his services in the matter.

"For the which act, not only the King's majesty, but also you shall have perpetual laud and memory of all them that be now, or hereafter shall be God's faithful people and the followers of his word. And this deed

[1] Cranmer, *Works*, Parker Soc., ii., 345–346.

[2] *I. e.*, Latimer.

you shall hear of at the great day, when all things shall be opened and made manifest. For our Saviour Christ saith in his Gospel that whosoever shrinketh from him and his word, and is abashed to profess and set it forth before men in this world, he will refuse him at that last day; and contrary, whosoever constantly doth profess him and his word, and studieth to set that forward in this world, Christ will declare the same at the last day before his Father and all his angels, and take upon him the defence of those men."[1]

So the "mischievous perversion" of the heretic who less than a year before had been burnt at the stake in Antwerp,[2] went forth with Cranmer's blessing to work its way among the English people, and Tyndale's translation, which had before been condemned, received now the sanction of authority, and permeated all future versions of the Bible in English. The result was not due to the Bishops as a whole, but to Cranmer, Cromwell, and Henry VIII., and of the three Cranmer, whose motives were unmixed with any considerations of worldly policy, deserves the greatest credit. This version was, however, too advanced for the government, and in 1538–9 an expurgated edition was printed in Paris, where finer type was available than in England. It is known as the Great Bible, and also, from the fact that the Archbishop wrote a preface for the 1540 and 1541 editions of it, as "Cranmer's Bible." In 1538

[1] *Works*, ii., 346–347.

[2] *Dict. Nat. Biog.*, lvii., 428, where the date of Tyndale's death is erroneously given as 6 August instead of 6 October.

Cromwell issued a fresh set of Injunctions,[1] ordering that a copy of this Bible "of the largest volume"[2] should be set up in every church where the people might most commodiously resort to it and read it, the cost of purchase being defrayed half by the parishioners and half by the incumbent.[3] The clergy were "expressly to provoke, stir, and exhort every person to read the same," but to avoid contention and altercation and to reserve disputed points for "men of higher judgment in Scripture." In other respects the Injunctions of 1538 were similar to those of 1536; every incumbent was to recite the *Paternoster*, Creed, and Ten Commandments in English, that his flock might learn them by degrees; he was to require some knowledge of the rudiments of the Faith before admitting candidates to the sacrament of the Altar, to keep a register of births, marriages, and deaths,[4] and to preach at least once a quarter.

The reasons which led Henry VIII. to permit

---

[1] Printed in Burnet, iv., 341–346.

[2] This expression may be explained by a letter from Grafton, the printer of this Bible, to Cromwell (Strype, *Cranmer*, ii., 729–732). Grafton complains that after he had spent 500*l.* on this edition other men "go about the printing of the same work again in a lesser letter to the intent that they may sell their little books better cheap than I can sell these great"; and the stipulation about "the greatest volume" was probably designed to protect the original printers from this piracy.

[3] For these editions see Dixon, ii., 77–79, and authorities there cited.

[4] Some hint that this invaluable reform was intended as early as 1536 apparently gave rise to the rumour in Lincolnshire that a tax was to be paid on each of these events.

these instalments of the Reformation were political rather than religious. The reading of the Scriptures, and the growing disbelief in Purgatory, tended to destroy what hold the Papacy still had over the minds of Englishmen and indirectly to reconcile them to Henry's own supremacy; the way was also paved for a better understanding with the Protestant princes of Germany whom Henry's political exigencies compelled him then to conciliate. Before the quarrel with the Emperor over Catherine of Aragon, the intense rivalry between Charles V. and Francis I. made England fairly secure; but the policy Henry pursued with regard to the Church involved the possibility of a Catholic coalition, and forced him to look beyond France for friends. These would naturally be found in the German Protestants, who, since 1530, had always been on the verge of war with their Catholic Habsburg rulers. In 1535 and 1536, English agents had been busy in Germany seeking for the basis of a political and theological union between England and the Lutheran states. Two years later the growing friendship of Charles and Francis, promoted by Paul III., threatened both English and Germans, and another effort was made to bring them together. This was Cromwell's favourite scheme, and Cranmer from very different motives threw himself eagerly into the work. He had since 1532 kept in communication with Lutheran divines, and his own theological opinions were nearer the Lutheran standpoint than those of any other Bishop in England. In 1536 Bucer dedicated to Cranmer his commentary on the Epistle to the Romans, prefixing a long letter which expressed the hope of Germany that the Archbishop of Canterbury would succeed in his efforts to reform the Church in England.[1] When the Protestant deputies, headed by Burckhardt, Vice-chancellor of Saxony, arrived in London in May, 1538, they found their chief support in Cranmer, and the Archbishop probably presided at the conferences between them and the English Bishops. The Germans demanded, as a preliminary to an alliance, the concession of the cup to the laity, the abolition of private masses, and permission for priests to marry; but the English Bishops refused to discuss these demands, saying that Henry VIII. was himself composing a reply. They wished to treat of the four disputed sacraments, matrimony, holy orders, confirmation, and extreme unction; but on these points they knew, says Cranmer, that the Germans would not agree with them, "so that I perceive," he writes to Cromwell, "that the bishops seek only an occasion to break the concord."[2] They were, however, better informed of Henry's mind than the Archbishop. It was not Cranmer, but Tunstall,[3] who was asked to assist the King; and his reply asserted the Catholic view of all the disputed questions. The concession of the cup to the laity, permission for priests to marry, and the abolition of private masses were

[1] Strype, *Cranmer*, i., 70.

[2] Cranmer, *Works*, ii., 379.

[3] Pocock's *Burnet*, i., 408; Gardiner seems also to have been consulted. The King's answer is printed by Pocock, iv., 373. See other documents relating to the German mission in Strype's *Ecclesiastical Memorials*, vol. i., App., Nos. 94–102.

all refused, and in October the Protestant envoys returned home empty-handed.

This rigid adherence to Catholic doctrine did not imply any slackening in Henry's pursuit of ecclesiastical property, or in his onslaughts on what he called superstitious practices; and in 1538–39 there was a regular campaign against the remaining monasteries, the shrines and relics of the saints, and wonder-working images. Cranmer himself suggested that royal commissioners should inspect the blood of S. Thomas in Christ Church, Canterbury, which he suspected to be but "a feigned thing, made of some red ochre or of such like matter."[1] The "blood of Hailes" suffered a similar inquisition, and the wonderful Rood of Boxley, an image whose eyes opened and shut, was exposed at Maidstone. These, we are told, were innocent toys never intended to deceive the most credulous folk,[2] and never put to such uses as the blood of S. Januarius at Naples. But, for innocent toys, their destruction provoked a somewhat excessive jubilation among the reformers. "Dagon," wrote one,[3] "is everywhere falling in England. Bel of Babylon has been broken in pieces"; and it is doubtful whether the Philistines looked upon Dagon and the Assyrians regarded Bel as nothing but innocent toys.

[1] *Works*, ii., 378.

[2] Bridgett, *Blunders and Forgeries*; Gairdner, *Church History*, p. 199.

[3] "Ruit hic passim Azzotinus Dagon; Bel ille Babylonicus jamdudum confractus est" (John Hoker of Maidstone to Bullinger in Burnet, vi., p. 194–195); cf. *Original Letters*, Parker Soc., ii., 609–610.

The surrender of the greater monasteries and the destruction of shrines like that of S. Thomas at Canterbury yielded Henry more solid gratifications than the burning of graven images. Rents from thousands of acres of monastic land went to fill the gaping void in Henry's exchequer, and cartloads of gold and jewels from the shrine of S. Thomas found their way to the royal treasure-house. This last outrage on Catholic sentiment precipitated the issue of the bull of excommunication which the Pope had long held in suspense over Henry's head. But its force was spent even before Henry's new treasures, and its main effect was to drive the King into the arms of Anne of Cleves. The Duke of Cleves was not exactly a Lutheran,[1] but he had reforming tendencies, heretical relationships, and claims on parts of the Netherlands; and Cromwell hoped, by marrying the King to Anne, to cement a political alliance between the German princes and England. The Emperor was passing through France on apparently intimate terms with Francis I.; and if, in their interviews at Paris, the two Catholic sovereigns agreed to obey the behests of their father the Pope, the English king would be placed in an awkward position. And so Henry consented, led on by Holbein's flattering portrait of Anne of Cleves and by Cromwell's extravagant praise of her charms,[2] to place his neck

---

[1] See Merriman, *Cromwell*, i., 246–247; *Cambridge Modern History*, ii., 236–237.

[2] Holbein's portrait now in the Louvre is here reproduced. Cromwell told Henry that every one praised her beauty, and that she excelled the Duchess of Milan "as the golden sun did the silver

once more under the matrimonial yoke; he hoped that his support of Cleves and other German princes would give Charles enough to do at home without troubling to execute Papal censures in England.

The event belied both Cromwell's and Cranmer's expectations, and brought their ideas of a religious reformation into violent conflict with those of their masterful sovereign. Cromwell's religious sincerity has recently been denied, mainly in order to enhance his reputation for unscrupulous political skill.[1] Probably some injustice has thereby been done him; his private friendship with advanced reformers,[2] and his hostility to Catholic prelates seem inconsistent with the theory that to him all religions were indifferent; his constant efforts to promote a union with Protestant princes give more support to his sincerity than to his sagacity, and one of the counts against him in the Act of Attainder was that he affirmed heretical doctrine condemned by the King to be good. About Cranmer's attitude there is no doubt; his statesmanship was not of a very high order, and he was little interested in the political aspect of affairs. His mind was bent on religious reform, and his theological opinions travelled slowly but steadily away from the Old in the direction of the New Learning.

---

moon." The portrait of the Duchess of Milan, now in the National Gallery, explains how chagrined Henry was when he saw Anne.

[1] Merriman, *Life and Letters of Thomas Cromwell*, 1902.

[2] *E. g.*, with Stephen Vaughan, for whom see *Dict. Nat. Biog.*, lviii., 179; the freedom with which Vaughan expressed Protestant opinions to Cromwell is incomprehensible unless he was sure of their favourable reception.

His zeal for the Reformation and his sanguine temperament sometimes led him to take a more optimistic view of its progress than the facts warranted; and in 1537 he rebuked a Kentish magistrate for asserting that the Ten Articles and the *Institution of a Christian Man* "allowed all the old fashion and put all the knaves of the New Learning to silence."

> "If," Cranmer went on, "men will indifferently read those late declarations, they shall well perceive that purgatory, pilgrimages, praying to saints, images, holy bread, holy water, holy days,[1] merits, works, ceremony, and such other be not restored to their late accustomed abuses; but shall evidently perceive that the word of God hath gotten the upper hand of them all."[2]

This dispute as to the real intention of Anglican doctrine was the first of a series which is not yet exhausted; and thus early it appeared that the Anglican settlement was to be a compromise between two opposing schools of thought, and a compromise so ambiguously and so skilfully expressed that each party could read into the terms its own individual meaning and turn them to its own purposes whenever it happened to be predominant.

Cranmer, however, still held to Catholic doctrine in its essential details. He, like the Church, recog-

---

[1] Cranmer himself complained to Cromwell that these superstitious holy-days were still observed at court (Strype, *Cranmer*, ii., 729).

[2] Cranmer, *Works*, ii., 349–356; in Pocock's *Burnet*, iv., 298–299, are printed "some considerations offered to the King by Cranmer, to induce him to proceed to a further reformation," but he had to wait till the reign of Edward VI.

nised no divorce, and set his face against the prevailing lax views on marriage which had been encouraged by the frequency of Papal dispensations from the canon law. He was often pressed by men of influence to grant similar dispensations himself,[1] but always refused. He wrote in disgust to Osiander about the immorality at which Lutheran divines connived when practised by Lutheran princes, and particularly with respect to the bigamous marriage which they, adopting a precedent set by a Pope, countenanced in the case of Philip of Hesse.

> "What excuse," he asked, "can you possibly offer for allowing divorce and remarriage while both the divorced parties are alive, or what is still worse, without any divorce at all, the marriage of a man to more than one wife? By the teaching of the Apostles and of Christ himself, marriage is only of one with one, nor can those who have been joined contract new unions except after the death of one or the other partner."[2]

He also still held the canonical doctrine that "such marriages as be in lawful age contracted *per verba de præsenti* are matrimony before God," and such solemn betrothals therefore invalidated any subsequent marriage with other persons.

Not less important was his assertion of the Catholic doctrine of the mass. He had already abandoned the Roman dogma of Transubstantiation; it is not affirmed in the Ten Articles of 1536, and in 1538 he

[1] *Cf.* Cranmer, *Works*, ii., 250–251, 329.

[2] *Cotton MS.*, Cleopatra, E. v. f. 111, printed in Strype, *Cranmer*, ii., 752–756, and Cranmer, *Works*, ii., 404.

wrote to Cromwell that Adam Damlip, the preacher of Calais, "taught but the truth" when he "confuted the opinion of Transubstantiation." But he was still a firm believer in the Real Presence; and when a Zwinglian, Joachim of Watt (Vadianus), whose acquaintance Cranmer seems to have made in 1532, sent him a treatise against that doctrine, he declared himself much displeased with the argument, and said he wished Vadianus had employed his study to better purpose.[1] Nor did he deny the necessity of recourse, in the last resort, to extreme penalties against obstinate disbelievers in the real presence. Toleration was in the sixteenth century no more a part of the orthodox Protestant creed than it was of Roman Catholicism; Protestants as well as Catholics thought that only one form of truth could be true, and that form must be preserved at all costs; and toleration was not conceded until the impossibility of forcing men to conform to one orthodox standard had been practically demonstrated. But Cranmer's mildness made him reluctant to persecute, and the tale of his victims is short. In 1538 one Atkinson[2] was accused before Cranmer of denying the sacrament of the altar; but he recanted and escaped with doing penance. In the same year Cranmer was joined with other Bishops in the proceedings against John Lambert, but Stokesley and

[1] *Cotton MS.*, Cleopatra, E. v. f. 111, printed in Strype, *Cranmer*, i., 94–95, ii., 740–742; Cranmer, *Works*, ii., 342–344; *Original Letters* (Parker Soc.), i., 11.

[2] The German envoys interceded in vain on Atkinson's behalf; *cf.* Cranmer, *Works*, ii., 372, and Mason, pp. 106–107.

Gardiner were the moving spirits, and Gardiner is said to have expressed discontent with the way in which Cranmer at Henry's command replied to Lambert's contentions. The King himself presided at Lambert's trial, and the sentence was read by Cromwell.[1] With regard to Anabaptists he probably felt less scruple; the recent excesses at Münster had shocked the whole of Europe, and the Lutheran elector of Saxony wrote to warn Henry VIII. against members of the sect who were flocking to England. The Archbishop was placed on a commission to deal with them,[2] but we have no details to show his personal connection with the burning of three Anabaptists on St. Andrew's Day, 1538,[3] and he was soon absorbed in an attempt to stem the tide of reaction which in the following year threatened to involve all reformers alike in a common fate.

---

[1] Cranmer was also concerned in the singular case of Friar John Forest, who is erroneously said (*Dict. Nat. Biog.*, xix., 435) to have been imprisoned in 1534 "on a charge of heresy, the basis of which was denial of the King's supremacy." The Act of Supremacy had not then been passed, and when it was, denial of the King's supremacy was not heresy but treason. The heresies for which Forest was condemned by Cranmer are given in Wriothesley's *Chronicle* (Camden Soc.), i., 79; his denial of the royal supremacy also involved him in a charge of treason, and at his execution he had to suffer the penalties for both crimes; he was hanged in chains for treason, and for his heresy a fire was lighted under him. It was not in accord with the refined cruelty of the age that a man should escape with one form of death when he had been condemned on two capital charges.

[2] Strype, *Cranmer*, i., 99.

[3] Wriothesley, *Chronicle*, i., 90.

CHAPTER V

CRANMER AND THE CATHOLIC REACTION

IT is a commonplace with historians to write of the last eight years of Henry VIII.'s reign as the first of those periods of reaction which have followed on each successive stage of England's progress from Roman Catholicism. The Lutheran tendencies of 1529–38 gave way to Catholic influence during the remainder of Henry's reign. The rapid Protestant advance of Edward VI. was succeeded by the violent Romanism of Mary. Elizabeth's reign was marked by a steady growth of Puritan feeling; and on its heels trod the High Anglican reaction of Laud and the other Caroline divines which culminated in the attempts of Charles II. and James II. to bring England again within the Roman fold. The revolution of 1688 was religious no less than political, and its effects upon the Church were the complete predominance of the State, the abeyance of Convocation, and the supremacy of Low Church and Latitudinarian views. Against this last phase Newman and Pusey raised their protest, and the movement which they started may not even now have reached its flood.

This oscillation which has characterised England's political and religious history affords ground for a convenient generalisation; but it must not be exaggerated, and too much stress has often been laid upon the variations in the ecclesiastical policy pursued by Henry VIII. The changes described in the last chapter did not mean to the King that doctrinal revolution which they seemed to imply to the Archbishop; and it is probable that Henry went no further in this direction "than the more enlightened popes and cardinals would have done."[1] He had himself, in 1538, drawn up the reply to the emissaries of the Schmalkaldic League, rebutting their arguments against communion in one element, clerical celibacy and private masses, points on which even good Catholics were then inclined to make concessions; and he was at the same time edifying the orthodox by creeping to the Cross on Good Friday, serving the priest at mass, and observing all other "laudable ceremonies." In spite of the store which he set upon his own private judgment, Protestant theology never made its way into Henry's heart or mind. He had abolished the Pope, but not Popery, wrote Bishop Hooper.[2] It would be truer to say that he had taken the place of the Pope in the English Church, and substituted a Royal for a Roman Catholicism.

In this religious conservatism Henry VIII. was at one with the mass of his people. The accumulated force of the habits, customs, and traditions of cent-

[1] Stubbs, *Lectures on Mediæval and Modern History*, 1887, p. 298.

[2] *Original Letters* (Parker Soc.), i., 36.

uries could not be destroyed at once, nor merely by preaching; and it is probable that the heart of the nation never went out to the Protestant cause until it had been sanctified by the blood of the Marian martyrs. In 1538–9 the majority of Englishmen were Catholic to the core.

"Who is there almost," complained a reformer in 1539, "that will have a Bible but he must be compelled thereto. How loath be our priests to teach the commandments, the articles of the Faith, and the *Paternoster* in English! Again how unwilling be the people to learn it! Yea, they jest at it calling it the New *Paternoster* and the New Learning."[1]

And there were parishes in which it was held to be more profitable for men's souls that they should spend their time praying on their beads than listening to the Scriptures. The popular feeling, which Henry VIII. had used as a lever and without which even he would have been powerless, was animosity towards the papal claims and towards the wealth and class privileges of the clergy, and not towards the doctrine of the Church. Now the papal jurisdiction had been abolished; the nobility and gentry had sated their envy of clerical riches by sharing the spoils of the monasteries; the commercial classes had been appeased by the prohibition of the more obnoxious forms of clerical trading, and by the limitation of the Church's power to prosecute for heresy; while the Catholic susceptibilities of the nation had been outraged by the irreverent extravagances into

[1] *L. and P.*, vol. xiv., pt. ii., p. 140.

which the more violent of the Protestant agitators had been led by their hatred of papal abuses. There was little desire to undo what had been done, and the reaction of the next two years only implied a cessation in the progress of the revolution; yet the predominant feeling in the nation was that things had gone far enough. Bucer believed that Gardiner had warned the King that if he proceeded further, commotions would occur, and that he would find the principal lords in the kingdom against him[1]; and Luther complained that although England had taken away the Pope's name and property, she was strengthening "his doctrine and abominations."[2]

In this condition of public opinion a general election took place in March, 1539. Its course was marked by an unusual amount of government interference, for the idea that there was no freedom of election in Tudor times, and that the House of Commons was an assembly of royal nominees, is a gross exaggeration.[3] The bribes or threats employed in 1539 were not, so far as the evidence enables us to judge, directed towards securing the return of royal nominees in preference to popular candidates, so much as towards promoting the election of one set of ministerial candidates rather than another; that is to say, Cromwell was nursing a party to overthrow

[1] *Corpus Reformatorum*, iii., 775.

[2] *L. and P.*, xiv., ii., 327; Luther, *Briefe*, v. 209; compare Luther's letter to the Elector of Saxony, 23 Oct., 1539, for some curious remarks on Henry VIII. and Gardiner. *Corpus Ref.*, iii., 796; *L. and P.*, xiv., ii., 379.

[3] See E. and A. Porritt, *The Unreformed House of Commons*, 1903.

Gardiner and Norfolk. The result was a striking illustration of the difficulty of packing a Parliament against the popular will; for the House of Commons, which Cromwell took particular pains to pack, passed without a dissentient voice the Act of Attainder against him, and left his rivals secure in royal favour. The Protestant policy which he and his adherents favoured received a sudden check, and the Act by which the Parliament of 1539 is best remembered is the ferocious Statute of Six Articles.

That this blow to the cause of religious reformation was severely felt by Cranmer, goes without saying, and his only ground for satisfaction was the knowledge that he had done his best to avert it. He was naturally a member of the Lords' committee appointed at the King's instance to devise some uniform standard of faith; but the committee, which represented in fairly equal proportion prelates of the Old and the New Learning, could come to no agreement; and after ten days' debate the Duke of Norfolk brought the question before the House of Lords itself.[1] There it was fully discussed for three days. Cranmer, assisted by Bishops Goodrich of Ely, Shaxton of Salisbury, Latimer of Worcester, Hilsey of Rochester, and Barlow of S. Davids, maintained the principles of the Reformation against Archbishop Lee of York and Bishops Gardiner of Winchester, Stokesley of London, Sampson of Chichester, Tunstall of Durham, Repps of Norwich, and Aldrich of Carlisle. Opinions among the Bishops were fairly balanced, but in the whole House the Reformers were in a

[1] *Lords' Journals*, vol. i., p. 109.

hopeless minority. "We of the temporality," writes a peer in describing the scene,[1] "have been all of one mind," and that mind was one of bitter hostility to the New Learning. At length the King himself intervened. There was little doubt as to which side he would take; he attached small weight to the views of his Bishops, whether Catholic or Protestant, when they conflicted with those of the laity; and when the weight of all the lay peers and of at least half the Bishops was thrown into one scale, when even Cromwell and Audley deserted the losing cause, it is doubtful whether Henry could have redressed the balance even had he agreed with Cranmer and been willing to risk his authority in a conflict with Catholic feeling. His object was to compel uniformity, and it was less dangerous to require the few than the many to submit. So, in the words of an admiring peer, the King confounded them all with his learning. Other persuasions may have been used; Cranmer is said to have refused to be confounded with learning, and to have submitted only when ordered by the King to withdraw.[2]

[1] *L. and P.*, xiv., 1040; Burnet, vi., 233; *Narratives of the Reformation*, p. 248.

[2] This assertion apparently rests on the uncorroborated statement of Foxe. In one point Cranmer carried the King with him, namely, that auricular confession was not enjoined by Scripture. Tunstall challenged this view, whereupon Henry wrote to him to say that his arguments were futile (Burnet, iv., 400–407). In 1549 Cranmer asserted that the Six Articles would never have passed unless the King had come personally into the Parliament house (*Works*, ii., 168). This assertion illustrates the sanguine way in which Cranmer underestimated the forces opposed to him.

This submission was in any case only partial, and on some of the points in dispute the Archbishop renewed the struggle in Convocation a few days later. The proposals were introduced not of course by Cranmer, who would never have done such violence to his convictions, but by Cromwell, who, as Vicegerent, took precedence of all the Prelates.[1] The assertion of the doctrine of Transubstantiation and of the perpetual force of vows of chastity seems not to have been challenged again. All the Bishops agreed that private masses might "stand with the Word of God," and that confession was "very requisite and necessary"; but Cranmer, Shaxton, Latimer, Hilsey, and Barlow reaffirmed that priests might lawfully marry, and Cranmer and Barlow contended that the sacrament should be administered under both kinds. In the Lower House of Convocation there were only two dissentients from the Six Articles, Cranmer's commissary and marriage-connection, Dr. Nevinson[2] and Dr. John Taylor, the future bishop of Lincoln.[3] The New Learning on the episcopal bench was the result of Cromwell's and Cranmer's patronage and of Henry VIII.'s political exigencies; it had taken little root as yet in the church, and the lower clergy were still unmoved by its power.

---

[1] For the debates in Convocation, see Wilkins's *Concilia*, iii., 845, and *L. and P.*, xiv., i., 1065.

[2] In *L. and P.*, xiv., i., 1065, the name is misprinted "Levynson."

[3] For Taylor, see the present writer in *Dict. Nat. Biog.*, lv., 430.

Rarely indeed has a measure been passed with such manifold signs of general approval as the "bloody whip with six strings." Henry VIII.'s apologists have cast the whole burden of responsibility upon the Catholic bishops, and clerical historians have retorted it upon Henry VIII. It is idle to exculpate the one or the other, but both put together need not bear all the blame. The Catholic bishops would have been powerless to carry the Act, and Henry VIII. would not have helped, unless the mass of the laity had been on the same side. It is an anachronism to represent the people of England in the sixteenth century as enamoured of either political or religious liberty. Toleration was shocking to the minds of the most enlightened; Sir Thomas More may not have committed the cruelties which Foxe alleges against him, but in theory at any rate he believed in religious persecution. As for the masses, they viewed with the utmost indifference the burning of martyrs for heresy and the torture of priests for treason, and the Act of Six Articles passed without a sign of popular protest.

The Act and the policy it implied involved one or two changes on the episcopal bench. Latimer was made to give up the See of Worcester and Shaxton that of Salisbury.[1] Cranmer, Barlow, Goodrich, and Hilsey were retained in their bishoprics, and so long as that was the royal pleasure they had no option but to remain. The modern practice of resigning

[1] Their resignation does not appear to have been voluntary, but to have been extorted or at least suggested by the King (Dixon, ii. 138–139).

distasteful and difficult posts would have consorted ill with the rigorous ideal of duty to the State which prevailed in the sixteenth century. Cranmer, like every one else in that age, admitted the right of the State or the Church to overrule individual conscience; and the tyranny of this political principle was not brought home to his mind till towards the end of his life. The harshness of the theory was, moreover, considerably modified in practice under Henry VIII. The Archbishop was not forced to make any alteration of view with regard to the doctrines laid down by the Act of Six Articles, nor was he required personally to execute its pains and penalties. It is one of the few admirable traits of Henry's character that, provided his ministers observed the outward form of his somewhat arbitrary laws, he did not seek to put further burdens on their conscience. We have it on Sir Thomas More's own authority,[1] that all the time that he was Chancellor the King did not employ him on business connected with the divorce of Catherine of Aragon, because he knew that More disapproved of it; and in the same way he did not expect Cranmer in person to handle the whip with the six bloody strings.

Under these conditions Cranmer remained at his post, not without benefit to the cause of the Reformation, for it was doubtless due to his and Cromwell's

[1] The King, says More, "only used in prosecuting the matter those whose consciences were persuaded, while those who thought otherwise he used in other business" (More, *English Works*, i., 424; Strype, *Eccl. Mem.*, I., ii., No. 48; *L. and P.*, 1534, p. 123). More also says that Henry's first lesson to him on entering his service was that he should look first to God, and after God to him.

influence that the penalties attached to the Act of Six Articles were not put in execution. In October, 1539, Burckhardt, the Lutheran envoy, wrote to Melanchthon, rejoicing that "the papistical faction had nowise obtained its hoped-for tyranny"; [1] they had only secured the statute, he said, and not its execution, and he had no doubt but that it would shortly be abolished. Gardiner and his allies had not yet won the victory; both he and the reactionary Bishop of Chichester were excluded from the Council, and Cromwell was planning that marriage with Anne of Cleves, which it was hoped would wed Henry VIII. indissolubly with the anti-Catholic cause.

Yet the Catholics were leaving no stone unturned to ruin the two protagonists of reform, and the peril in which Cranmer stood is illustrated by a curious tale related to Foxe by the Archbishop's secretary, Morice.[2] After the passing of the Act of Six Articles, Henry VIII., who was genuinely interested in theological questions, sent to Cranmer and asked him to give him in writing a statement of the reasons which had led him to oppose the measure. When the manuscript was completed Cranmer entrusted it to Morice, who happened to be crossing the Thames in a wherry, while a bear was being baited in the water. The animal broke loose, capsized Morice's boat, and the manuscript went floating down the river. It was recovered by the keeper of the Princess

[1] *L. and P.*, XIV., ii., p. 149.

[2] It is reprinted in the present writer's *Tudor Tracts*, 1903, pp. 35 *et sqq.*

Elizabeth's bears, a strenuous Catholic; he perused the book, and, convinced that he could now put a spoke in the Archbishop's wheel,[1] refused to surrender his treasure at any price. The next day he went to the Council chamber to deliver what he considered damning evidence of Cranmer's heresy to Sir Anthony Browne or Bishop Gardiner. But Morice had warned Cromwell beforehand, and Cromwell, summoning the bearward, made him relinquish the manuscript and soundly rated him for withholding it from its proper owner.

The Archbishop, however, was not to enjoy the advantage of Cromwell's protection much longer. Anne of Cleves landed at Dover in December, 1539, and on the 29th of that month Cranmer met and entertained her at Canterbury. But the lady whose beauty had been extolled by Cromwell and flattered by Holbein was not to Henry's taste, and he talked of renouncing the marriage. He rudely described his bride as a "Flanders mare," and sullenly asked Cromwell if he must really put his neck under the yoke.[2] He affected to doubt whether she really was

[1] By the Act of Six Articles it was heresy to speak against the first of them, and treason to speak against the rest; so that Cranmer, by committing his arguments to paper, was rendering himself liable to both these penalties. That he did it by the King's command might have been no more protection to him than the King's licence was to Wolsey when accused of a breach of *Præmunire;* for Henry had already, when it suited his purpose, adumbrated the modern constitutional doctrine that the royal licence or command was no bar to prosecution for a breach of statute law.

[2] "My Lord," said Henry to Cromwell, "if it were not to satisfy the world and my realm, I would not do that I shall do this day for none earthly thing" (*L. and P.*, xv., 824).

free from her alleged precontract with the son of the Duke of Lorraine; but Cranmer argued that the engagement had not gone far enough to prevent her marriage with Henry. Fear lest her repudiation should throw her German friends into the arms of Charles V. and Francis I., and leave England without an ally, induced the King to complete the match; and on 6 January Cranmer married the pair at Greenwich.[1] Closer acquaintance only increased Henry's disgust, while soon an incipient breach between Charles and Francis showed that the plain Anne of Cleves and the distasteful German alliance might both be discarded with safety.

The result was fatal to Cromwell, but it need hardly be said that the failure of the Cleves marriage was not the only cause of the minister's fall. The non-execution of the Act of Six Articles and the continued immunity which Protestant preachers enjoyed exasperated the Catholic party and braced it to make one more effort. The changes on the episcopal bench in 1539-40 were all in their favour. Two reactionaries, Bell and Capon, took the places of Latimer and Shaxton at Worcester and Salisbury. Stokesley, the truculent Bishop of London, died in September, 1539, but his See was taken by the still more strenuous Bonner. Heath, Queen Mary's future Chancellor, succeeded the reforming Hilsey at Rochester, and another Catholic, Skip, stepped into Bonner's shoes at Hereford.[2] A royal

[1] Hall, *Chronicle*, p. 836.

[2] See Le Neve, *Fasti.*, ed. Hardy, and the *D. N. B.* for all these prelates.

commission was sent to purge Calais of the heresy which Cranmer's commissary had encouraged there, and fingers were pointed at Cranmer himself. Nor was he more popular in the country than at the Court; when he summoned a popular London preacher, Dr. Watts, to account for his Catholic doctrine, ten thousand citizens are said to have assembled to know the reason why[1]; and the popular temper of the time is illustrated by the fact that persecution of heretics was rarely so severe as in 1539-40, when the administration of heresy laws had been largely confided to secular hands.[2]

All this was of evil omen to Cromwell. Whatever his private religious views may have been, he had become identified with a Protestant policy, and the fight between him and his foes was in effect a struggle between Reformer and Catholic for control of the government. The match was sadly unequal. Cromwell had no real friend but Cranmer, and the Archbishop's political influence was never very considerable. Melanchthon and the Lutheran princes of Germany might write in Cromwell's praise, but Henry paid more heed to the opinions of Francis I. and Charles V., who both detested the upstart Vicegerent. During his mission to Paris in February, 1540, Norfolk was warned by the French king of the evil impression produced by Cromwell's dealings,[3] and Norfolk, like every other English noble, hated Cromwell even more than he had hated

[1] *L. and P.*, XIV., ii., p. 280.

[2] Dixon, *History*, ii., 135-136.

[3] *L. and P.*, xv., 785.

Wolsey. In this matter, as in that of the Six Articles, the temporal peers were all of one mind. Cromwell's power had no root except in the royal favour, and Henry was beginning to wonder whether his minister's great abilities were worth the friction which his retention involved. The struggles in the Council were becoming a public danger; now one and now the other faction gained the upper hand. In April, 1540, Marillac, the French ambassador, wrote that Cromwell was tottering to his fall, and cynically commiserated Cranmer and the other divines who, having taught the lords to spoil the monasteries, were now threatened with ruin themselves.[1] Gardiner had been readmitted to the Council, and there was a plan for making the Catholic Tunstall Vicegerent.[2] But the end was not yet. A few days later Cromwell was created Earl of Essex, two of his satellites[3] were made secretaries of State, his enemy, the Bishop of Chichester, was sent to the Tower, and it was rumoured that Cranmer would begin a course of sermons at St. Paul's Cross to obliterate the effect of those delivered by Gardiner in the previous Lent. Nor would Cromwell stop there. There were five bishops, he said, who ought to be sent to the Tower like Sampson of Chichester; every day, wrote Marillac, new accusations were discovered, and things were brought to such a pass that either Cromwell's or Gardiner's party must succumb.

[1] Ribier, *Lettres*, etc., Paris, 1666, i., 513.

[2] *L. and P.*, XIV., pt. ii., p. 141; XV., 486.

[3] Thomas Wriothesley, afterwards Earl of Southampton, and (Sir) Ralph Sadleir.

The Bishops were in a state of "envy and irreconcilable division, and the people in doubt what to believe."[1] The tension was too great to last; if some solution were not speedily found there would be open disruption.

Then Henry struck as "remorselessly and suddenly as a beast of prey."[2] On the 10th of June Norfolk accused Cromwell of treason; the whole Council joined in the attack, and the Vicegerent was stripped of the Garter and sent to the Tower. A vast number of crimes were laid at his door. He was "the most false and corrupt traitor, deceiver, and circumventor against your most royal person and the imperial crown of this your realm that hath been known, seen, or heard of in all the time of your most noble reign." He had done innumerable acts without the sovereign's knowledge or licence, and had boasted that "he was sure of" the King. Being a "detestable heretic," he had "secretly set forth and dispensed into all shires" a "great number of false, erroneous books," sowing disbelief in the Sacrament of the Altar "and other articles of Christian religion most graciously declared by your majesty by the authority of Parliament," and had averred that it was as lawful for every Christian man to be a minister of the said Sacrament as it was for a priest. He had released heretics from prison, saved them from punishment, and rebuked their accusers. He was, in fact, the prime cause of all the heresy and schism in the land; in defence of it he said he would

---

[1] *L. and P.*, xv., 737.

[2] Brewer in *L. and P.*, iv., Pref., p. dcxxi.

THOMAS CROMWELL, EARL OF ESSEX.

BY HOLBEIN, PROBABLE DATE ABOUT 1537. PICTURE IS NOW AT TYTTENHANGER PARK, AND IS REPRODUCED BY PERMISSION OF THE COUNTESS OF CALEDON AND MESSRS. GOUPIL.

fight the King in person, and he hoped that if he lived a year or two longer, the King would be powerless to resist; finally he had held "your nobles of your realm in great disdain, derision, and detestation."[1]

All this and much more was set down in an Act of Attainder which passed both Houses of Parliament without opposition. The only voice raised in Cromwell's favour was Cranmer's. He wrote to the King, "with timidity," says Lingard, "boldly considering the times," says Lord Herbert, on Cromwell's behalf.[2] It was not of much use to address Henry in hectoring tones, and whether Cranmer's letter was bold or timid, his was now, as it was in the case of Anne Boleyn, the only plea which any one ventured to urge in favour of mercy. In neither instance did it prove of any avail. Cromwell, like the Countess of Salisbury in the previous year, was not even accorded a form of trial. Parliament condemned him unheard, and on the 20th of July he was beheaded on Tower Hill.[3]

The last service the King required of him was that he should contribute his share of evidence

[1] Burnet, iv., 415–423.

[2] *Works*, Parker Soc., ii., 401.

[3] The expression that Cromwell died by the bloody laws which he himself made is often misunderstood as meaning that he invented the use of Acts of Attainder. That of course was not the case. Acts of Attainder were in use before Cromwell's time, but even in Henry VIII.'s reign they were usually passed in addition to, and not as a substitute for, legal trials. Their motive was to render the nation an accomplice in all the King's acts of severity, to make out that these executions were not merely the deeds of the King or of a

towards the divorce of Anne of Cleves.[1] That the moving cause in that measure was Henry's disgust with his wife and dislike of the German alliance admits of no doubt; but neither was a sufficient legal justification, and it is necessary to examine the legal grounds upon which Cranmer, Convocation, and Parliament based the dissolution of the marriage. The law which had to be administered was of course the Roman canon law which had not been abolished with the Roman jurisdiction, but remained in a state of suspended animation, capable of being repudiated or enforced as circumstances might require. According to that law, the validity of a sacrament depends upon the "intention" of the minister; for instance, an Anglican clergyman might administer the Eucharist with all due Roman forms, but unless he believed in Transubstantiation his administration would not be efficacious, because his "intention" would be defective. Marriage is a sacrament which the parties minister to themselves,[2] and if there is a defective intention on the part of either the marriage may be invalid. Henry VIII. therefore set to work to prove that his "intention" in marrying Anne of Cleves had been defective; that the matrimony was no more than a form which circumstances had compelled him to adopt. Hence the depositions of

---

jury which might be packed, but of the whole nation represented in the High Court of Parliament. What Cromwell did was to secure condemnation of the Countess of Salisbury by an Act of Attainder *without* the usual trial, and this was the measure meted out to him.

[1] *L. and P.*, xv., 823–824; Merriman, *Cromwell*, ii., 268–272.

[2] See T. Sanchez, *De Matrimonio*, 1739, bks ii. and iv.

Cromwell and other courtiers parading Henry's expressions of reluctance and disgust on the eve of his marriage.[1] Probably the depositions are substantially true, but they do not prove that the pressure of external danger was so great as to render the King's "intention" sufficiently defective to invalidate his act.[2] That was a question of state which Henry claimed that he alone could decide.

None the less the divorce was a scandal only rendered possible by the survival of the grotesque requirements of the canon law; and the whole Church and people of England must share the opprobrium which primarily attaches to the King. It was Gardiner and not Cranmer who "explained the cause of the nullity of the marriage in a lucid speech" before Convocation.[3] The decree of invalidity was subscribed by Gardiner, Tunstall, and Bonner, as well as by Cranmer; it was signed by nineteen Bishops and by a hundred and thirty-nine other divines,[4] who apparently thought it a venial offence to strain the marriage law a point or two if by so doing they could get rid of an unpopular Queen and an undesirable policy. In the sixteenth century, when the interests of the State overrode every other consideration, it would have seemed pedantry to take any other course. Happily, so far as Anne of Cleves was concerned, there was more of comedy than of

[1] Printed in Strype, *Eccl. Memorials*, I., ii., 452–463.

[2] In comparatively recent years the Pope annulled the marriage of the Princess of Monaco, who pleaded that she had no "intention" of marrying, but had been forced into it by Napoleon III.

[3] Wilkins, *Concilia*, iii., 851; *L. and P.*, xv., 860.

[4] The list is given in Burnet, iv., 431, and in *L. and P.*, xv., 861.

tragedy. There is no reason to suppose that her separation from Henry was a great blow to her affections. She was liberally endowed with estates to the then enormous value of four thousand pounds a year. She was richer and freer than she had been in Cleves; she was probably more happy and certainly far more secure than she would have been as Henry's wife. She lived on excellent terms with him and with his successors, and when she died in 1558 was buried in Westminster Abbey.[1]

While Cranmer must share in the responsibility for whatever illegality there may have been in Anne's divorce, he is exempt from the blame of having sought to bring it to pass. That rests mainly upon Gardiner and the Duke of Norfolk. It was they who deliberately used the charms of another woman to stimulate Henry's repugnance to Anne and resolve to put her away. The lady selected was Catherine Howard, Norfolk's niece, and it was under the Bishop of Winchester's roof that a familiarity first grew up between her and the King.[2] The Bishop, writes one of Bullinger's correspondents, very often provided feastings and entertainments for the pair in his palace at Southwark.[3] The first official intimation of the favour in which she was held was the grant to her of the goods of two escaped malefactors in April, 1540, two and a half months before Anne's divorce.[4] Other tokens fol-

[1] See Bouterwek, *Anna von Cleve*.

[2] *Dict. Nat. Biog.*, ix., 304.

[3] *Original Letters*, Parker Soc., i., 202.

[4] *L. and P.*, xv., 613 [12].

lowed, and on the 28th of July,[1] nineteen days after Convocation had pronounced the marriage with Anne of Cleves invalid, Henry privately wedded Catherine Howard at Oatlands.

Thus was completed the triumph of the Catholic party. It was not so absolute as some desired, for Cranmer still remained Primate of England, Audley was still Lord-Chancellor, and other statesmen of reforming proclivities, such as the future Protector Somerset, were growing in influence; and it is a common error to suppose that the ferocious penalties of the Six Articles were enforced with any persistence.[2] Yet enough had been done to show the helplessness of the reformers. Norfolk, who openly expressed a partiality for burning heretics, was the Queen's uncle and the King's chief minister, while Gardiner represented Henry's predominant theological mood. Continental Protestants were aghast at the repudiation of Anne of Cleves, and the burning of men like Barnes, Gerrard, and Jerome; and

[1] This is the date given by Dr. Gairdner in *Dict. Nat. Biog.*, ix., 304, but in his *Church History*, 1902, p. 218, he gives 8 August, the day on which Catherine was publicly proclaimed Queen.

[2] Canon Dixon (Vol. II., caps. x., xi.) first examined this misconception satisfactorily; cf. *L. and. P.*, 1543, pt. i., Pref., p. xlix.; pt. ii., Pref., p. xxxiv.; *Original Letters*, ii., 614, 627; S. R. Maitland, *Essays on the Reformation* (ed., 1898). In 1540 Henry ordered "that no further persecution should take place for religion, and that those in prison should be set at liberty on finding security for their appearance when called for." (*L. and P.*, xvi., p. 271.) Cranmer himself wrote that "within a year or little more" Henry "was fain to temper his said laws, and moderate them in divers points; so that the statute of Six Articles continued in force little above the space of one year." (*Works*, ii., 168.)

they likened Henry VIII. to Nero. Englishmen, wrote one of Bullinger's correspondents, were when subject to the Pope not under such a yoke as they now were, when all their property and life itself was at the King's disposal; "a man may now travel from the east of England to the west, and from the north to the south without being able to discover a single preacher who, out of a pure heart and faith unfeigned, is seeking the glory of our God. He has taken them all away."[1]

Furiously beat the waves of reaction upon the chief remaining pillar of the Reformation in England, and many were the attempts to procure Cranmer's downfall. He had foes at Court, foes on the episcopal bench, among the squires of Kent, within the precincts of his own cathedral and the walls of his own house. The prebendaries of Canterbury had a special and private grudge against their Archbishop. For, when the chapter was reconstructed after the dissolution of the monasteries, Cranmer had urged that "not only the name of a prebendary" should be "exiled his Grace's foundations, but also the superfluous conditions of such persons." The prebendaries, he said, "spent their time in much idleness, and their substance in superfluous belly cheer"; they were commonly "neither learners nor teachers, but good marianders." Corrupt themselves, they seduced younger men from "abstinence,

[1] *Original Letters* (Parker Soc.), i., 204-206. The statement is, of course, a slight exaggeration. As will be seen later on, there was some preaching in Kent under Cranmer's protection which was scarcely in accord with the letter or the spirit of the Six Articles.

study, and learning," to follow their own appetite and example. St. Paul made no mention of prebendaries, and it would be well for religion, thought the Archbishop, if the four hundred pounds destined to support twelve idle prebendaries were devoted to the maintenance of twenty divines at ten pounds and forty scholars at ten marks apiece.[1] This was in 1539, before the fall of Cromwell and the triumph of reaction; but the new foundation was not established by royal charter until April, 1542. Cranmer's influence was then under a shadow, and his advice was not taken either with regard to the extinction or selection of prebendaries. He had proposed for dean the Protestant preacher Dr. Crome; but the dean selected was that accomplished trimmer, Dr. Nicholas Wotton[2]; and among the twelve chosen prebendaries there was only one, the future Bishop Ridley, who made any mark as a Reformer. Cranmer does, indeed, appear to have obtained the King's permission to appoint three of the New as well as three of the Old Learning to be select preachers in his cathedral.[3] But the impartiality of this arrangement did not tend to unity nor improve the Archbishop's relations with his Catholic chapter; and the diocese was soon rife with recrimination in which clergy and laity both took part. The country gentry and the Justices of the Peace were largely Cath-

[1] Cranmer, *Works*, ii., 396–397.

[2] For Wotton see the present writer in *Dict. Nat. Biog.*, lxiii., 57–61.

[3] This was one of the sore points with the prebendaries—they considered such a step to be the means of setting divisions among them, but Cranmer declared that it was the King's will.

olic, and among them was Sir John Baker, possibly the Justice with whom Cranmer had carried on the controversy noticed in the preceding chapter[1]; he was also Chancellor of the Exchequer, and apparently hoped to supplant the Protestant Audley as Lord Chancellor of England.[2] Another Catholic magnate of Kent was Sir Thomas Moyle, who represented the county in the Parliament of 1542, and was chosen Speaker that year. They hoped by means of the Statute of Six Articles to rid the county of heretics; and they as well as the clergy looked to Bishop Gardiner as the champion of their cause.

Returning in September, 1541, from an embassy to the Diet of Ratisbon, Gardiner paid a visit to Canterbury; and while there he seized the opportunity to sound his namesake, William Gardiner, one of Cranmer's Catholic prebendaries. The prebendary told a grievous tale; he himself was suspect for his preaching, while men like Edmund Scory, the future Bishop of Rochester, and Lancelot Ridley, cousin to the future Bishop of London, disseminated unsound doctrine. One Catholic prebendary and two preachers were already in durance for their maintenance of the faith.[3] The bishop lis-

[1] See above, p. 120.

[2] Baker had also served on the commission appointed to inquire into the doings of Cranmer's commissary at Calais.

[3] Some of the Catholic preaching appears to have been extraordinary. Serles, for instance, was charged with saying that as Adam was expelled from Paradise for meddling with the tree of knowledge, "so we, for meddling with the Scripture" (*L. and P.*, 1543, ii., p. 304). A young layman was reported as saying that "the Bible was made by the Devil." (*Ibid.*, p. 308.)

tened sympathetically; he rebuked Ridley, and encouraged William Gardiner to send him any further complaints he might have to make against Cranmer. Nor was it long before the bishop heard from his confidant again. Serles and Shether, two of the divines imprisoned by Cranmer, refused to plead their cause before him, and were sent back to prison. Prebendary Gardiner at once bespoke the powerful bishop's aid, but an order had already come from Court to Serles to submit himself to his metropolitan's authority,[1] and "wily Winchester," as Foxe loved to call the bishop, was too wary to oppose a mandate from the King.

So Serles and Shether were left to Cranmer's mercy; and their punishment, combined with Ridley's and Scory's immunity, was declared by another of Cranmer's enemies to be the origin of the "Prebendaries' Plot" against the Archbishop.[2] There were other causes at work in the minds of Serles and his friends. Cranmer had threatened to hold them as cheap as they held him and to break their bond of resistance. His see should be godly and quietly governed, and if restraint was put on Reformers by the Six Articles, Catholics at least

---

[1] *L. and P.*, xv., 1189.

[2] *Ibid.*, XVIII., ii., p. 361. The full story of this "Plot of the Prebendaries" was first rendered accessible by the publication in 1902 of MS. 128 in Corpus Christi College Library in Cambridge, in vol. xviii. of the "Letters and Papers." This MS. contains a number of depositions, etc., and even in Dr. Gairdner's abbreviation it occupies eighty-eight closely printed pages. Strype had previously printed a small portion, but the above account is based entirely on the depositions, etc., in *L. and P.*

should not return to the fleshpots which had really been left behind. The Justices of the Peace and the Catholic clergy thought he passed that limit of action, and secretly if not covertly encouraged the spread of heresy. He received, it was said, letters once a month from Germany, and thought German divines good judges of theology; he had maintained that image and idol were but the Latin and Greek for the same evil thing.[1] His commissary at Calais, John Butler, and his commissary in Kent, Dr. Nevinson, were both suspected of doubting the truth of Transubstantiation. Nevinson had, much to the scandal of the orthodox, released a notorious heretic in the person of Joan Bocher,[2] and although he was married, he had been chosen as proctor in Convocation for the diocese. His wife was daughter of Cranmer's sister, who was accused of having two husbands alive. Such were some of the tales which found their way into the receptive ears of the Bishop of Winchester.

Serles meanwhile was waiting his turn. At last, in March, 1543, he persuaded Dr. John Willoughby, vicar of Chilham, that it was his duty as royal chaplain to bring these Kentish scandals to the knowledge of the King. Willoughby refused to go alone, so the pair rode together to London on Friday, March the 16th, with a list of charges against the Archbishop. It seemed a propitious moment, for a heresy hunt was in full swing in other parts of the kingdom, and the victims were not confined to men

[1] *L. and P.*, XVIII., ii., p. 329.

[2] She was afterwards burned in 1550.

of low degree. The Dean of Exeter, two gentlemen of the Court,—Thomas Sternhold, the author of the metrical version of the Psalms, and Sir Philip Hoby, afterwards a statesman of repute,—were sent to prison[1]; and Dr. John London, Warden of New College and Dean of Christ Church, Oxford, had made a great impression on the King by detecting the poison of heresy among the royal choir at Windsor.

It was to Dr. London that Serles and Willoughby first resorted. They found that prelatical scoundrel puffed up with his Windsor success and eager for further triumphs. He told them to fear not, took their articles, dressed them up, showed them to some of the Privy Council, and then sent Serles and Willoughby on to Bishop Gardiner, who also gave them words of encouragement. The next step was to clothe the charges in legal form and to obtain the signature of sufficient witnesses; and with this object Dr. London sent Serles and Willoughby back into Kent. But now a fit of caution seized the prebendaries; tale-bearing was well enough, but to set one's hand to a slander and perhaps be tried on its truth was quite another matter, and Willoughby returned empty-handed. Thereupon the zealous Dr. London bade him tell Sir Thomas Moyle that the Justices of the Peace in Kent would be held liable if such evil practices were not brought to light, and that they would never have occurred had the Justices done their duty. Moyle then set to work with his colleagues to obtain the

[1] *Acts of the Privy Council*, 1542–1547, pp. 97, *et. sqq.*

requisite subscriptions from the prebendaries and parish clergy. When these had been extracted the prebendaries themselves were summoned to London by Dr. Nicholas Wotton, the Dean of Canterbury, about St. George's Day, the 23rd of April. Moyle was now busy with his parliamentary duties,[1] and the management of the affair was left to Sir John Baker, who had the advantage of Bishop Gardiner's advice. Gardiner thought the articles "well enough," and the conspirators were confident that a general commission would be sent down into Kent to deal with the accusations. They now directed their efforts towards excluding Cranmer from the commission; it was hoped that Gardiner himself would be placed at its head and that its members would include the very prebendaries who were specially aggrieved against the Archbishop.[2] On the 4th of May they had so far succeeded that the Privy Council passed a resolution that "if the King should be so content" a commission should be sent into Kent to examine "generally all abuses and enormities of religion." It was probably something more than a coincidence that, on the following day, the *King's Book of Religion*, which was to confound all heretics, was "read in the Council Chamber before the nobility of the realm."[3]

It would have gone ill with Cranmer and the cause of the Reformation in England had that commission with Gardiner at its head, and with Henry VIII.'s

[1] He was Speaker in the 1543 Parliament.

[2] *L. and P.*, XVIII., ii., 327.

[3] *Acts of the Privy Council*, i., 126, 127.

authority at its back, been let loose in Kent. But the plotters little knew their King; Henry had many failings, but no monarch had a keener insight into men's minds or less liking for being made the tool of others. What reception he gave to this demand of the Privy Council and to the accusations against Cranmer is not known. He kept his counsel and his sentiments to himself,[1] until one day, as he was being rowed past Lambeth Palace in his barge, he espied the Archbishop standing on the edge of the steps. Calling to him, he made Cranmer take a seat beside him. "Ha, my chaplain," he said, "I have news for you; I know now who is the greatest heretic in Kent"; and he pulled out of his sleeve the articles against Cranmer and his preachers signed by the Justices and prebendaries. The Archbishop demanded the appointment of a commission to inquire into their truth. "Marry," said Henry, "so will I do; for I have such affiance and confidence in your fidelity, that I will commit the examination hereof wholly to you and such as you will appoint." Cranmer demurred because he, being the accused, would not be an indifferent judge. Henry would listen to no objection. "It shall be no otherwise," he said, "for surely I reckon that you will tell me the truth; yea of yourself, if you have offended. And therefore make no more ado, but let a commission be made out of you and such other as you shall

[1] This was his habit: "Three may keep counsel," he once said, "if two be away; and if I thought that my cap knew my counsel, I would cast it into the fire." Never, says Brewer (*L. and P.*, iv., Pref., p. dcxxi.), "had the King spoken a truer word, or described himself more accurately."

name, whereby I may understand how this confederacy came to pass."[1]

Here was a bolt from the blue; instead of a commission presided over by Gardiner to search out Cranmer's misdeeds, came one presided over by Cranmer to inquire into the "confederacy" of the plotters! Cranmer, however, was but a poor inquisitor; either unsuspectingly, or with an over-nice desire to be impartial, he nominated as his assessors his chancellor and his registrar, both of them secret "fautors of the papists," as Morice calls them, and the enquiry made no progress, though the commission sat for six long weeks. Then through the intervention of Sir William Butts, the King's favourite physician, and Sir Anthony Denny, his favourite gentleman of the chamber, a more expert investigator was appointed in the person of Sir Thomas Leigh, who had enjoyed a long practice as a visitor of monasteries, and was now summoned from York to lay bare the Kentish plot. Under his vigorous hands the tale was soon unrolled. It was in vain that the prebendaries laid their heads together and then separately tried to shift the blame from one to another, or that the Justices sought the help of the clerk of the peace to divert the scent by drawing up indictments against the heretics. Disaster after disaster attended their cause; Dr. London was convicted of perjury and died miserably in prison[2]; and the Bishop of Winchester's nephew and secretary, Germain Gardiner, who drew up one copy of the articles against Cranmer, was executed on a

[1] *Narratives*, p. 252.

[2] Hall, *Chron.*, p. 859.

charge of denying the royal supremacy. Cranmer's rebellious clergy were more fortunate. A few weeks' or months' confinement was the only penalty they paid; not one appears to have suffered the loss of any preferment, or to have been exempted from the general pardon passed as an Act of Parliament in the following spring. The principal effect of this plot and of the zeal of the heresy-hunters was certainly undesigned; for Parliament in 1544 sought to prevent malicious accusations of heresy by providing that no one should be arraigned except on the oath of twelve accusers, nor for any offence committed more than a year before, and that no one should be arrested for heresy except on the warrant of two of the Privy Council.

Possibly the ease with which the Archbishop's enemies escaped encouraged further delation. At any rate, in the 1544 or 1545 session of Parliament, Sir John Gostwick complained in the House of Commons of Cranmer's preaching. Gostwick was probably the mouthpiece of the Archbishop's old enemies, the Justices of Kent, for he himself represented Bedfordshire and had not heard the sermons of which he complained. Henry was moved to wrath. "Tell that varlet Gostwick," he said, "that if he do not acknowledge his fault unto my Lord of Canterbury . . . I will sure make him a poor Gostwick, and otherwise punish him to the example of others" —a threat the force of which Gostwick could well appreciate.[1] He hastened to Lambeth and was so

[1] Gostwick had profited enormously by the dissolution of the monasteries and by holding the treasurership of First-fruits and Tenths.

penitent that Cranmer not only forgave him, but interceded with the King on his behalf. Henry was not so easily mollified, and it was with difficulty that he could be persuaded to grant his pardon on Gostwick's promise never to meddle with Cranmer again.[1]

The third attempt to ruin the Archbishop was the most nearly successful, and is the best known because of the dramatisation of the story in Shakespeare's *Henry VIII.*[2] On this occasion the Council went so far as to demand Cranmer's committal to the Tower. The King demurred, but was persuaded to consent by the argument that no one would dare to witness against so powerful a personage unless he were in the Tower. Even so, Henry's consent was feigned or he soon repented of giving it; he sent for Cranmer about eleven o'clock of the same night, and informed him of what had occurred. Cranmer thanked the King for his warning, and expressed

---

[1] Dr. Gairdner suggests that this attempt was the occasion of Henry VIII.'s remarkable sermon addressed to the Houses of Parliament at the close of the session in 1545, the substance of which is printed in Hall's *Chronicle* (ed. 1809, pp. 864–868), in Lord Herbert's *Life and Reign of Henry VIII.* (1672, pp. 598–601), and in the present writer's *Henry VIII.*, pp. 282–4.

[2] Act V., sc. i., ii. This is not the place to discuss the question whether Shakespeare or another wrote these scenes; the dramatist, whoever he was, took his story from Foxe, who had it from Cranmer's secretary, Morice. Morice's original narrative is printed in *Narratives of the Reformation* (Camden Soc., 1859, pp. 254–258), and although Foxe took some liberties with Morice's MS. most of the details and many of the phrases in Shakespeare are incorporated from Morice. The date given in the play for the incident, viz.,

himself only too glad of an opportunity to answer whatever might be laid to his charge; he was very well content, he said, to go to the Tower, "so that he might be indifferently heard."

"O Lord God," exclaimed Henry, "what fond simplicity have you so to permit yourself to be imprisoned that every enemy of yours may take vantage against you. Do you not think that if they have you once in prison, three or four false knaves will soon be procured to witness against you and to condemn you, which else now being at your liberty dare not once open their lips or appear before your face. No, not so, my Lord, I have better regard unto you than to permit your enemies so to overthrow you. And therefore I will that you to-morrow come to the Council, who no doubt will send for you; and when they break this matter unto you, require them that being one of them you may have thus much favour as they would have themselves, that is, to have your accusers brought before you; and if they stand with you without any regard of your allegations, and will in no condition condescend unto your requests, but will needs commit you to the Tower, then appeal you from them to our person, and give to them this ring by which they shall well understand that I have taken your cause into my hands from them, which ring they well know that I use it to no other purpose but to call matters from the

1533, about the time of Queen Elizabeth's birth, is of course an instance of poetic licence. It may have occurred in 1545, but certainly not later, as Dr. Butts, who plays an important part in it, died in that year, while Morice's language implied that it was the last attempt against Cranmer made in Henry VIII.'s reign. It would seem to be a more likely occasion for Henry's allocution to Parliament in 1545 than Gostwick's puny attack.

Council into mine own hands to be ordered and determined."[1]

By eight o'clock the next morning Cranmer was summoned to the Council, and by a refinement of malice he was made to wait outside the door for nearly half an hour surrounded by serving men and lackeys. His faithful secretary, who tells the story, sped at once to Dr. Butts, who first considerately came to keep the Archbishop company and then informed the King. "What," exclaimed Henry, "standeth he without the Council chamber door? Have they served me so? It is well enough; I shall talk with them by and by." Presently Cranmer was called into the Council room and charged with infecting the whole realm with heresy. No plea to be confronted with his accusers could avail; he must go at once to the Tower. Then the Archbishop produced Henry's ring. Russell swore his customary oath: "Did I not tell you, my Lords," he said, "what would come of this matter? I knew right well that the King would never permit my Lord of Canterbury to have such a blemish as to be imprisoned, unless it were for high treason"; and they went with fear and trembling into Henry's presence. "Ah, my Lords," broke out the King, "I had thought that I had a discreet and wise Council, but now I perceive that I am deceived. How have ye handled here my Lord of Canterbury? What! make

[1] Other instances of Henry's using a ring for this purpose are quoted in Nichols's notes to the *Narratives of the Reformation*, pp. 56, 256; and the reader will remember the story of Queen Elizabeth and the Earl of Essex.

ye of him a slave, shutting him out of the Council chamber amongst serving men? Would ye be so handled yourselves? I would you would well understand that I account my Lord of Canterbury as faithful a man towards me as ever was prelate in this realm, and one to whom I am many ways beholding by the faith I owe unto God; and therefore whoso loveth me will regard him hereafter." Norfolk tried to make excuses and pretended that their design was only to send the Archbishop to the Tower in order that he might have the greater glory of a triumphant acquittal. "Well," said Henry, "I pray you use not my friends so. I perceive well enough how the world goeth among you. There remaineth malice among you one to another; let it be avoided out of hand, I would advise you."[1] And from that time, continues Morice, no man ever more durst spurn against the Archbishop during King Henry's life.

The confidence which Henry VIII. reposed in Cranmer was, indeed, the envy of the Archbishop's friends and wormwood to his enemies. "You were," said Cromwell to him, "born in a happy hour; for do and say what you will, the King will always take it well at your hand. And I must needs confess that in some things I have complained of you unto His Majesty, but all in vain, for he will never give credit against you, whatsoever is laid to your charge; but let me or any other of the Council be complained of, His Grace will most seriously chide and fall out with us. And therefore you are most happy if you can keep you in this estate."[2] Henry indeed could not

[1] *Narratives*, pp. 254–258.

[2] *Ibid.*, pp. 258–259.

easily afford to dispense with Cranmer; there was no prelate in England who could have filled his place. Gardiner was able enough in worldly matters, and he had hitherto proved sufficiently pliant, but he had not the advantage of Cranmer's learning nor his simplicity of character. "My Lord of Canterbury," said Henry to Gardiner, when they were seeking to combat Cranmer's denial that the "canons of the Apostles" were of as good authority as the four evangelists, "is too old a truant for us twain"[1]; and even those who most dislike Cranmer's later theology are thankful that the task of moulding the English liturgy fell into his hands and not into those of the Bishop of Winchester. Tunstall was perhaps the best alternative, being as mild, respectable, and tolerant as Cranmer himself[2]; but Tunstall again had spent in the study of law and pursuit of diplomacy the time which Cranmer devoted to scriptural and ecclesiastical learning, and there was nothing to be gained from a personal point of view by his substitution for Cranmer as Primate. Moreover, any unnecessary change was to be avoided; the King was too wise and too conservative to provoke wanton

---

[1] *Narratives*, p. 250.

[2] For Tunstall, see the present writer in *Dict. Nat. Biog.*, lvii., 310–314. In 1539 Gardiner was said by a Reformer to be the "wittiest, the boldest, and the best learned of his faculty," but to be of "very corrupt judgment," though Tunstall had done more harm to the cause of the Reformation by his "stillness, soberness, and subtlety"; he added the pregnant remark that "by such bishops as these came nothing but *translatio imperii*, so that they make of the King as it were a pope" (*L. and P.*, 1539, ii., p. 141.)

disorder when the essence of his contention was that his measures only effected the restoration of an older, better, and more legitimate form of church government; and the only unnatural changes in the *personnel* of the episcopate during his reign were the execution of Fisher for treason and the compulsory retirement of Shaxton and Latimer for heresy. Cranmer's humility no doubt gratified the King's autocratic temper, but his simplicity and single-hearted devotion to the anti-papal cause enhanced his estimation in Henry's eyes. There was in him no touch of the self-seeking ambition which ruined Wolsey and Cromwell. Cranmer almost alone of Henry's advisers refused to join in the general scramble for wealth,[1] and the King was often impressed by virtues he did not himself possess. So, too, the Archbishop's obvious defencelessness against the wiles of his enemies was a recommendation to the protection of a monarch who loved to put down the mighty from their seats and to exalt the humble and meek. What would they do, he once asked, with Cranmer when he was gone?[2] And his warning to the Archbishop that he would in the end be sorely tested if he "stood to his tackling," was emphasised by his substitution of three pelicans for

[1] "We," wrote Sir William Petre, one of Henry's secretaries of State, "which talk much of Christ and his Holy Word, have I fear me used a much contrary way; for we leave fishing for men, and fish again in the tempestuous seas of this world for gain and wicked mammon." (Quoted in P. F. Tytler, *Edward VI. and Mary*, i 427.)

[2] *Narratives of the Reformation*, p. 254.

three cranes on Cranmer's coat-of-arms; for he would have, like the pelican, "to shed his blood for his young ones brought up in the faith of Christ."[1]

[1] "The 'pelican in her piety' had been long a recognised emblem of the Passion of Christ, and there is an old distich:

> 'Ut pelicanus fit matris sanguine sanus
> Sic sumus sanati nos omnes sanguine Nati.'

It afterwards became a favourite device in religious heraldry, and Cranmer was not the first prelate who adopted it. A pelican on an azure field was borne by Richard Fox, Bishop of Winchester, who died in 1528 . . . and these arms are still used by Corpus Christi College of his foundation at Oxford. Similar arms were assumed by several of Queen Elizabeth's Bishops, either (says Strype) to imitate Cranmer or to signify their readiness to shed their blood for the Gospel" (Chester Waters, *Memoirs of Cranmer*, pp. 382–383).

CHAPTER VI

CRANMER'S PROJECTS DURING HENRY'S LAST YEARS

EAGER as his enemies were to undermine Cranmer's influence with the King, they yet were often glad to employ it as a screen for themselves, and to thrust upon the Archbishop unpleasant and dangerous duties; and during the last years of Henry's reign, though Cranmer's chief labours were spent in quiet preparation for religious reform, he was more than once required to take an important part in secular matters. He had already been made the Council's mouthpiece on one perilous occasion. In 1533 Henry was boiling over with fury at the Princess Mary's stubborn refusal to relinquish her title and recognise the validity of her mother's divorce. It was, according to Chapuys, the imperial Ambassador, Anne Boleyn who had worked him into this state of feeling, and so exasperated was he that he meditated sending the Princess to the Tower as a disobedient subject. The Council were fully alive to the consequences which would probably follow such a proceeding, but they shrank from pointing them out to Henry, fearing that wrath of the King which Wolsey and Warham and Norfolk declared to be death. So the burden was laid upon Cranmer's shoulders, and the "timorous" Archbishop interceded for Mary as he did for Anne Boleyn and for Cromwell when no other durst open his mouth. In this case his pleadings succeeded, though Henry is said to have prophesied that his intervention would "be to his utter confusion at length"—a remarkable prediction if it is true.[1]

A still more trying ordeal was imposed upon Cranmer in 1541. Henry VIII. was satisfied from every point of view with his marriage to Catherine Howard; and on All Saints' Day, 1541, he ordered his chaplain, the Bishop of Lincoln, to make prayer and give thanks with him to God for the good life he was living and hoped to live with his present Queen.[2] Twenty-four hours later Cranmer had to communicate to him the news of Catherine Howard's infidelity. Details of her misconduct before marriage had come to the Archbishop's ears during Henry's absence in the north of England; investigation left no doubt as to the correctness of the charges, and it became some one's duty to inform the King. Councillors' hearts quailed at the thought, and with one accord they importuned Cranmer to undertake the task. The King was deeply cha-

[1] Morice in *Narratives of the Reformation*, p. 259; the phrase is in a later hand than Morice's and may be a prophecy after the event. Morice appears to have written "one of them should see cause to repent."

[2] *L. and P.*, 1540–1541, No. 1334; Nicolas, *Proceedings of the Privy Council*, vii., 352.

Copyright Photo., Walker & Cockerell.

QUEEN CATHERINE HOWARD.

PAINTED IN THE SCHOOL OF HOLBEIN.

grined; men whose own morality is not above reproach are often the more scrupulous about the prenuptial morals of their wives, and Henry was so overwhelmed by the early indiscretions of his Queen that he shed tears and was thought to have gone mad.[1] Cranmer was sent to obtain her confession and to hold out hopes of mercy, and it is possible that Catherine would have escaped with a divorce, had not proofs of her misconduct after marriage come to light during a later stage of the enquiry. This offence was high treason, and as such it passed out of Cranmer's jurisdiction. Parliament intervened, and having secured the King's permission, passed an Act of Attainder to which the royal assent was given by royal commission, professedly to spare the royal feelings.[2] Thus ends the tale of Cranmer's share in the matrimonial troubles of Henry VIII., for Catherine Parr, his last wife, albeit a lady inclined to religious reform, was married to the King by Bishop Gardiner.[3]

The selection of the Bishop of Winchester to officiate at this ceremony, which took place at Hampton Court on 12 July, 1543, may be connected with the circumstances that Cranmer was still nominally suffering under the imputation of heresy brought against

[1] *L. and P.*, 1540–1541, Nos. 1403, 1426.

[2] This is believed to have been the origin of the practice since grown common of giving the royal assent to Acts of Parliament by commission.

[3] Catherine Parr, it may be remembered, had already had two husbands, and was to have a fourth after Henry's death, so that she was almost as much married as the King himself.

him by his prebendaries, and that Henry had been annoyed by the discovery of heresy at Windsor. But the cross-currents in Henry's Court were so numerous and so fluctuating that it is impossible to construct the history of the time on the theory that any religious or political principle was all-powerful at any particular moment. Individual ministers apparently enjoy the confidence of the Crown as fully when they are hostile as when they are friendly to the main drift of national policy; and, indeed, before the Cabinet system had been evolved, there was no objection to the government's being administered by men of divergent principles. Hence Cranmer seems to have been as actively employed in the Council during the period succeeding Cromwell's fall as he had been before. From 1540 to the end of the reign, except during his laborious investigation into the Plot of the Prebendaries, he was a regular attendant at its meetings. In the autumn of 1541, when the King was absent in the north, the Archbishop's name heads the list of those councillors who were responsible for the direction of affairs in London; and again in 1544, when Henry crossed the Channel to wage war in person against the King of France, Cranmer is first in the Council of Regency appointed to advise the Queen. In July, 1541, he was selected to harangue the French ambassador on the advantages of peace between France and England and on the evil effect which would be produced if the French continued some offensive fortifications they had begun near Calais; and in the following month he remonstrated with Chapuys about the treatment of English commerce in the Netherlands.[1] In November, 1542, after the battle of Solway Moss, the Earl of Cassilis, the chief of the Scottish prisoners, was entrusted to the Archbishop's care at Lambeth, and his intercourse with Cranmer is said to have induced the Earl to adopt the New Learning and thus to have contributed to the furtherance of the Reformation in Scotland.

To the cause of religious reform Cranmer was, in spite of its official unpopularity, still devoting in private his vast industry and extensive learning. Probably he did not expect much from the prevalent mood of the King and the people, but he believed that the time for a further reformation would come; he knew that the opportunity, when it came, could not be effectively used without previous preparation, and during the latter years of Henry VIII. he was quietly maturing plans which came to fruit in the reign of Edward VI. He drew up at least two schemes of church service which were afterwards used as the basis of the First Book of Common Prayer,[2] and also drafted a scheme of canon law, for the reform of which three Acts of Parliament were passed in 1534, 1536, and 1544[3]. But the commission, the appointment of which was then sanctioned, was not actually selected until late

[1] *L. and P.*, 1540–41, Nos. 1011, 1085.

[2] Wood, *Scottish Peerage*, i., 330; Le Bas, *Life of Cranmer*.

[3] During the Convocation of 1544 there was "a secret discussion about asking the King to establish ecclesiastical laws" (Wilkins, *Concilia*, iii., 868). Cranmer's collection may be connected with this discussion, but nothing came of the proposal.

in the reign of Edward VI.[1]; and the consideration of Cranmer's other drafts may be conveniently postponed until their connexion with the First Book of Common Prayer has to be discussed.[2] The same may be said of Cranmer's labours on the *Book of Homilies.* He had apparently begun to work on them as early as 1539,[3] but it was not till 1543 that the *Homilies* were submitted to Convocation.[4] Even then they were not published nor apparently approved, and their issue was one of Cranmer's earliest measures in the reign of Edward VI.

In some minor questions, however, Cranmer was able to get his way even in the reign of Henry VIII. The modification of the Act of Six Articles already mentioned was doubtless furthered by him. In July, 1541, he drew up, with Henry's acquiescence, a proclamation abrogating a few superfluous saints' days and abolishing certain "childish superstitions."[5] In the following October he was authorised to enjoin the removal of shrines and relics which were superstitiously revered, and to prohibit the offering of lights and candles "except to the Blessed Sacrament."[6] In 1542 he defeated Gardiner's attack upon the English Bible. Convocation had declared that the version known as "Cranmer's Bible" could not be retained without scandal unless it were revised and corrected. The task of revision was entrusted to a committee headed by Tunstall and Gardiner, and Gardiner produced a long list of

---

[1] See below, pp. 213, 214.

[2] See below, pp. 213, 214.

[3] *L. and P.*, XIV., i., 466.

[4] *Ibid.*, 1543, i., 167.

[5] *Ibid.*, 1540–41, Nos. 978, 1022, 1027.

[6] *Ibid.*, No. 1262.

words which should remain in Latin or else be translated in a more Catholic sense. But three weeks later Cranmer came down with a message from the King to the effect that the revision of the Bible should be entrusted to the universities of Oxford and Cambridge. The bishops all protested, except Cranmer and his brethren of Ely and St. Davids, that Convocation was better fitted for the task than the universities, *i. e.*, that the voice of authority should prevail over that of learning[1]; but the protest was unavailing, and as the universities were not after all consulted, Cranmer's Bible escaped its Catholic revision.

The Archbishop is also believed to have prevented an official recognition of the numerous existing forms of church service. A committee of divines had for some time been engaged in drawing up a "Rationale of Rites and Ceremonies," in which they contented themselves with commending without amending those in use.[2] Gardiner's hand has been traced in this production, which, according to Foxe, was "confuted" by Cranmer. At any rate, it never received the sanction of Convocation, and in February, 1543, Cranmer announced it as the King's wish that mass-books, antiphoners, and portuises should be newly examined and purged of all mention of the Bishop of Rome and of "all apocryphas, feigned legends, superstitions, orations, collects, versicles, and responses"; and that the names of all saints not mentioned in "the Scriptures or in the authentical Doctors should

[1] *L. and P.*, 1542, No. 176.

[2] Collier, ii., 191; Dixon, ii., 313, n.

be abolished and put out of the same books and calendars."[1]

Less successful were Cranmer's efforts to stamp his individual impress upon the manual of faith, which, published under the title, *A Necessary Doctrine and Erudition for any Christian Man*, was known as the "King's Book" to distinguish it from the "Bishops' Book" of 1537,[2] and epitomised the prevailing theology of the latter years of Henry's reign. The "Bishops' Book" had been too advanced for many Bishops and possibly for the King himself; and since Cromwell's fall the episcopal bench had been labouring at its revision. Questions as to the origin, nature, and number of the sacraments, as to the origin and nature of the episcopal authority, of Holy Orders, and of the power of princes in the Church, were submitted to the Bishops and other divines; and various replies have survived. Henry himself took part in the discussion, and we have a document containing the King's own annotations on some of the conclusions put before him. There is also a copy of the "Bishops' Book" with numerous emendations in Henry's hand and answers to them in the Archbishop's.[3] These are interesting as a

[1] Wilkins, *Concilia*, iii., 863. The Bishops of Ely and Salisbury were entrusted with this task with the help of six members of the Lower House of Convocation, but the Lower House did not co-operate, and the purgation apparently was not carried out, or was limited to the omission of the word "Pope," to the suppression of the office and name of Thomas Beket, and to the correction of typographical errors (Gasquet and Bishop, *Edward VI. and the Book of Common Prayer*, p. 4, n.).

[2] See above, pp. 108–109.

[3] Cranmer, *Works*, ii., 83.

conclusive refutation of the idea that Cranmer never ventured to express different opinions from those of his sovereign; for in this document it is seldom that the Archbishop agrees with the King; some of the royal phrases, says Cranmer, "obscure the meaning" of the text; others are "superfluous" and "were better out"; some, again, "diminish the goodness of God," and others are "not grammar." The "preter tense," he reminds the King, "may not conveniently be joined with the present." "I cannot perceive," he bluntly says of two other suggestions, "any manner of consideration why those words should be put in that place." And so on throughout the book Cranmer's comments proclaim the freedom with which he could speak his mind to the King, and remind us of the testimony of Erasmus to the urbanity and unruffled temper with which Henry was in the habit of conducting his theological disputations.

In the result, however, it is fairly clear that, while Cranmer's literary taste left its mark upon the form of the "King's Book," the doctrine it inculcated represented the views of the Catholic rather than those of the Reforming party; and the book may perhaps be regarded as a fair epitome of the Anglo-Catholic faith which most Englishmen of the year 1543 held, and to which, with one important exception, not a few Anglicans would wish to return to-day. That exception is due to the decay of monarchy and the development of democratic views. In 1543 there was no question of an independent Church; the only alternatives were a Church dominated by the King and a

Church dominated by the Pope; and Gardiner and Cranmer vied with each other in zeal for the royal supremacy. All were agreed that the *selection* of bishops belonged to the prince,[1] and that no ecclesiastic could act without the prince's permission; the election by chapters was tacitly regarded as an empty form. Cranmer and Barlow went farther than this; they considered that this royal appointment conferred *potestas ordinis* as well as *potestas jurisdictionis*, that consecration was not required, and that the King was *summus episcopus*, from whom the clergy derived the whole of their powers; and as a logical corollary of this position they denied that Holy Orders were a sacrament.[2] This was Lutheranism pure and simple; it met with the decided opposition of the great majority of the English divines, and was consequently not adopted in the "King's Book."

[1] Canon Dixon thinks it significant that Gardiner either did not receive, or returned no answers to, the questions circulated on these points, but his silence is probably due to his absence in Germany in 1541.

[2] See Cranmer's and Barlow's answers in Burnet, iv., 443 *et seq.*, and compare Dixon, ii., 303-307. "This," says Cranmer, "is mine opinion and sentence *at this present;* which nevertheless I do not temerariously define, but refer the judgement thereof wholly unto your Majesty." His convictions were not settled on the point, and in 1548 he reverted to the more orthodox view of ordination, deriving the "ministration of God's word" from the imposition of hands by the Apostles and their successors. The change was probably due (*a*) to the fact that the exercise of royal power by the Council in Edward VI.'s minority made it more difficult to believe in the royal power to confer spiritual privileges, and (*b*) Cranmer was then turning from the Lutherans to the Zwinglians, who had no such regard as the Lutherans had for the prince as *summus episcopus.*

This "third English Confession," as Canon Dixon calls it, consisted of an exposition of the Creed, of the Ten Commandments, of the Sacraments, and of the Lord's Prayer and other select passages from Scripture. It was much more detailed and explicit than the "Bishops' Book" in its assertions about the sacraments. It uses several of the Latin words which Gardiner recommended in preference to the English translations adopted in Cranmer's Bible. It is definitely committed to the doctrine of Transubstantiation, to the Invocation of Saints, and, of course, to the celibacy of the clergy.[1] It was carefully revised by Convocation during the spring of 1543, and the King himself wrote a Preface reproving diversities of opinion and the improper use of the Scriptures in much the same terms as he afterwards used in his farewell to Parliament in 1545. On 6 May, 1543, it was read to the Peers in the Council chamber,[2] and it was issued from the press on the 19th. Parliamentary approval was expressed in the first Act passed that year, and great expectations

[1] Canon Mason (pp. 115–117) seeks to show that the "King's Book" was essentially Cranmer's work and "a reforming work." Of course it indicated no idea of repairing the breach with Rome, restoring the monasteries or the worship of saints like Thomas Beket, but the contention that it marks an advance upon the "Bishops' Book" of 1537 rests upon the assumption that the latter implied the acceptance of all the old theology that was not expressly repudiated, and that its *omissions* have no particular significance. But it was of these large omissions that the Catholic party complained, and the filling them up in 1543 in a Catholic sense left no room for such interpretations as Cranmer had put upon the "Bishops' Book" in his letters to the Justice of Kent (see above, p. 120).

[2] *Acts P. C.*, 1542–47, p. 127.

were entertained of it. The King, said his Council, had "set forth a true and perfect doctrine for all his people."[1]

This much-trumpeted solvent of all religious difficulties has long passed into that limbo which only theological antiquaries explore. But soon afterwards Cranmer in the privacy of his study, and without any of the pomp and parade which ushered the "King's Book" into the world, was toiling at a document every phrase of which has become a household word wherever the English tongue is spoken. The use of litanies had early grown up in the Western Church, and from the fact that they were sung in procession they were often themselves called processions.[2] In his later years Henry not infrequently ordered special processions for special occasions. There had been one in 1543 on account of the wet harvest, but owing, complained the King, to the fact of its being in Latin the people "have used to come very slackly to the procession"; and in June, 1544, when he was about to invade France, he ordered a litany to be drawn up in English and to be used frequently "not to be for a month or two observed and after slenderly considered."[3] This

[1] *L. and P.*, 1543, i., 534.

[2] Hence Wriothesley's phrase "a solemn *procession upon their knees* in English" (*Chron.*, i., 186), which now sounds strange. There were other processions besides the Litany. See Gasquet and Bishop, *Edward VI. and the Book of Common Prayer*, p. 54. Calfhill (*Works*, ed. Parker Soc., p. 194) says that litanies were used long before processions. See other references to the subject in Gough's *General Index to the Parker Society's Publications*.

[3] Cranmer, *Works*, i., 494.

litany was issued by the King's printer on 16 June, and a contemporary chronicler describes it as "the godliest hearing that ever was in this realm."[1] The important point about it was its appearance in the vernacular tongue, for the use of English in the church services was still suspect; and one of the charges brought against Dr. Ridley by the Kentish clergy was that the *Te Deum* had been sung in English in his parish church.[2] There is, however, no evidence that this litany was of Cranmer's composition,[3] nor was it the famous English Litany which has survived. For in October, 1544, four months after its publication, the Archbishop writes to the King[4] to say that in obedience to Henry's commands he has translated certain Latin processions into English, using therein "more than the liberty of a translator," because many of the Latin processions were barren and little fruitful. Some, therefore, he had left out entirely; others he had added, and in many he had made partial alterations. The whole was to be sung

---

[1] Wriothesley's *Chronicles*, i., 148.

[2] *L. and P.*, 1543, ii., 306.

[3] Strype (*Cranmer*, i., 184) thinks that it was, but he confuses the two litanies of 1544 and 1545. So do Burnet and apparently his latest editor, Pocock, who (*Hist. Ref.*, iii., 389) says that the litany of June, 1544, was included in the Primer of 1545. There is a much more considerable confusion in Blunt's *Reformation* (8th ed., 1897, i., 498–499), where, in representing the Litany as the work of a Committee of Convocation, he appears to be confusing it with the "King's Book." Canon Dixon and Dr. Gairdner seem to be correct in distinguishing between the litanies of 1544 and 1545, and Wriothesley also distinguishes them, though not clearly.

[4] Cranmer, *Works*, ii., 412.

or chanted; "but in mine opinion, the song that shall be made thereunto would not be full of notes, but, as near as may be, for every syllable a note; so that it may be sung distinctly and devoutly." The revision of the Litany or the setting of the "devout and solemn note" which Cranmer desired, appears to have taken some time; for it was not till June, 1545, that the Primer containing this litany was published.[1] In the following August injunctions[2] were sent to the various Bishops to see that it and no other was sung or said in all the churches in their dioceses on Sundays and festivals, and it was first used at St. Paul's on St. Luke's Day, the 18th of October.[3]

Such was the inception of "the most exquisite of English compositions."[4] That it was not in all its parts original was natural, for in this as in all his works Cranmer sought not to uproot the old and begin a new edifice upon a different foundation, but to repair, restore, and improve; and he used all the old material that could be wrought into his new and finer Litany. That his Litany was immeasurably superior to the old will scarcely be denied. The Roman Litany consisted largely of the phrase "Ora pro nobis," repeated afresh after each of a series

[1] Wriothesley, *Chron.*, i., 156. Primers were collections of prayers intended not for public, but for private use. English Primers in MS. had existed long before the Reformation, and eight have been enumerated of earlier date than 1460 (Dixon, ii., 360).

[2] Cranmer, *Works*, ii., 495-496.

[3] Wriothesley, *Chron.*, i., 161.

[4] Gairdner, *Hist. of the English Church*, 1902, p. 230, n.

of saints' names[1]; and even the litanies included in Marshall's and Hilsey's[2] Primers of 1535 and 1539 were bald and unrhythmical. These were all transformed by Cranmer, who, albeit no musician, had a wonderful ear for English prose, into the beautifully smooth and rhythmic cadences of the present English Litany. And apart from its literary charm, the Litany has proved so admirable a vehicle for religious devotions and aspirations that its phrases have won their way into the hearts and minds of millions who do not profess and call themselves members of the English Church. It has stood the test of time better than any other part of the Church Service Book, itself one of the least perishable of human achievements; and it has remained almost unchanged from the day that Cranmer penned it to the present. The petitions to the Virgin, angels, patriarchs, etc., to "pray for us,"[3] which Cranmer inserted after the invocation of the Trinity, were left out in all the editions of the Book of Common Prayer; and the prayer to be delivered "from the tyranny of the Bishop of Rome and all his detestable enormities,"[4] was properly and significantly omitted

[1] *E. g.*, "Sancta Maria Magdalena, ora pro nobis,
Sancta Maria, ora pro nobis,
Sancta Katherina, ora pro nobis,
Sancta Margaretha, ora pro nobis,
Sancta Helena, ora pro nobis."

[2] For Marshall, see the present writer in *Dict. Nat. Biog.*, xxxvi., 250, and for Hilsey, Bishop of Rochester, see *ibid.*, xxvi., 433. Hilsey's Primer was corrected by Cranmer (*Works*, ii., 392).

[3] These petitions were not strictly "invocations."

[4] This was the one jarring note in Cranmer's Litany (Gairdner, *History*, p. 230, n.).

from the edition of 1559 and was never restored; for the rest, there have been only slight verbal alterations, and those not always improvements.[1]

The Parliament which met in the autumn of 1545, soon after the first general celebration of the English Litany, was marked by another blow, if not for the Reformation, at least against the old system. An Act was passed abolishing chantries or the endowments of priests to say masses for the souls of the departed. The measure could scarcely, as Dr. Crome afterwards pointed out, be reconciled with a belief in Purgatory, and incidentally it did not a little to undermine that article of the Catholic faith; but it originated in no more lofty motive than the necessity of meeting the expenses of the war which England waged with France from 1544 to 1546, and the desire of the King to reserve to himself and his friends the profits of a confiscation which the descendants of chantry founders had already begun to effect for their own private gain. There was little opposition, and even Gardiner subsequently expressed his approval of the act; but Cranmer and other friends of education regretted that these funds were not appropriated to some national object instead of going, as they mostly did, to swell the pockets of the landed gentry.

A more singular incident than the continued pillage of the Church distinguished this session of Parliament. A bill for the extinction of heresies, which presumably must have been more ferocious than the

[1] See Parker's *First Prayer-Book of Edward VI.*, Oxford, 1877, pp. 268–275.

Act of Six Articles, was introduced into the House of Lords and read no fewer than five times.[1] This protracted procedure indicates a considerable divergence of opinion among the Peers, but in its final form their Lordships passed the bill unanimously, and it was then sent down to the Commons. Whether it expressed the views of the King or not, we do not know. If it did not, the Lords were curiously independent in passing it; but if it did, the Commons showed a still more significant independence of both King and Lords by rejecting the bill.[2] This incident can hardly have been anything but a blow to the reactionary party and a foreshadowing of the tendency which the House of Commons, at least, would show in the coming reign. Indeed, the old system was crumbling away before the inroads of the New Learning even while Henry VIII. succeeded in maintaining the principal outworks intact; and this last Parliament of Henry's reign sanctioned two other small measures quite inconsistent with previous Catholic practice. By the first, the Knights of St. John, whose Order had been dissolved some years before, were released from their vows of celibacy; the second enacted that ecclesiastical jurisdic-

[1] *Lords' Journals*, i., 269–271. The now-established limitation of three readings for bills was not then the rule in either House of Parliament; Cranmer was one of the peers to whom the bill was committed after the first reading, and then again after the second.

[2] It is possible that this difference of opinion between the two Houses was the real occasion for the sermon with which Henry VIII. closed the session on Christmas Eve, 1545. In any case the incident is one of those which show that Parliament was not the servile edict-registering body it is often said to have been.

tion might be exercised by married doctors of civil law.[1]

Encouraged perhaps by these symptoms and by Gardiner's absence,[2] Cranmer seems to have obtained from the King an expression of opinion in favour of the demolition of roods "in every church," and of the abolition of bell-ringing upon All Hallow night, of the covering of images during Lent, and of creeping to the cross. Cranmer drew up a letter to this effect to be signed by the King,[3] but in the interval Henry received despatches from Gardiner averring that any further alteration in religion or in ceremonies would frustrate the negotiations then proceeding between England, the Catholic Emperor, and the King of France. Henry was, in fact, still at war with France and nervous lest his quondam ally, Charles V., should join the enemy. Gardiner's representa-

---

[1] The encroachments of the Civil Law upon both the Canon and the English Law was one of the characteristic features of Henry VIII.'s reign (see Maitland, *English Law and the Renaissance*, 1901). Civil Law was the Emperor's law and Canon law the Pope's law. Henry boasted that England was an Empire and his an imperial throne. The Civil Law with its absolutist maxims appealed strongly to him and to many Tudor statesmen and thinkers, including Francis Bacon; and but for the defeat of the Spanish Armada we should probably have had a *droit administratif* in England not unlike that of France.

[2] He was on an embassy to Charles V. from October, 1545, to March, 1546.

[3] A curious illustration of Cranmer's caution is his pleading that if creeping to the cross were abolished it should only be after the reasons for the change had been explained to the people lest they should think it implied some diminishing of Christ's honour (*Works*, ii., 415).

tions were quite enough to make him change his mind, for the proposed reforms, even in the eyes of a Reformer, must have appeared of slight importance compared with the necessity of preserving the Emperor's friendship.

They would, moreover, have offended the Catholic party at home, which gave abundant signs of vitality and power during the last year of Henry's reign. Lord-Chancellor Audley, who with Cromwell and Cranmer had formed a sort of reforming triumvirate at Henry's Court, had died in 1544, and his place had been taken by Wriothesley, afterwards Earl of Southampton, who, although a *protégé* of Cromwell and a foe of Gardiner, had on Cromwell's fall abjured his radical opinions and devoted himself with zest to the task of crushing heresy. He found a worthy colleague in the Solicitor-General, Sir Richard Rich,[1] and the pair, aided by the influence of Norfolk, whose taste for burning heretics ceased only with his death, were responsible for the renewed persecution that broke out in 1546. Gardiner, too, returned in March, and though his memory has perhaps been burdened with an unfair load,[2] his influence with the King can hardly be regarded as a force tending towards lenity. In April the celebrated preacher, Dr. Crome, delivered at St. Paul's Cross the sermon above referred to, pointing out

[1] For Wriothesley and Rich see the present writer in *Dict. Nat. Biogr.*, lxiii., 148–154, and xlviii., 123–127.

[2] S. R. Maitland, in his *Essays on the Reformation*, made a clever but not altogether convincing effort to clear Gardiner from the aspersions of Foxe.

the inconsistency of the abolition of chantries with a belief in Purgatory. He was called before the Council and forced to make two recantations. A like fate befell two others, a third was burnt, and Latimer himself was sent to prison.[1] In June followed the trials of Anne Askew and Shaxton, the former Bishop of Salisbury. Shaxton made a pitiful abjuration, but no threats and no torture could shake the constancy of Anne. She was racked in the Tower by Wriothesley and Rich, and then in July was burnt at Smithfield in the presence of Wriothesley, Norfolk, the Lord Mayor of London, and many peers and aldermen. In the same month proclamations were issued for the seizure and burning of all copies of Tyndale's and Coverdale's New Testaments and of all the works of Frith, Wycliffe, George Joy, William Roy, Barnes, William Turner, and Richard Tracy.[2]

It was the expiring effort of reaction in Henry's reign, and Fortune's wheel came round once more. Peace was concluded with France in June, and the Emperor was involved in war with the Schmalkaldic League of Protestants. Their envoys besought the King for aid, and Henry was dallying with a proposal for a Christian league against the Emperor, the Pope, and the Council of Trent.[3] It was the policy of Cromwell revived, and Henry invited the German princes to send him the names of ten or twelve of their learned men that he might choose a

[1] Wriothesley, *Chron.*, i., 167–168.

[2] Lives of all these Reformers will be found in the *Dict. Nat. Biogr.*

[3] See A. Hasenclever, *Die Politik der Schmalkaldener*, 1902.

few with whom to confer on religion. A stranger proposition followed. In September, 1546, a French ambassador, the Admiral d'Annebaut, came to England, and he, Henry VIII., and Cranmer discussed the prospects of a further reformation in both kingdoms. The King, says Cranmer, leaning on his and the Admiral's arms, was

"at this point not only within half a year atter to have changed the mass into a communion . . . but also utterly to have extirped and banished the Bishop of Rome and his usurped power out of both their realms and dominions. And herein the King's Highness willed me to pen a form thereof to be sent to the French King to consider of. But the deep and most secret providence of Almighty God, owing to this realm a sharp scourge for our iniquities, prevented (for a time) this their most godly device and intent, by taking to his mercy both these princes." [1]

The war of domestic faction was also going ill for the Catholics. In November Gardiner had a violent quarrel with the future Duke of Northumberland [2] and a dispute with Henry over an exchange of lands. One or the other affair caused his ab-

[1] Foxe on Morice's authority in *Acts and Monuments*, ed. Townsend, v., 563-564. The story is corroborated by a letter from Hooper written in the latter part of December, 1546, to Bullinger: "The bearer will inform your excellence of the good news we received yesterday from Strasburgh. There will be a change of religion in England, and the King will take up the gospel of Christ, in case the Emperor should be defeated in this most destructive war; should the gospel sustain a loss he will then retain his impious mass."—*Original Letters*, Parker Soc., i., 41.

[2] Odet de Selve, *Corresp. Politique*, 1886, p. 51.

sence from the Council, and there is no record of his attendance between the middle of November and the middle of January, though, according to Foxe's story, he used to accompany members of Council to the door of the Council chamber to make people think he was in as good credit as ever. Finally, the ruin of Surrey, the poet, and his father, the Duke of Norfolk, decisively turned the balance in favour of the Reformers. "Nor," wrote one of Bullinger's correspondents, "is any one wanting but Winchester alone, and unless he also be caught, the evangelical truth cannot be restored."[1] Gardiner was not yet to be laid by the heels, but the chief influence in the Council had passed to the future Protector Somerset, whose wife had already betrayed her own and her husband's theological predilections by secret support of Anne Askew; and in the final draft of Henry's will, which was drawn up on St. Stephen's Day, 26 December, the Bishop of Winchester was excluded from the Council of Regency appointed to govern the realm during the nonage of Edward VI.

The sands in the glass of Henry's life were now fast running out, and rumours of his death were rife at the beginning of January, 1547; but the end did not come until the early hours of the 28th. In his last moments the King turned towards him who had been his best friend in life; and feeling that his strength was ebbing he sent late at night to fetch Cranmer from Croydon. When the Archbishop reached Whitehall the King was no longer able to speak; all he could do was to stretch out his hand to Cranmer

[1] *Original Letters*, Parker Soc., ii., 638, 639.

and reply with an affirmative grasp when the Archbishop urged him to call upon Christ's mercy and give some token that he trusted in the Lord. So died Henry VIII., and the last support of which he was conscious on earth was the hand of the man whose only support he himself had been in the time of trouble. Faithless to many, to Cranmer the King was true unto death; and from that day to his own last agony the Archbishop left his beard to grow in witness of his grief.

CHAPTER VII

CRANMER AND THE FIRST BOOK OF COMMON PRAYER

WHILE Cranmer was soothing the last moments of Henry's life, two ministers were pacing up and down the gallery outside the chamber of death, busily discussing plans for dividing the mantle of the dying King. One was the Earl of Hertford, better known as Protector Somerset, the brother of Queen Jane Seymour; and the other was Sir William Paget, the King's Secretary, and one of the astutest politicians of the age. On Monday morning, the 31st of January, Lord-Chancellor Wriothesley announced to Parliament the demise of the Crown, and in the afternoon the first meeting of the Council of Regency was held in the Tower. Cranmer's name as Archbishop of Canterbury naturally headed the list of members; but he had no political ambitions or taste for political intrigue, and though his voice was more potent in the affairs of the Church, his political influence does not appear to have been any greater in the reign of Edward VI. than it had been under Henry VIII. There is little doubt that he welcomed the appointment of Hertford to the Protectorship, for the Earl was probably the statesman of the time with whom the Archbishop was in the fullest agreement and sympathy. He was a man of large and noble ideas, but these were little in harmony with the prevailing temper of the times.[1] He believed in civil and, as far as possible, in religious liberty; and not one instance of death or torture for religious opinion stains the brief and troubled annals of his rule. He has been denounced as a "rank Calvinist,"[2] apparently on no other ground than that Calvin once wrote him a letter,[3] and has been accused of feverish zeal for a Protestant revolution on the entirely erroneous assumption that he was responsible for the policy of the Second Book of Common Prayer and the Second Act of Uniformity.[4]

A week after Hertford's election as Protector, Paget read to the Council a list of honours which Henry VIII. had intended conferring upon the executors of his will.[5] Only about half of these were carried into effect; but Hertford became Duke of

---

[1] On the character of Somerset and his policy, see the present writer's *England under Protector Somerset*, 1900, or, more briefly, in vol. ii., chap. xiv., of the *Cambridge Modern History*, 1904.

[2] N. Pocock in *English Hist. Rev.*, x., 418.

[3] See British Museum, *Stowe MS.*, 155, f. 9.

[4] These of course were passed in 1552 after Somerset's death. He was deprived of the Protectorate in 1549, and cannot be held responsible for acts of the Government after that date; he must be judged by the Reformation so far as it had proceeded by October, 1549.

[5] There is no evidence that these intentions were fabricated; the ruling faction would not then *proprio motu* have conferred an earldom on Wriothesley, nor invented instructions which they did not mean to carry out.

Somerset, Wriothesley Earl of Southampton, and Lisle (the future Duke of Northumberland) was created Earl of Warwick. Preparations were then made for the coronation of Edward VI. The ceremony was performed by Cranmer in Westminster Abbey on Sunday, the 20th of February; and the Archbishop has been blamed for lending his help to an assertion of Tudor absolutist tendencies by presenting Edward as King before exacting the oath to observe the liberties of the people.[1] He seems indeed to have considered the forms of the coronation as somewhat empty and as conveying no privilege or power; but technically, at any rate, popular assent had already been given to Edward's succession through the mouth of Parliament in the reign of Henry VIII., when the crown had been settled on him by statute.[2] Edward VI. was therefore the first King of England who came to the throne with a parliamentary title,[3] and no dissent in the audience at Westminster could have affected the validity of an Act of Parliament.

The coronation of Edward VI. was speedily followed by the fall of Lord-Chancellor Wriothesley,

[1] Hallam, ed. 1884, i., 38, n.; Dixon, ii., 413. Cranmer's address at the coronation is printed in his *Works*, ii., 126–127; but the original is lost, and I doubt the authenticity of the speech as printed.

[2] 35 Henry VIII., c. i.; Henry VIII. himself had no power to leave the crown away from Edward, but only to decide the claims of Mary and Elizabeth, whose legitimacy was uncertain.

[3] The cases of Henry IV. and Henry VII. are not parallel, because in 1399 and 1485 Parliament only gave its assent to a fact already accomplished by unparliamentary methods.

who was convicted of an unconstitutional and illegal act in issuing a commission out of Chancery without a warrant from the Council. Wriothesley, as we have seen, had been closely identified with the repressive measures of Henry's last years, and his removal from the Council materially smoothed the path of religious reform. Such a policy was both natural and inevitable considering the constitution of the new Government and the circumstances in which it was placed. It was known before the end of Henry's reign that the Protector was "well disposed to pious doctrine and abominated the fond inventions of the Papists"[1] He had long "not only favoured, but also furthered the truth of God and his glory in most dangerous times"[2]; and the ruin of Norfolk and Surrey, the exclusion of Gardiner[3] and Thirlby from the list of Henry's executors, and now the degradation of Wriothesley left the Catholic party without a leader. Tunstall and Sir Anthony Browne were respectable Catholics, but neither had the force of character to stem the tide, which even the sluice-gates of the Six Articles had barely enabled Henry VIII. to check.

That ferocious statute and, indeed, all the heresy laws ceased to be operative with Somerset's acces-

[1] *Original Letters*, i., 256.

[2] Brit. Mus., *Royal MS.*, 17, C. v., quoted in Gasquet and Bishop, p. 158.

[3] There is no valid reason for believing that his exclusion was not the deliberate act of Henry VIII. See *England under Protector Somerset*, pp. 21–23.

sion to power; and the pent-up flood spread tumultuously over the land. The majority of Englishmen probably had no keen desire for doctrinal change, but zeal and energy were on the side of the Reformers, and the overwhelming need for a practical reformation was ever before the eyes of the Government. So much minute criticism has of late been expended upon the lives and characters of the leading Reformers, that the forces which made reform inevitable have been completely left out of sight, and the supremely inadequate theory has gained ground that the whole movement originated, first, in Henry VIII.'s desire for Anne Boleyn, and, secondly, in the greed of the laity for the spoils of the Church. Those motives did exist; but great revolutions do not arise from petty causes, and the magnitude of the Reformation measures the strength of the forces which brought it to pass. The state of the Church not only provoked its loss of power and privilege, but threatened the nation with ruin; and the Reformation was an essential condition of the greatness of modern England. There is no need to rely for proof of the wide-spread corruption upon the fervid invectives of Latimer or the strident censures of Foxe; dry and musty records are far more conclusive and eloquent, and the recently published[1] register of the visitation of the Bishopric of Gloucester in 1551 will perhaps be found sufficient for our purpose. Three hundred and eleven clergy were then examined; one hundred and seventy-one could not

[1] By Dr. James Gairdner in the *English Historical Review*, January, 1904, pp. 98–121.

repeat the Ten Commandments in English, ten could not say the Lord's Prayer, twenty-seven could not tell who was its author, and thirty could not tell where it was to be found; sixty-two incumbents were absent, and most of them were pluralists who did not reside in the diocese. There is no reason to suppose that the clergy of Gloucester were more ignorant than their brethren elsewhere; and the weakness of the Church is really no mystery. The condition of the clergy thus affords some excuse for a Government which sought to reform them, and helps to explain the contempt in which they were held by a laity growing in knowledge.

In reality the Council of Edward VI. found it necessary to restrain rather than to stimulate the ardour of the Reformers; and one of its earliest acts was to compel the wardens and curate of a London parish church to restore the images they had removed.[1] The new-found liberty of the people, in fact, degenerated into licence, and every parish church was liable to become the scene of religious experiment. The destruction of images proceeded so fast, and was in many districts so popular, that the Council was afraid to enforce a general restoration. Later in 1547 it was driven to issue a Proclamation against the rough treatment which priests experienced at the hands of London serving-men and apprentices,[2] and to send round commissioners to make an inventory of church goods in order to stay the extensive embezzlement practised by local

[1] *Acts P. C.*, 1547–50, p. 25.

[2] *Ibid.*, p. 521.

magnates. In 1548 the Government put forth further Proclamations[1] denouncing unauthorised innovations, silencing preachers who urged them, and prohibiting the eating of flesh in Lent; and endeavoured to stop the growing practice of divorce. The first Act of Parliament passed in the new reign was directed, not against Catholics, but against those who impugned or spoke "unreverently" of the Sacrament of the Altar. Convocation thought the moment had come for recovering the position from which Henry VIII. had driven it, and petitioned[2] either that ecclesiastical laws should be submitted for its approval, or that the clergy should be readmitted to their lost representation in the House of Commons.

All this should tend to modify the idea that the new Government under the inspiration of Cranmer or the Protector rushed headlong into a policy of rash religious revolution without the least justification of popular support. Cranmer indeed is reported as saying that it was better to have attempted a reformation in Henry's reign than during the minority of Edward, for no one would have ventured to oppose Henry.[3] The remark is characteristic of the Archbishop's tendency to rely on a stronger power; but the words that follow show that Cranmer was afraid of the effects of a drastic reformation and not of the middle course which the Protec-

---

[1] Strype, *Eccl. Mem.*, II., ii., 346.

[2] Wilkins, *Concilia*, iv., 15; Cardwell, *Synodalia*, ii., 419; Makower, *Const. Hist. of the Church of England*, p. 207.

[3] Cranmer's *Works*, ii., 416, n.

tor actually pursued[1]; and Gardiner, probably not without some reason, insinuated in his letter[2] to Somerset that the Protector was encouraged in his measures by the Archbishop himself. The young King's minority was a great disadvantage, particularly as it gave the opponents of reform a plausible though not a sound constitutional argument against any change. The King, they maintained, was *personally* Supreme Head of the Church, and during his nonage that authority was in abeyance; it could not be exercised by the Council or Protector in his name. This argument proved too much, for Gardiner, Bonner, Tunstall, Thirlby, and all the Catholic bishops had, albeit reluctantly, taken out new licences for the exercise of spiritual jurisdiction at the commencement of the reign; and if the royal supremacy was in abeyance these licences were all invalid. It was impossible to set up a distinction between the Supreme Head's power to confer ecclesiastical jurisdiction and his power to effect ecclesiastical changes: if the one could be exercised in his minority, so could the other. Constitutionally, too, the argument was quite unsound. At no period in English history has it been admitted that the royal authority was legally any the less during a

[1] "Therefore," he continues, "the Council *hath* forborne especially to speak thereof, and of other things which gladly they would have reformed in this visitation [1547], referring all those and such like matters to the discretion of the visitors."

[2] Foxe, ed. Townsend, vi., 42; in his reply to Gardiner the Protector said he was "pressed on both sides," and there can be no doubt that he and the Government policy down to 1549 represented a *via media* between two extremes,

minority or during a period of royal insanity than when the King was of full age and sound mind.[1] To countenance such a theory would be to clog the wheels of government and impair the security of the State just when it would naturally be most liable to danger; and a Government could only adopt such a view in a suicidal frame of mind. The Council felt that the question was crucial and fundamental; and its measures against Gardiner and Bonner were mainly directed towards extorting from them an acknowledgment that the King's authority was as great as if he had reached maturity.[2]

Fortified by this conviction, by the expressions in favour of further reform which Henry had used in the previous autumn, and by the presumption arising from the fact that Henry had entrusted the education of his son exclusively to men of the New Learning, Cranmer and the Council undertook the task of carrying out those projects which had been suggested or begun under Henry VIII. The tendencies of the Government were not obscurely indicated by the sermons which Bishop Barlow, Dr. Nicholas

---

[1] Henry VIII. and his Parliament had done something to encourage this unconstitutional view by enacting that Edward might on reaching his twenty-fourth year annul all acts passed during his minority. Hence the King of France made difficulties about concluding treaties with the new Government on the ground that they might be considered null in after years.

[2] A consistent Roman Catholic like More would have agreed with the Council on the ground that at no time of his life could a temporal sovereign be supreme head of the Church; but Gardiner and Bonner had given away the best part of their case by acknowledging Henry's supremacy.

Ridley, and Cranmer's commissary, Dr. Glazier,[1] preached during Lent, 1547, at St. Paul's Cross against images and other ceremonies; and the part that Gardiner would play under the new *régime* was revealed when he protested that there was no authority for making the changes suggested by Barlow until Edward VI. came of age. But the first avowed indication of the Government's policy was the publication of Udall's edition of Erasmus's *Paraphrase*[2] of certain portions of the New Testament, of Cranmer's *Book of Homilies*, and of a number of *Injunctions* which were enforced in a general visitation of the realm.

None of these measures can be described as revolutionary. Erasmus's *Paraphrase* was obviously not a Protestant document; Udall's edition had been prepared in the reign of Henry VIII. and the Princess Mary herself had taken a hand in the translation.[3] Gardiner, indeed, attacked it vehemently because the version, like "Cranmer's Bible," embodied translations nearer the original sense than the Latin words with their accretion of mediæval ideas; but on the question of scholarship his authority would hardly be preferred to that of Erasmus, whose "great

[1] Dixon and Dr. Gairdner say Glazier preached at Court, but their authorities, Stow, Burnet, and Strype, say St. Paul's Cross.

[2] Most bibliographical works and other authorities (including the *D. N. B.*, lviii., 7) say this *Paraphrase* did not appear until 1548, but Gardiner, writing on 14 October, 1547, says both it and the *Homilies* "flowed abroad by liberty of the printers" before that date. It was probably issued with the *Homilies* and *Injunctions* on 31 July, 1547.

[3] Udall's Preface.

faults" he denounced. He was on firmer ground when he showed that the *Paraphrase* and the *Homilies* did not on some points agree.

The latter production was an old scheme of Cranmer's. He had been engaged on it as early as 1539,[1] and in 1543 a collection of *Homilies* had been submitted to Convocation without obtaining its approval.[2] The present volume consisted of twelve discourses which explained the proper use of the Scriptures and the main points of the Christian Faith, such as good works and charity, denounced the sins of perjury, apostasy, and adultery, and concluded with an exhortation to obedience and a warning against religious contention. Cranmer was probably responsible for the authorship of several and the tone of all, and they were directed, on the one hand, against superstitious practices, and, on the other, against the preaching of the "hot-gospellers."[3] On the whole they were rather practical than doctrinal treatises, and the dogmas of the Six Articles were not directly impugned. They did not on that account escape Gardiner's censure, and he attacked especially the Homily on Salvation, which, he complained, excluded charity from the work of justification, while Bucer singled it out for special

---

[1] *L. and P.*, XIV., i., 466.

[2] See above, p. 166.

[3] Three, on Salvation, on Faith, and on Good Works, are printed in Cranmer's *Works*, ii., 128–149; probably he edited the others. He wrote to Gardiner, asking him to assist in their preparation, and indicating apparently that part of their design was to correct rash innovations in preaching. (Dixon, ii., 426.)

commendation.[1] On this point, indeed, Cranmer seems to have outrun the views of the Council, for in the *Injunctions* which were issued at the same time it was asserted that the charity which consisted in relieving the poor was "a true worshipping of God, required earnestly upon pain of everlasting damnation." [2]

These *Injunctions*, which were based upon Cromwell's, were even more largely concerned with conduct than the *Homilies*. There was to be at least one sermon a quarter in every parish church[3]; the *Paternoster*, the Creed, and the Ten Commandments were to be learnt by all people; children were to be properly educated and trained to some honest means of livelihood; the sacraments duly administered; a Bible and *Paraphrase* of Erasmus to be provided in every church, and a register of weddings, christenings, and burials kept; every incumbent was to devote a portion of his income to the maintenance of some scholar at school or at a university, and the parishioners were to do their part by contributing to the relief of the poor; the sale of benefices was to be punished by deprivation of the presentee and by forfeiture of the presentor's patronage. There were also injunctions against the superstitious use of im-

[1] Foxe, *Acts and Monuments*, vi., 45; Strype, *Eccl. Memorials*, II., i., 50.

[2] Cardwell, *Documentary Annals*, p. 18; the *Injunctions* with the articles or questions which the visitors were to put to incumbents are printed by Cardwell, pp. 4–31.

[3] That such an injunction should have been necessary proves that Latimer's famous invectives against "unpreaching" clergy were not exaggerated.

ages, the veneration of relics, and the celebration of "feigned" miracles; but the principal innovations appear to have been the abolition of processions, the reading of the Gospel and the Epistle in English, and the saying or singing of the Litany in English by the priests and choir kneeling "in the midst of the church."[1]

There was little in these *Injunctions* that was not admirable and in keeping with that aspiration for a purging of the practice of the Church which supplied the moral force of the Reformation. They express, in fact, an ideal of conduct to which the Church has not yet attained, and the sale of livings, for instance, has shocked the devout and defied the reformer from that day to this. The halting success which attended these efforts was largely due to the fact that creed and not conduct has ever been the cry of religious parties. Nine parts out of ten in these *Injunctions* related to conduct; yet with one accord Catholics and Protestants neglected these nine parts, on which they agreed, in order to fight over the tenth, on which they differed.[2] The detail to which Gardiner objected most strongly was the injunction that every incumbent should obtain and diligently study the recently published *Paraphrase*

---

[1] Cardwell, p. 14; *cf.* Gasquet and Bishop, p. 54. The motive given for the change was "to avoid all contention and strife . . . by reason of fond courtesy and challenging of places in procession, and also that they may the more quietly hear what is said or sung to their edifying."

[2] Dr. Gasquet and Mr. Bishop admit that these *Injunctions* contain "reasonable and salutary provisions."

of Erasmus. He had, he said, favoured Erasmus before he read this book; but now he agreed with those who said that Luther only hatched the eggs which Erasmus laid.[1] On broader grounds the Bishop of Winchester attacked the *Injunctions*, the *Homilies*, and the *Paraphrase*—in short, the whole policy of Cranmer and the Government—as being unconstitutional; and his letters to the Protector on this question contain one of the most interesting constitutional arguments propounded in Tudor times.[2] It is in effect a plea that the King's authority in the Church ought to be and was subject to similar limitations as those which the common law imposed upon his prerogative in the State. These *Injunctions*, he said, were mere royal commands; they were not based upon statutory authority, and could not have the force of law. Obedience to them might involve him in a peril like Wolsey's, who found that the royal permission to execute legatine jurisdiction could not protect him against the statute of *Præmunire*. There was much plausibility and some force in this argument, and it is a pity that Gardiner forgot his own lesson so conveniently in the earlier days of Queen Mary[3]; but statesmen in power do not always observe the excellent maxims they enunciate in opposition. Nor, indeed, was Gardiner's reasoning really sound.

[1] Foxe, vi., 47.

[2] *Ibid.*, vi., 42–52.

[3] The mass was then re-established without any statutory authority, and the laws of the preceding reign were treated as null before they were repealed by the Parliament.

Wolsey could legally be condemned to the penalties of *Præmunire*, because Henry VIII. had no statutory authority to license his exercise of legatine jurisdiction. But the Act of Supremacy and the subsequent legislation of Henry's reign had given the King legal authority to reform any ecclesiastical abuses that he thought needed reformation.[1] The Royal Supremacy was in fact to be really royal and not parliamentary. The Popes had not been fettered by common-law restrictions; they claimed absolute authority in the Church, and so far as jurisdiction went, the whole of that authority had been bestowed on Henry VIII. Gardiner, in fact, had welcomed the exercise of these powers when they went to restrain heretics; he viewed them in a different light when they were employed to effect a reformation, and his resistance to authority involved his incarceration in the Fleet prison. Bonner courted a similar fate, but he soon admitted that his protest against the visitation afforded a bad example, and was released in time to take part in the Parliament which met in November.[2]

Convocation assembled at the same time, and the occasion is remarkable as being one of the few

---

[1] See above, p. 88.

[2] Dr. Gairdner, p. 254, thinks he remained in prison till released by the general pardon, passed as the last act of the session, but several votes of his are recorded in the *Lords' Journals: e. g.*, p. 308, on 15 December he voted against the first draft of the Chantries Act, and on the 10th he voted against the Bill for Administration of the Sacrament. He was also in his place at the meeting of Parliament on 4 November. It was Gardiner who was released by the operation of the general pardon.

instances since 1529 in which the clerical and lay representatives of the nation have been of one mind with regard to theological questions. Convocation unanimously recommended at Cranmer's instance[1] the administration of the Communion in both elements,[2] and by a majority of fifty-three to twenty-two votes it petitioned for the repeal of all enactments prohibiting the marriage of the clergy.[3] The former recommendation was embodied in a bill and passed through both Houses of Parliament, having been incorporated in the House of Lords with another bill directed against irreverence towards the Sacrament. The object of this incorporation, which was due to Somerset, was no doubt to conciliate the Catholic bishops; but in this it failed, for the bishops of London, Norwich, Hereford, Worcester, and Chichester all voted against it.[4] The second measure was not so fortunate; a bill with the singular title, "that lay and married men may be priests and have benefices," was passed in the House of Commons, but it only reached the House of Lords

[1] Strype, *Cranmer*, i, 221.

[2] This was no novelty, for, apart from primitive practice and the Utraquists of Bohemia, the Cistercians are said to have commonly administered the Communion in both elements, and the same practice is alleged to have been countenanced in a provincial constitution of Archbishop Peckham. (Foxe, vi., 237.)

[3] Strype, *Cranmer*, i., 222.

[4] *Lords' Journals*, and Gasquet and Bishop, pp. 69–72. Strype (*Eccl. Mem.*, II., i., 97) thinks this Act "so properly and well expressed" that the "penning thereof" must have been done by Cranmer himself, and later on he "conjectures" that it was "of Cranmer's procuring and drawing up, too." There is nothing improbable in the suggestion, but I know of no evidence for it.

on the last day of the session (24 December), and proceeded no further.[1]

More important was another act of this session, "occasioned," says Bishop Burnet, "by a speech that Archbishop Cranmer had made in Convocation."[2] Therein he had exhorted the clergy to study the Scriptures and consider "what things were in the Church that needed reformation"; to which reply was made that so long as the Six Articles remained in force, it was perilous to express an opinion. The difficulty was reported by Cranmer to the Council, which thereupon is said to have given orders for the drafting of a bill to repeal these Acts. This bill, which produced some lively debates in both Houses of Parliament, and was under discus-

[1] *Lords' Journals*, i., 311; this singular phrase is not an echo of the "universalist" theory of the priesthood which attracted many adherents in Germany in 1525. All it meant was that marriage should be no bar to ordination. This bill apparently did not, like the Act of the succeeding year, permit the marriage of priests already in orders and can hardly have been satisfactory to Cranmer.

[2] *Hist. Ref.*, ii., 92; this is an exaggeration of Cranmer's share in the Act. It was mainly due to the Protector. Convocation met on 5 November, when its only business appears to have been the election of a Prolocutor. It then adjourned till the 18th; but meanwhile the Act of Repeal had been introduced into the House of Lords on the 10th. Yet there is some truth in Burnet's story, for on 9 December a deputation of the clergy waited on Cranmer to learn "what indemnity and impunity this house shall have to treat of matters of religion in cases forbidden by the statutes of the realm to treat" (Strype, *Cranmer*, i., 222). Presumably Convocation did not enjoy or understand parliamentary privilege; the Six Articles would have been perpetual had it been treason or felony to discuss their repeal in Parliament. The Act of Repeal was then awaiting its third reading in the House of Commons.

sion nearly the whole of the session, is one of the most remarkable in English history. It not only destroyed at a blow almost the whole of Henry VIII.'s repressive legislation, but established for the first time a considerable measure of freedom of opinion and freedom of the press. Treason was reduced to the moderate definition which was laid down by Edward III. and is still the law with slight modification. All heresy Acts from the days of Richard II. were repealed, all felonies created by Henry VIII. were abolished, and no one was to be condemned for any sort of treason unless he was charged within thirty days of the date of the offence, and either confessed or was accused by two sufficient and lawful witnesses.[1] The Act giving the King's Proclamations the force of law was also repealed, and that enabling the King to annul laws on reaching the age of twenty-four was modified. With the exception of the Royal Supremacy, which was still to some extent[2] guarded by penalties of treason, there was to be full liberty to discuss religious questions and to print in English the Scriptures and all kinds of theological treatises. It was, in fact, an attempt to settle the great question of the Reforma-

[1] Hallam and all other authorities have written as though this clause first appeared in the Act of 1552. For a more detailed description see the present writer's *England under Protector Somerset*, pp. 59–67.

[2] It was no longer treason to deny the Royal Supremacy by "open word" (a limitation which would have enabled Sir Thomas More to escape), but it was still treason to do so in writing. The Papacy was, in fact, to be excluded from the argument, the real question at issue being between Protestant and Anglo-Catholic.

tion by public discussion; and the only restriction imposed on the liberty of the press was the salutary provision, which was enacted in 1548 and still remains in force, that every publication must bear the name and address of the printer and the publisher.

In two other measures which came before this session of Parliament Cranmer took an active part. On the 15 December, 1547, he with the Bishops of London, Ely, Norwich, Hereford, Worcester, and Chichester, voted against the Chantries Bill[1] on its fourth reading, and his influence is illustrated by the fact that even at that late stage of the proceedings an amendment was introduced into the bill to meet his criticisms. What they were precisely is not known; but Cranmer voted for the bill in its final form, though all the other malcontents persisted in their opposition. To him also the Lords committed a bill for abolishing the pretence of electing Bishops by their Chapters and providing for direct nomination by royal letters patent. This was really nothing more than a recognition of the *fait accompli;* for Henry VIII.'s Parliament had empowered him to nominate in case the Chapter omitted to elect his candidate within twelve days, and had made rejection of the royal candidate an offence against *Præmunire;* nor,

---

[1] See *England under Protector Somerset*, pp. 123–129. The chief misconceptions about this Act arise from exaggerating its scope. It did not confiscate all the property of guilds, nor did it abolish masses for the dead; all it did was to abolish certain perpetual foundations and transfer the revenues to the King for the express purpose of founding schools. See, on its secular aspect, Ashley, *Economic History*, ii., 139, *et sqq.*, and, on its religious aspect, Gasquet and Bishop, pp. 82–83.

in fact, has there been a single instance since the Reformation of successful resistance to the royal dictation. But Cranmer's emendation of the bill does not appear to have pleased the Lords, and on the following day it was entrusted to a committee consisting of Bishop Tunstall and Goodrich, the chief Baron of the Exchequer, and the Attorney-General.[1]

So far as legislation went, the results of Edward VI.'s first year certainly indicated no violent change with the past; to eager Reformers they seemed not only moderate but meagre. The clergy were still in the bonds of celibacy, the change in the method of appointing bishops was only one of form, and even the grant of the cup to the laity was a concession at which the Popes had connived in Bohemia and which many good Catholics had been willing to make in Germany.[2] For the rest, it might seem that Parliament wished the nation to argue the matter out for itself. But Cranmer and the Government thought it their duty to give the nation a lead, and even on occasion to require that the lead should be followed in the interests of peace and quietness. From the beginning of the reign the Royal Chapel had afforded an example for others to imitate.

[1] Canon Dixon (*Hist.*, ii., 459, note) says that the bill "owed its final form" to Cranmer, but he has overlooked this second commission; See *Lords' Journals*, 15 and 16 December, 1547. The Act was, of course, repealed in Mary's reign, and excepted in 1559 from Elizabeth's general repeal of Mary's ecclesiastical legislation; so the system of *congé d'élire* was restored and remains in force, giving to the Chapters the shadow of a power, the substance of which is retained by the Crown.

[2] See *Cambridge Modern History*, ii., 240.

Compline was there sung in English on Easter Monday, 1547, the sermon was preached, and the *Te Deum* sung in English on 18 September to celebrate the Protector's victory at Pinkie over the Scots; and at the opening of Parliament on 4 November the *Gloria in Excelsis*, the Creed, and the *Agnus* were all sung in the vernacular tongue. At the same time Thomas Sternhold,[1] a gentleman of the Court, who had been in trouble in 1543 for advanced religious views, was engaged in composing a metrical version of the Psalms in English, designed both to promote their vogue and to supplant the "lewd" and offensive ballads which found too much favour with reformers of the baser sort.

So, too, Cranmer had no mind to be idle till Parliament met again, and he believed that the vast powers conferred by the Act of Supremacy imposed a moral obligation upon the Government to lead the people along what it considered the strait and narrow way. The services of the Church had not been touched by Parliament, but soon after it rose the Archbishop submitted to his colleagues a series of questions intended to elicit their opinions on the subject of the mass or communion service.[2] This transformation had been one of the projects considered by Henry VIII. in the last year of his life, and only prevented, according to Cranmer, by his death. Parliament and Convocation had now both enjoined the administration of the Sacrament in

---

[1] See *Dict. Nat. Biogr.*, liv., 223.

[2] The date must have been between 20 December, 1547, and 7 February, 1548; see Gasquet and Bishop, p. 84.

both elements, and it fell to the Bishops to draw up some form for the rite. If it had been the intention of Henry VIII. to change the mass into a communion service, that intention was certainly not carried into effect at this juncture, for the result of the deliberations of the divines was the retention of the old mass,[1] with the addition of a communion service for the laity. "It would almost seem," say two Catholic writers, "that the action of two minds working with different intentions is to be traced in the composition of this Order of Communion."[2] Cranmer's was the mind working for reform, and his answers to the questions circulated[3] among the Bishops are, with one exception, in favour of innovation. He objected to the terms "oblation and sacrifice," declaring that the mass was only a "memory and representation"[4] of the Sacrifice of the Cross. Its virtue was limited to the receivers of the communion, and the laity derived no benefit from private masses performed by priests; these he thought should cease, and by securing that the laity

[1] *I. e.*, the private masses performed by the priest in which no layman communicated. There might be several of these daily, and they were the special aversion of reformers in all countries, implying as they did that each mass was a sacrifice, performed by the priest for the laity, whose participation was unnecessary, although the communion *might* be administered to them at any mass (Gasquet and Bishop, p. 91).

[2] *Ibid.*, p. 93, n.

[3] The original of these questions is in the library of Corpus Christi College, Cambridge. (MS. 105, ff. 230–231); the answers with the questions are printed by Burnet (ed. Pocock, v., 197–217) from a Lambeth MS.

[4] Burnet, v., 201.

should only communicate on certain public occasions, of which due notice was to be given, he prepared the way for their abolition.

Cranmer's propositions were supported in the main by Ridley, now Bishop of Rochester, Holbeach of Lincoln, Barlow of St. Davids, and by Drs. Cox and Taylor; but the majority took the Catholic view, and the Protector was averse to violent measures. The chief point was the language to be used. The Catholics disliked the adoption of English, as separating the ceremony in England from the manner and custom of other countries. That objection would have been fatal to much else in the Reformation; but Cranmer himself doubted the wisdom of using English "in certain mysteries," and he agreed with Tunstall's proposal that Latin should be retained in the mass, but that certain prayers in English might be added to instruct and stir the popular devotion. One other cautious change was tacitly admitted under the guise of a warning to Reformers; those who were content with the general confession were required not to be offended with others who practised also auricular and secret confession to the priest.[1] This Order of Communion was printed on the 8th of March, 1548, and issued on the 15th with an injunction that it should be adopted by Easter following. Its object, like that of all the early measures of Edward's reign, was to open the door to the New Learning without shutting it in the face of the Old,

---

[1] The Act of Six Articles, which insisted upon auricular confession, had of course already been repealed.

BISHOP HUGH LATIMER.

and to carry the whole nation as far as possible slowly and cautiously along the path of Reform.

The same spirit of compromise pervaded the various Proclamations issued during the spring of 1548. On the 16th of January, for instance, a Proclamation appeared lamenting the lax observance of Lent and enjoining respect for the old fast-days; but a few days later the Council resolved to discountenance the burning of candles on Candlemas Day, the use of ashes on Ash Wednesday and of palms on Palm Sunday, as well as creeping to the Cross on Good Friday, and the taking of holy bread and holy water, changes to which Cranmer had nearly obtained the consent of Henry VIII. But again, on the 6th of February, a Proclamation censured innovations begun by parish priests on their own authority, while on the 11th the Council ordered the removal of all images, under the impression that this drastic measure would cause less disturbance than the perpetual contention as to whether they were abused or not.

But the mind of the Government—which, speaking generally of religious matters at this time, means that of Cranmer and the Protector—was not so ambiguous as, in the vain hope of peace and quietness, it was made to appear. It was with the connivance of these two that Latimer, who since his release by Henry's death had been living with Cranmer at Lambeth, began a course of sermons at St. Paul's Cross in January, 1548; in them he lashed not merely the "unpreaching prelate" of the Old, but the greedy landlord of the New Learning, against whom the Protector was about to launch his ill-fated but generous crusade. On 12 May at Westminster the whole communion service was said in English; and the fact that the sermon was preached by a royal chaplain suggests that the alteration was not viewed with disfavour in government circles. It is possible, too, that in the Royal Chapel a form of service something like that afterwards enforced by the first Act of Uniformity was in use as early as August, 1548. There is, however, no evidence to prove that the simultaneous exclusion of Latin from the services at St. Paul's and the cessation of private masses there and in various London parishes was due to any other influence than the zeal of the Protestant Dean[1] and popular pressure. Protestant principles were in fact making rapid strides, and a Government which sympathised with the Reformation could hardly be expected to set its face like adamant against all change, still less to check it by the methods of Henry VIII., when those methods had been made illegal by Parliament. A caution was, however, issued in May to the licensed preachers to restrain them from advocating further innovations and to exhort them to rebuke the innovators.

This popular agitation encouraged or compelled the Government to meditate further projects. Somerset was probably more concerned to keep the peace than to attempt the perfection of religious truth; and the complaint of a reformer that the Protector preferred watching the builders at Somerset House to hearing sermons should do something to relieve

[1] William May; see *Dict. Nat. Biogr.*, xxxvii., 146.

his memory of the charge of religious intemperance which it has long unjustly borne. Cranmer had no such worldly distractions; his mind was advancing with the times, and in the great controversy about the Eucharist which was now tending to overshadow all other religious questions he had not only gone as far as Luther, but was beginning to look in the direction of Zwingli. In this he reflected the temper of a large and growing body of English Reformers, and the year 1548 saw a great outburst of Protestant theology. Books poured from the press[1] controverting and ridiculing the Catholic doctrine of the mass, some of them respectable arguments, but most appeals to the crowd couched in coarse and ribald terms. There was a repetition of the ferment which pervaded Germany from 1521 to 1525[2]; and while Protestant tracts multiplied, scarcely a voice was raised on the Catholic side.[3] Cranmer himself joined in the fray by publishing an English translation of the Lutheran Catechism of Justus

[1] Between twenty and thirty such books against the mass are known to have appeared in England in 1548, and probably there were many more.

[2] See the present writer in the *Cambridge Modern History*, vol. ii., chap. v.

[3] This disproportion has been explained on the theory that the Government rigidly controlled the press, encouraged the Protestant writings, and suppressed Catholic productions. But this was not the case; the Government had given up the control of the press by the Act of 1547, and it was not till 13 August, 1549, that the Council, threatened by revolts in the East and in the West, ordered that no book should be printed without the licence of one of the Secretaries of State or of William Cecil (*Acts P. C.*, 1547–1550, p. 312). Moreover, the disproportion was just as great in Germany, where all

Jonas, but this book struck dismay into the hearts of those Zwinglians who had begun to entertain hopes of the Archbishop's conversion.

"This Thomas," wrote one to Zwingli's successor, Bullinger, "has fallen into so heavy a slumber that we entertain but a very cold hope that he will be aroused even by your most learned letter. For lately he has published a catechism, in which he has not only approved that foul and sacrilegious transubstantiation [1] of the Papists in the holy supper of Our Saviour, but all the dreams of Luther seem to him sufficiently well-grounded, perspicuous, and lucid." [2]

Another of Bullinger's correspondents excepted Cranmer and Latimer from the bulk of the learned and the nobility who shared Zwinglian views. "As to Canterbury," he continued, "he conducts himself in such a way . . . that the people do not think much of him and the nobility regard him as lukewarm. In other respects he is a kind and good-natured man." [3] These complaints were merely due to the restraint which Cranmer placed upon himself

the licensing powers were in the hands of Catholics. Gasquet and Bishop (pp. 122, *et sqq.*) give some specimens of these books. The tract *John Bon and Master Parson*, which they had not been able to find (p. 121, n.), is printed in the present writer's *Tudor Tracts*, 1903, pp. 159–169.

[1] This, of course, is a mistake, but advanced Reformers, and Cranmer himself at a later date, saw little difference between Transubstantiation and the Real Presence.

[2] *Original Letters*, Parker Soc., pp. 380–381.

[3] Barth. Traheron to Bullinger, 1 August, 1548. (*Original Letters*, i., 380.) For Traheron see the present writer in *Dict. Nat. Biogr.*, lvii., 148.

and to his reluctance to enunciate private opinions before he could adopt them in public practice. For in reality at least one phrase in his translation of the Catechism indicated a departure from the Lutheran creed; and he implied in his answer to Gardiner, printed in 1551, that shortly before the publication of the Catechism he had abandoned "that error of the real presence."[1]

This union of Cranmer with the forces of popular enthusiasm and the more interested desires of the nobility made it very difficult for the Protector to hold the balance even between Anglo-Catholic and Protestant. The pressure which he told Gardiner was being put upon him from both sides in 1547 now grew very unequal, and it required some skill and some rigour to prevent dangerous friction between the two parties. The Government was keenly alive to the disruptive effects which disputes over the Eucharist had produced on the Continent; and although the English Constitution enjoyed better guarantees of stability than those of Germany or Switzerland, the fear of religious war was ever present to the minds of England's rulers in the sixteenth century. In 1548 feeling was so acute that disputes whether there should be mass or not led to blows being exchanged in St. Paul's and other London churches; and the French ambassador, probably with some exaggeration, declares that there were daily fights on the subject. If unity was to be preserved, there must be some sort of uniformity; and

---

[1] Cranmer, *Works*, i., 374.

pending the production of one uniform order, a compromise and a standard which all should be persuaded or compelled to observe, the Council imposed silence on the disputants, especially with regard to the doctrine of the mass.[1]

Uniformity was the natural outcome of separation from Rome, for in an universal church there is more room for local option than in a national church, especially when that national church was anxious to define the boundaries which marked it off from the Roman church on one hand and the various Protestant churches on the other. If there was to be anything national about the church it was scarcely permissible that one diocese or one parish should approximate to the Roman use, while the next diocese or parish might follow that of Geneva, Wittenberg, or Zurich. There was more latitude in Germany, where a national system could not be said to exist either in religion or politics; but the results of German diversity scarcely recommended its adoption elsewhere. And so the progress towards uniformity began almost as soon as the connexion with Rome ceased. The Ten Articles of 1536 and the Six of 1539 were both assertions of the right, and indications of the intention of England to select her own formularies of faith and make them uniform. So, too, in 1543, Convocation had recommended the uniform adoption of the Sarum Use throughout the

[1] On 23 September even licensed preachers were prohibited for the time from preaching anything except the Homilies. Gardiner's failure to observe silence on the mass was one of the causes of his imprisonment in the Tower, 30 June, 1548.

province of Canterbury; and the task of compiling a Book of Common Prayer out of the various service-books in use had occupied much of Cranmer's time during the later years of Henry VIII. There was need of reform as well as of uniformity; the latter was felt mainly in England, but the defects of the current service-books were patent to Roman Catholics, and the reformed Breviary which Cardinal Quignon dedicated to Paul III. in 1535 anticipated not a few of the changes effected by the first English Book of Common Prayer.[1]

The Breviary of Cardinal Quignon and the Sarum Use were the basis of two schemes of Office[2] drawn up by Cranmer probably between 1543—when Convocation or the King or both ordered a revision of the service-books,—and 1547, when Convocation demanded the production of the results of the labours of those who had been engaged in this task. These two schemes mark two successive stages in the evolution of the First Book of

[1] The similarities between Quignon's work and the Preface to the First Book of Common Prayer were originally pointed out by the Rev. (Sir) William Palmer (1803–1885) in his *Origines Liturgicæ*, published in 1832. Quignon was a Spanish Franciscan and a friend and confidant of Clement VII. and Paul III.; many references to him will be found in the *Letters and Papers of Henry VIII.*, and in the *Calendar of Spanish State Papers*.

[2] The MS. is in the British Museum (*Royal MS.*, 7, B. iv.); it has been printed and exhaustively discussed in Gasquet and Bishop's *Edward VI. and the Book of Common Prayer*, 1890, the most valuable of all works on the subject, to which reference should be made for an account of the difference in detail between the various documents. The MS. is mainly in the hand of the Archbishop's secretary, Ralph Morice, and the corrections are in Cranmer's own.

Common Prayer. The first has been described as "Sarum material worked up under Quignon influence," while the latter "comes nearer to the form of morning and evening prayer in the first printed Prayer Book of Edward VI." The chief feature of interest about the second scheme is that it marks the transition from the ancient arrangement of the Office to the order adopted in 1549. *Compline* and the four *Hours* "prime, terce, sext, and none" were omitted altogether, and it is possible that upon this draft was modelled the form of service, from which *Compline* was omitted, used in the Chapel Royal in 1548, and recommended by Somerset in a letter of September the 4th to the Vice-Chancellor of Cambridge as a model for use in College chapels.

However that may be, there was a considerable step between the second of Cranmer's draft schemes and Edward VI.'s First Book of Common Prayer. The petition of Convocation in 1547 for the production of the schemes was not conceded, and it was not till September, 1548, that the final stage in the evolution of the Book of Common Prayer was commenced. The work is usually supposed to have been done by a body of Bishops[1] called the "Windsor Commission," and their names have been variously given by different historians, who in this connexion gener-

---

[1] The "other divines" who are said to have existed are not as a rule mentioned in contemporary references which speak only of "bishops"; see Gasquet and Bishop, p. 178. But on the other hand, Somerset in his letter to Cardinal Pole writes "as well bishops as other equally and indifferently chosen of judgment." (Pocock, *Troubles Connected with the First Book of Common Prayer*, p. x.)

ally confuse the Order of Communion with the First Book of Common Prayer. But these lists have not been traced to any authentic source, and a thorough search has failed to reveal any trace of a formal commission. It is, however, fairly certain that some Bishops did assemble first at Windsor and then at Chertsey Abbey in September and October, 1548, and deliberate upon the controversies raging with so much fury; and we have their own assertion for the fact that a draft Book of Common Prayer was submitted for their approval. It does not appear, however, that they had much share in drawing up this document, and one of the Catholic Bishops subsequently complained in the House of Lords that the book had been materially altered since he had subscribed to it. The only prelate who refused his assent was Bishop Day of Chichester, but the Catholics subscribed mainly for the sake of unity and not because they agreed with all its particulars. Their subscriptions were much like the "*nolens volo*," by which Tiptoft[1] once expressed his concurrence in an Ordinance of the Privy Council.

The Book, in fact, was, in the form in which it came before Parliament, to all intents and purposes the work of Cranmer. Not only was the doctrine of Transubstantiation—in which Cranmer had ceased to believe ten years before—excluded, but that of the Real Presence was implicitly rejected. The elevation and adoration of the Sacrament were left out, the

---

[1] John, Baron Tiptoft (1375?–1443). See the present writer in *Dict. Nat. Biogr.*, lvi., 409–411, and Nicolas, *Proceedings of the Privy Council*, vol. ii., Pref., p. liv.

word *oblation* was studiously avoided, and Bonner asserted that there was "heresy in the book" because the elements were still described as bread and wine after the completion of those ceremonies which implied to a Catholic their transubstantiation. The commendations of the Zwinglian party confirmed the criticisms of the Catholics. "You must know," wrote Traheron to Bullinger, "that Latimer has come over to our opinion respecting the true doctrine of the Eucharist, together with the Archbishop of Canterbury, and the other bishops, who heretofore seemed to be Lutherans."[1] "Even that Thomas [Cranmer] himself," remarks another correspondent, "by the goodness of God and the instrumentality of that most upright and judicious man, master John à Lasco, is in a great measure recovered from his dangerous lethargy."[2]

Such were Cranmer's views in the autumn of 1548, but they are not an accurate indication of the doctrine[3] of the First Book of Common Prayer, for the Archbishop's scheme was subjected to criticism in both Houses of Parliament and emerged from the ordeal a compromise between the two parties.

[1] *Original Letters*, p. 322; this letter is dated 28 September, and the editor adds "1548," but the correctness of this I doubt. The reference to "painful events" applies better to 1549 than to 1548.

[2] *Ibid.*, p. 383. Cranmer himself attributed his change of view to Ridley and not to John à Lasco, for whom see *Dict. Nat. Biogr.*, and Hermann Dalton's *Lasciana* and *Life of à Lasco*. Still there is probably some truth in the above statement, as à Lasco passed the winter of 1548–49 with Cranmer at Lambeth.

[3] This doctrine is only a matter of inference; the Book of Common Prayer is a manual of devotion, not of doctrine, and nice definitions of dogma agree ill with the devotional spirit.

In this work of modification Convocation seems to have had no hand[1]; but both Houses of Parliament asserted a voice in the matter. The Commons were urged by Traheron[2] to tolerate "no ambiguity in the reformation of the Lord's Supper; but it was not in his power to bring over his old fellow-citizens to his views." Apparently in this instance the conservative feeling of the Lower House resisted the more radical spirit of the Lords, for there Cranmer and Ridley, we are told by Traheron, argued so well on behalf of the Zwinglian view that "truth never obtained a more brilliant victory. I perceive that it is all over with Lutheranism, now that those who were considered its principal and almost only supporters have altogether come over to our side."[3]

"The palm," echoes Peter Martyr to Bucer, "rests with our friends, but especially with the Archbishop of Canterbury, whom they till now were wont to traduce as a man ignorant of theology, and as being conversant only with matters of government; but now, believe me, he has shown himself so mighty a theologian against them as they would rather not have proof of, and they

---

[1] A whole literature has grown up round this disputed and intricate point; the scanty evidence we have is contradictory. See Joyce, *Acts of the Church*; Dixon, *History*, iii., 5, *et seq.*; Gasquet and Bishop, chap. x.

[2] How Traheron got elected is not revealed by the *Official Return of M. P.'s*, but his friend Hilles expressly states that he was one of the burgesses. (*Original Letters*, i., 266.)

[3] *Orig. Letters*, i., 323. Traheron probably heard the debate in the Lords, being no doubt one of the M. P.'s who, according to Peter Martyr, went up every day to hear the debate in the House of Lords. *Ibid.*, ii., 469.

are compelled, against their inclination, to acknowledge his learning and power and dexterity in debate. Transubstantiation, I think, is now exploded, and the difficulty respecting the presence is at this time the most prominent point of dispute; but the parties engage with so much vehemence and energy as to occasion very great doubt as to the result; for the victory has hitherto been fluctuating between them." [1]

A brief report [2] of this great debate has come down to us, and from this authentic record we learn the gist of Cranmer's views. "Our faith," he declared, "is not to believe Him to be in bread and wine, but that he is in heaven; this is proved by Scripture and Doctors till the Bishop of Rome's usurped power came in." Later on in the debate he said, "I believe that Christ is eaten with the heart. The eating with our mouth cannot give us life, for then should a sinner have life. Only good men can eat Christ's body; and when the evil eateth the Sacrament, bread and wine, he neither hath Christ's body nor eateth it." That is to say, the presence in the Eucharist was a spiritual presence conditioned by the faith of the recipient. Ridley was somewhat more guarded in his admissions; the bread, he said, remained bread after consecration, "still the bread of communion is not mere bread, but bread united to the divinity." The common bread, he explained, is made a divine influence.

---

[1] *Original Letters*, ii., 469–470.

[2] Extant in British Museum *Royal MS.*, 17, B. xxxix., and printed in Gasquet and Bishop, pp. 397–443; for a further exposition of Cranmer's views see the following chapter.

PIETRO VERMIGLI, COMMONLY KNOWN AS PETER MARTYR.

FROM THE PAINTING NOW IN CHAPTER-HOUSE ROOM AT CHRISTCHURCH, OXFORD. BY PERMISSION OF THE DEAN AND FELLOWS.

Such were the answers which Cranmer gave to the three questions propounded in the debate: whether there was a real presence in the sacrament, whether evil men received "that body," and whether there was transubstantiation. In each case his reply was in the negative. In the last two questions he carried the majority with him, but, as Peter Martyr indicates, the great point at issue was the real presence, and in regard to that the result did not correspond with Traheron's triumphant pæan over the rout of the Lutherans. The debate described above took place on 14–17 December, 1548, but the Act of Uniformity imposing the First Book of Common Prayer did not pass the House of Lords till four weeks later.[1] The interval was used to modify Cranmer's draft of the Book of Common Prayer so as to secure a majority of episcopal votes in its favour. This was regarded as of much importance by the Protector, and his success enabled the Government to maintain in its subsequent disputes with Bonner and the Princess Mary that the measure had received the sanction of the Church. A majority of prelates would not, however, have voted for the doctrine laid down by Cranmer, and various alterations were introduced to modify Catholic hostility. The most important, perhaps, was the substitution of the phrases "sacrament of the body" and "sacrament of the blood"

[1] That is, on 21 January, 1549; it did not receive the royal assent until 14 March, 1549; on this much-disputed date see the present writer in *English Historical Review*, xvi., 376–379 and Canon Maccoll's preface to the 10th edition of his *Reformation Settlement* (1902).

for "bread" and "wine" in the last rubric of the communion; and the change was doubtless designed to meet Bonner's complaint that the use of the words "bread" and "wine" in this conjunction was heresy.

In its final form the First Book of Common Prayer was a blow to the extreme Reformers. "The foolish Bishops," wrote Traheron to Bullinger, "have made a marvellous recantation."[1] Hooper described the Book as "very defective and of doubtful construction and in some respects indeed manifestly impious."[2] Dryander remarked that with regard to the Lord's Supper "the book speaks very obscurely, and however you may try to explain it with candour, you cannot avoid great absurdity. The reason is that the bishops could not for a long time agree among themselves respecting this article." Some concessions, wrote Bucer and Fagius, "have been made both to a respect for antiquity and to the infirmity of the present age"; and they instanced the vestments enjoined for the celebration of the Eucharist, the use of candles and the chrism, and the commemoration of the dead. The Book was, in fact, neither Roman nor Zwinglian; still less was it Calvinistic, and for this reason mainly it has been described as Lutheran. Richard Hilles, a well-informed layman, compared the communion service with that adopted in the Nürnberg churches and in some of the churches of Saxony. But the resemblance was due not so much to conscious imitation

[1] *Original Letters*, i., 323.

[2] *Ibid.*, pp. 232–3, 266, 350–1, 565.

as to the common conservatism which characterised the Lutheran and Anglican service-books, and led to the retention in them of many Catholic usages which Reformed churches in Europe rejected. The Anglican was, in fact, the most conservative of all the liturgies produced by the Reformation. The Sarum Use was its basis, but Cranmer's extensive acquaintance with contemporary liturgies enabled him to select the best from an enormous range of material. His indebtedness to the Breviary of Cardinal Quignon has already been mentioned; with all the more important Lutheran service-books he was familiar; and his correspondence with his wife's uncle, Osiander, and with Zwinglian divines such as J. de Watt (Vadianus) kept him in touch with the trend of every variety of continental opinion. Perhaps the clearest traces of foreign influence may be found in the similarities between the Baptismal Office of the First Book of Common Prayer and the *Pia Consultatio*, compiled by Bucer and Melanchthon and published under the authority of Hermann von Wied, the reforming Archbishop of Cologne, in 1543. But Cranmer also laid under contribution the liturgies of the Greek Church, numerous editions of which had been printed before 1548, and possibly of the Mozarabic or ancient rite of Spain.[1]

[1] The two similarities alleged between the English Book of 1549 and the Mozarabic Use are in the words of institution of the sacrament and the form of blessing the font. The first appears rather to have been derived from a contemporary liturgy; and Gasquet and Bishop (p. 185 n.), while admitting "that the form must have been derived either directly or indirectly from the Spanish Liturgy" point out that printed copies of this liturgy were scarcely accessible

Quite apart from conflicting views in the English Church and Parliament which made compromise essential, it was not likely that a liturgy derived from such various sources would embody or emphasise one clear, definite, dogmatic system; nor is a liturgy the proper vehicle for the assertion of dogma. The value of the English Book of Common Prayer is not to be compared with that of the Augsburg Confession or the Longer and Shorter Catechisms: it was different in kind, but not less in degree. The Prayer Book is not a creed nor a battle-cry, and it provokes the spirit of devotion rather than that of debate; it is religion and not theology. To it the Anglican Church owes the hold she retains on the English people. They are not attracted merely by the fact that the Church is established by law; it may be doubted whether her catholicity allures the bulk of the laity, and assuredly her standard of preaching is not the force which keeps men from joining other communions. But the Book of Common Prayer is unique, a *κτῆμα ἐς ἀεί*. Amid the

in 1549. But they have already suggested that similarities might be derived from *personal* intercourse, and here is perhaps the key of the puzzle. A reformer, known as Dryander or Duchesne, but whose real name was Francis Enzinas, was born at Burgos in 1515; he would certainly be familiar with the Mozarabic Use. In 1548 he came to England and was entertained by Cranmer for some time at Lambeth until he received an appointment at Cambridge. From him the Archbishop probably derived his knowledge of this usage. (See *Original Letters*, i., 348 n.; ii., 535; Cooper, *Athenæ Cantabr.*). On the general question the words of the liturgist Daniel may be quoted: "Perpauca inde (*i. e.*, ex Ægyptiis, Africanis, Gallicanis, Mozarabis) desumpta sunt, plurima ex Romanis liturgis, singula ex Reformatis"—*Codex Liturg. Eccl. Univ.*, iii., 349.

fierce contentions of the churches it gave the Church of England unity, strength, and a way to the hearts of men such as no other Church could boast. That the English Church survived was due in no small measure to the exquisite charm of her liturgy; and that was the work of Cranmer. He borrowed and learnt and adapted from various sources, but whatever he touched he adorned. Under his hands the rudest and simplest of prayers assumed a perfection of form and expression, and grew into one of the finest monuments of sacred literary art.

CHAPTER VIII

THEOLOGICAL VIEWS AND CONTROVERSIES

PURE theology occupies a smaller space in Cranmer's life than in that of other great Reformers, such as Luther, Zwingli, or Calvin; he founded no church and gave his name to no doctrinal system. His work was rather to reform a church, and he laboured under conditions unlike those which determined the thoughts and actions of his contemporaries in Europe. No one will dispute the vast importance of the religious issues which agitated civilisation in the sixteenth century, but it is impossible to understand the history of that epoch if it is treated from an exclusively theological point of view. Religious forces are potent indeed, but it is doubtful whether religion has fashioned nationality so much as nationality has moulded religion. If religion had been the one supreme test, it would have divided Europe into Catholic and Protestant parties, and not into Catholic and Protestant nations. Religion, in fact, was not so dominant in the sixteenth as it had been in the twelfth century, and the age was really one of secularisation. There was no Crusade, nor in any single instance was there an effective coalition of Catholic or of Protestant powers for any object whatever; and when wars of religion did come in the seventeenth century, it was France a Catholic power, which caused the Protestant victory. Political conditions exercised incalculable influence over the results of the religious movement; Protestantism broke in vain against the national temper of Spain, and it was national feeling in Germany which gave effect to Luther's protest. Political conditions, too, differentiated the Reformation in England from that in Germany and in Switzerland. Zwinglianism and Calvinism are republican because the Swiss cantons were republics; Lutheranism became a territorial religion because territorialism was the effective political principle then existent in Germany. The Church *in* England became the Church *of* England because a strong national monarchy grasped the sceptre which was slipping from the hands of the Papal hierarchy.

The predominance of the State in England was unfavourable to the influence of the Church and to the free development of religious speculation, while the loose and impotent political organisation of Switzerland and Germany stimulated independent thought. There the seat of authority was, if not empty, poorly filled; and in the early years of the Reformation, at least, its direction fell into the hands of religious leaders. Hence Luther and Zwingli were able to develop a theology which would soon have been checked in England. Their rulers were weak and not theologians. Henry VIII. was strong and a theologian with emphatic views of his own. In England a reformation could only be effected by the State and through the instrumentality of an Archbishop, who was not merely Primate of the Church but constitutionally the first adviser of the Crown; a position which, while it conferred honour and dignity, also imposed restraints. It not only bounded his liberty of action, but affected his point of view. To Luther truth could be the only consideration; Cranmer had also to consider how truth could be translated into action and imposed on a doubting people; to him compromise was essential, for he was a statesman as well as a theologian; he lived and moved in a practical sphere in which ideals and abstractions could play but a limited part.

Another difference arises from this process of reformation by government instrumentality. Luther's Ninety-five Theses were his own individual act; the Confession of Augsburg was the work of Melanchthon; but the Ten and the Forty-two Articles, the First and Second Books of Common Prayer, were the acts of a government and not the manifestoes of an individual or even of a party. In these documents Cranmer's voice sounded the dominant note, but all in varying degrees are of composite authorship and represent the working of several minds. Like the policy of modern cabinets, they may not embody any one man's ideal, and caution should be observed in any attempt to deduce therefrom the nature of private convictions. Particularly is this the case when the expressions of this composite and collective opinion are directed primarily towards the reformation of abuses and regulation of worship, and not towards the definition of dogma. Had the Reformation in England been guided by Calvin or Luther, or by a series of ecclesiastical councils, it might have produced religious war, but would probably have propagated a more definite theological system. A layman is not necessarily a bad theologian, but a statesman must economise truth and compound with the forces of darkness.

Circumstances thus turned Cranmer away from abstract speculation, and on its speculative and philosophical side his theology is not distinctive. Metaphysics lay quite beyond his mental horizon; and he has little or nothing to say on the tremendous issues involved in the relations between the will of man and the will of God. Probably he thought these vast realms a trackless waste on which it would be rash to enter. Caution was a marked characteristic of Cranmer's typically English mind; although it was open to many influences, no single idea took exclusive possession; truth shone into it through various media, and the light it received was a blend less clear but more soft than the rays which pierced the brain of Luther or Calvin. The same is true of Anglican doctrine; the strict alliance of Church and State was by no means an unmixed blessing, but it acted as some protection from the fierce glare of some theological dogmas; and when Lutheran, Zwinglian, and, lastly, Calvinistic rays did break in upon the English Church they were so combined and modified that a sort of spectrum analysis is required to distinguish them one from another. And if the light was moderate, the heat was also less; for the passion which loosed England from Rome was a political sentiment rather than a religious enthusiasm like that aroused by Predestination or Justification by Faith; and Cranmer's theology by itself would not have generated sufficient force to drive the engine of Reform.

Cranmer himself appears to have reached his convictions by the intellectual path of reason rather than through the sensational "experiences" which led to Luther's revolt. His repugnance to the old religious system did not, it would seem, arise from its failure to satisfy the spiritual needs of a clamant conscience, but from the dissonance between the Scriptures and the Papacy. It was the study of the Scriptures and not the wrestling of the spirit that first aroused Cranmer's doubts. To the Scriptures he had devoted his time from his early days at Cambridge, and throughout his life their influence over his mind was ever-increasing. His career was a troubled but constant journeying away from the papal towards the evangelical position; and the decrees of Popes and of General Councils, and even the words of the Fathers, gradually receded into the distance. Yet Cranmer never reached the extreme of Zwinglianism. He did not condemn all that was not in the Bible, for an Archbishop could scarcely do that with consistency; and he had little patience with those who objected to kneeling because it was not enjoined in the Scriptures. So, too, he always attached a great, though lessening, value to the

Fathers as interpreters of the words of Christ and of the Apostles.

The Bible was Cranmer's Ark of the Covenant, and his lack of the speculative instinct saved him from the temptation to lay impious hands upon it. He could make effective use of the contradictions between the various decrees of the Popes; but he seems to have been happily blind to the difficulties presented by the text of the Scriptures. In this respect he was less acute or less frank than Luther, who admitted the discrepancies between the Synoptists and the Gospel of St. John, and between Stephen's account of Jewish history and that recorded in the Old Testament.[1] Still farther was Cranmer from the mental attitude of Carlstadt, who doubted the Mosaic authorship of the Pentateuch, and believed that the original form of the Gospels had not been preserved intact.[2] His interest in textual criticism of the Scriptures was conditioned by the support which it gave to attacks on the Papacy. This was the natural position for a practical man engaged in a life-and-death struggle; it is scarcely the business of such an one to exhibit the defects in the weapon with which he defended himself and attacked his enemies; and Cranmer was too busy wielding the sword of the Gospel to spend much time in displaying its flaws.

The application of the Scriptural test to the problems of the time was with Cranmer a slow and

[1] H. E. Jacobs, *Luther*, p. 351.

[2] For Andrew Bodenstein, or Carlstadt, see the present writer in *Cambridge Modern History*, ii., 165.

gradual development; but it was none the less an independent process, anterior to and not consequent upon the action of the State. For years before the divorce of Catherine of Aragon he had prayed for the abolition of the papal jurisdiction; and before the Government had taken any action with regard to the doctrine or the practice of the Church, his faith in papal theology had gone the way of his respect for papal law. Whether his visit to Rome in 1530 produced as deep an impression as Luther's did, we do not know; but at least it did nothing to alter the tendencies of his mind. It is obvious that in 1532 he no longer believed in compulsory celibacy for the clergy; and his intercourse with the Lutheran divines during his embassy to Germany in that year had probably confirmed his doubts of other orthodox views. As soon as he became Archbishop he began to agitate for an authorised version of the Scriptures in English, and the Ten Articles of 1536 were evidence of the distance he had already travelled from later Catholic doctrine. He had in 1537 already rejected the abuses of "Purgatory, pilgrimages, praying to saints, images, holy bread, holy water, holy days, merits, works, ceremony, and such other."[1]

Of these changes the most important was the denial of Purgatory, for it was belief in its existence and in the power of the clergy to redeem men's souls from its pains that gave the Roman Church its hold over the popular mind. The claim was not capable of practical or ocular refutation; and the

[1] Cranmer, *Works*, ii., 351.

fear that, however successfully the priest might be restrained in this world, he might have the last word in the other, was, next to the impression that the priest was endowed with the miraculous power of "making God," the greatest obstacle in the path of the Reformation. Hence the importance of Luther's dogma of Justification by Faith, which made priestly intercession a work of supererogation; and hence that dogma was so far accepted by the English Church as to undermine the belief in Purgatory. Cranmer himself went farther in this direction than most English Reformers, and the views he expressed in 1547 in his *Homily of Salvation*[1] are scarcely distinguishable from Luther's own; "faith," he wrote, "doth not exclude repentance, hope, love, dread, and the fear of God, to be joined with faith in every man that is justified, but it excludeth them from the office of justifying. . . . Nor that faith also doth not exclude the justice of good works, necessarily to be done afterward of duty towards God . . . but it excludeth them, so that we may not do them to this intent, to be made good by doing of them."

Cranmer's attitude towards other theological questions (except the Eucharist) may best be indicated by summarising his replies to the series of interrogations put to the bishops by Henry VIII. about 1541.[2] He did not materially vary from the

[1] This homily is printed in *Works*, ii., 128–134; Cranmer was almost certainly its author. His "Notes on Justification," consisting of passages from the Scriptures, the Fathers, and the Schoolmen, are printed in *Works*, ii., 203–211, and in Jenkyns, ii., 121 *et sqq.*

[2] Burnet, iv., 443-496.

position he then held, and his answers illustrate not only the difference between him and the Roman Catholics, but that between him and both High and Free churchmen of to-day. With regard to the nature, number, and authority of the sacraments he said that the Scriptures "sheweth not what a sacrament is," nor how many sacraments there were; while the "ancient doctors" described a sacrament as *sacræ rei signum, visibile verbum, symbolum, atque pactio, quâ sumus constricti*, and applied the name to many more than the orthodox seven; he knew no reason why the word should be attributed to the seven only, for that number of seven was "no doctrine of Scripture, nor of the old authors." Questioned whether the *thing* was there, though the name was absent, he replied that Baptism and the Eucharist were the only two things in Scripture which could be regarded as sacraments; penance was in Scripture "a pure conversion of a sinner in heart and mind," and there was no mention of its conventional tripartite division into contrition, confession, and satisfaction; matrimony, confirmation, and extreme unction were not sacraments; nor was there any allusion in Scripture to "confirmation with chrism, without which it is counted no sacrament."

The interrogations then pass on to the debatable ground of the ecclesiastical power of princes. Was it for lack of commission from a Christian king that the Apostles took upon them to make bishops? or had they authority given of God? Cranmer drew up a long reply. All Christian princes, he said, have committed to them immediately of God the whole cure of all their subjects, as well concerning the administration of God's Word for the cure of the soul as concerning the ministration of things political and civil governance.[1] So under them they have both civil and ecclesiastical ministers, who are appointed by their laws and orders. In the admission of many of these officers divers comely ceremonies and solemnities were used, but they were not necessary, and their omission would not invalidate the appointment; nor was there any more divine promise of grace to be given "in the committing of the ecclesiastical office" than in that of the civil office. It was the lack of authority from a Christian king that compelled the Apostles to appoint ministers of God's Word.

To further questions Cranmer answered that in the beginning there was no distinction between priest and bishop, and that while a bishop might make priests, so might princes and governors, "and the people also by their election." "In the New Testament he that is appointed to be a Bishop or Priest needeth no consecration by the Scripture, for election or appointing thereto is sufficient"; a Christian prince was also bound, in case ecclesiastics failed, to teach and preach the Word of God and to make and constitute priests. A man was not bound by Scripture "to confess his secret deadly sins to a

[1] These views appeared to be derived from Marsiglio of Padua who anticipated by two centuries the Tudor theory of Church and State (*cf.* Dunning, *Ancient and Mediæval Political Theory*, pp. 242–3). Marsiglio's *Defensor Pacis* was printed in England in 1536, with Cromwell's approbation (see the present writer in *D. N. B.*, s. v. "Marshall, William," xxxvi., 250).

priest"; nor did Scripture command or forbid a bishop or priest to excommunicate; such powers depended entirely upon the laws of the country where he lived.

Many of these points are of merely antiquarian or academic interest, and their importance is slight compared with that of Cranmer's views on the Eucharist. The doctrine of Transubstantiation he had abandoned early, though the exact date of the change cannot be ascertained. In 1538 he wrote to Cromwell[1]:

"As concerning Adam Damplip of Calais, he utterly denieth that ever he taught or said that the very body and blood of Christ was not presently in the sacrament of the altar, and confesseth the same to be there really; but he saith that the controversy between him and the prior was because he confuted the opinion of transubstantiation, and therein I think he taught but the truth.'

But he was yet far from the Zwinglian position;

"for," he wrote in 1537[2] to the Zwinglian J. de Watt, "unless I see stronger evidence brought forward than I have yet been able to see, I desire neither to be the patron nor the approver of the opinion maintained by you. And I am plainly convinced . . . that the cause is not a good one."

The doctrine of the Real Presence was, he thought, proved by "evident and manifest passages of Script-

[1] *Works*, ii., 375.

[2] *Ibid.*, ii., 343.

ures," and "handed down to us by the Fathers themselves and men of apostolical character from the very beginning of the Church"; and "our gracious Lord would never have left his beloved spouse in such lamentable blindness for so long a period."

The last was a two-edged argument for a Reformer to use, and the time came when Cranmer himself rejected the Real Presence in spite of the manifest passages in Scripture, the Fathers, and men of apostolical character. This development was, however, slow, and its history has been obscured by a remark of Cranmer's during his examination before Bishop Brooks in 1555.[1] "You, master Cranmer," said Dr. Martin[2] to him, "have taught in this high sacrament of the altar three contrary doctrines, and yet you protested in every one *verbum Domini*." "Nay," replied Cranmer, "I taught but two contrary doctrines"; and his remark has been considered[3] a decisive refutation of the idea that he had passed through a Lutheran phase in his transition from papal to Zwinglian doctrine. It is perhaps a little loose to identify the High Anglican doctrine of the Real Presence with the Lutheran dogma of Consubstantiation; but that Cranmer at one time believed in the Real Presence while he disbelieved in Tran-

[1] Foxe, viii., 56.

[2] Thomas Martyn, or Martin, was a zealous Roman Catholic civilian who took a prominent part in the proceedings against the Marian martyrs; he was, however, unmolested in Elizabeth's reign, and was even given some legal work by the Government; see *D. N. B.*, xxxvi., 320.

[3] Wordsworth, *Eccl. Biogr.*, iii., 550; *cf.* Jenkyns iv., 95, and Cranmer, *Works*, ii., 218.

substantiation is certain. That is the only inference possible from his letters to Cromwell and Watt quoted above; and in the preface to his *Answer to Dr. Richard Smith* he wrote that he was "in that error of the *Real Presence*, as I was many years past in divers other errors, as of *Transubstantiation*," thus clearly distinguishing between the two. His answer to Dr. Martin may have been misreported, or his memory may have deceived him; but there is a third explanation. Proceeding to define the two "contrary doctrines" he had taught, he indicates "the Papists' doctrine" as one, and the view he then held as the other. He had come to regard the Real Presence no less than Transubstantiation as "Papists' doctrine," and the same identification is made in the preface to his answer to Gardiner.

Yet Cranmer would not have called the Real Presence "Papists' doctrine" at any time between 1538 and 1548. He believed it himself throughout that decade, and assuredly he then was no papist. Down to the eve of the debate on the Sacrament in December, 1548, he was regarded by the Zwinglians as a lukewarm Lutheran, though nearly a year before he had described the mass as "a memory and representation,"[1] and the description of him as a Lutheran merely means that he was neither papist nor Zwinglian. The means of Cranmer's conversion have been already discussed[2]; the results were apparent in the debate on the Sacrament and in Cranmer's controversies with Bishop Gardiner and with Dr. Richard Smith; in these books he gives the fullest account

[1] Burnet, v., 201.

[2] See above, p. 216.

of his belief on the question and of the reasons which led him to hold it.

The First Book of Common Prayer had embodied a compromise on the Eucharist between the views of Cranmer and those of the Catholic bishops. The phraseology employed was capable of a Catholic and of a Protestant interpretation, and both sides asserted that theirs was the only true gloss. But the political events of 1549 had substituted an aggressive for an accommodating government, and it was with the good wishes if not at the instigation of the ruling Protestants that Cranmer set to work to prove that the Protestant view was correct. His book was entitled *A Defence of the True and Catholic Doctrine of the Sacrament*, and it was published in 1550.[1] In it Cranmer took occasion to impugn some assertions made by the Bishop of Winchester in his sermon before the King on 30 June, 1548, and Gardiner, although he was now in prison, found means to take up the cudgels in his own defence. His book was entitled *An Explication and Assertion of the True Catholic Faith touching the most blessed Sacrament of the Altar with Confutation of a book Written against the Same.* Gardiner affected to believe that the *Defence*, although published under Cranmer's name, was not by him because it was inconsistent with the views which the Archbishop

[1] The origin of his book is also attributed to the publication of Gardiner's *Detection of the Devil's Sophistry*, a treatise against Protestant views of the sacrament, but this had been published four years before in 1546. A Latin version of the *Defence* by Sir J. Cheke was published abroad in 1553.

had previously expressed on the subject. Another attack on Cranmer was made by Dr. Richard Smith, who is extravagantly described by Anthony Wood as "the greatest pillar of the Roman Catholic cause in his time."[1] The Archbishop replied to both in *An Answer*, published in 1551, in which are also incorporated his original treatise and Gardiner's rejoinder. The whole volume is more than three times the size of this present one, so that it is impossible to follow even in outline the threads of Cranmer's argument or to do more than give a brief indication of his conclusions.

From the point of view of mental equipment Gardiner was scarcely a match for the Archbishop. He had no claim to Cranmer's learning, and although, as he acknowledges, his skill in debate had earned him the name of "sophister," he complains that Cranmer overcame him with sophistry; and Sir Thomas More had once confessed himself staggered by the subtlety of Cranmer's arguments. Nevertheless Gardiner had a great deal of rough common sense, and he presented the Catholic view with no little ability, and considerable moderation. "I know,"

[1] Smith had been first Regius Professor of Divinity at Oxford; he repudiated his Romanism in 1547, but in 1549 had a famous argument on the Sacrament at Oxford with Peter Martyr. He then fled to Louvain, whence his answer to Cranmer was published. He was restored to his professorship under Mary, and preached at Latimer and Ridley's martyrdom from the text, "If I give my body to be burnt, and have not charity, it profiteth nothing." The fact suggests that Smith himself had little charity; neither did he give his body to be burnt, but again recanted in 1559, was deprived of his professorship on the ground of adultery, and was made chancellor of Douay University; see *D. N. B.*, liii., 101–102.

he writes,[1] "by faith Christ to be present [in the sacrament], but the particularity how he is present, more than I am assured he is truly present, and *therefore in substance* present I cannot tell; but present he is, and truly is and verily is, and . . . *therefore in substance is, and, as we term it, substantially is present.*" The words in italics represent the position which Cranmer challenged; and they have the merit of avoiding the vague term *real*. For spiritual things are as real as things material; and in this sense Cranmer strenuously asserted the Real Presence in the Sacrament. "As for the real presence of Christ in the Sacrament," he writes, "I grant that he is really present . . . that is to say in deed, and yet but spiritually."[2] That *real* did not involve a *corporal* presence; and Gardiner's *therefore* begged the question. "Doth not God's word," asked Cranmer, "teach a true presence of Christ in spirit where he is not present in his corporal substance? As when he saith: 'where two or three be gathered together in my name, there am I in the midst of them.' And also when he saith: 'I shall be with you till the end of the world.' Was it not a true presence that Christ in these places promised? And yet can you not of this true presence gather such a corporal presence of the substance of Christ's manhood as you unlearnedly contrary to the Scriptures go about to prove in the sacrament."[3]

Cranmer's thesis is, "that as no Scripture, so no ancient author known and approved hath in plain terms your transubstantiation; nor that the body

[1] Cranmer, *Works*, i., 59. [2] *Ibid.*, i., 127. [3] *Ibid.*, i., 61.

and blood of Christ be really, corporally, naturally, and carnally under the forms of bread and wine; nor that evil men do eat the very body and drink the very blood of Christ; nor that Christ is offered every day by the priest a sacrifice propitiatory for sin."[1] His doctrine, he maintained, "was never condemned by no council, nor your false papistical doctrine allowed, until the devil caused Antichrist, his son and heir, Pope Nicholas II.,[2] with his monks and friars, to condemn the truth and confirm these your heresies."[3] Elsewhere he declares that Pope Innocent III. was "the chief author of your doctrine both of transubstantiation and of the real presence."[4] By "real presence" Cranmer generally means a corporal presence, which Luther asserted when he declared that "the mouth eats the body of Christ bodily." Cranmer believed "that Christ giveth himself truly to be eaten, chewed, and digested; but all is spiritually with faith, *not with the mouth*."[5] Here was a clear repudiation of Lutheran doctrine, and Gardiner made a good forensic use of the discrepancy between the two Reformers. He complained that the Archbishop sought to prejudice his opponent's case by calling the Real Presence a Papistical dogma, whereas others held it who were no Papists,—for instance, Luther and himself.

[1] *Works*, i., 13.

[2] Nicholas II. was Pope from 1058 to 1061.

[3] *Works*, i., 14.

[4] *Ibid* i., 65; Innocent was Pope from 1198 to 1216.

[5] *Ibid.*, i., 15; the eating of God as a means of salvation was not, of course, originally a Christian idea; it is found in some very primitive religions.

Cranmer retorted that he called it Papists' doctrine because Papists invented it, not because Papists and no one else believed in it; and he pointed out that Luther was not a good witness for Gardiner to allege, because Luther, while holding the Real Presence, denounced more emphatically than any other Reformer the doctrine of Transubstantiation, in which Gardiner believed.

Having thus repudiated both Lutherans and Papists, Cranmer showed that he did not sympathise with the extreme Zwinglian view, that the bread and wine were "bare tokens," and nothing more. "They be," he writes,[1] "no vain or bare tokens (for a token is that which betokeneth only and giveth nothing, as a painted fire, which giveth neither light nor heat); but in the due ministration of the sacraments God is present, working with his word and sacrament." The bread and wine "have promises of effectual significance."[2] "As the bread is outwardly eaten indeed in the Lord's supper, so is the very body of Christ inwardly by faith eaten indeed of all them that come thereto in such sort as they ought to do, which eating nourisheth them into everlasting life."[3] "I do not say that Christ's body and blood be given to us in signification, and not in deed. But I do as plainly speak as I can, that Christ's body and blood be given to us in deed, yet not corporally and carnally, but spiritually and effectually."[4]

This is the gist of Cranmer's teaching. There is

[1] *Works*, i., 11.
[2] *Ibid.*, i., 36.
[3] *Ibid.*, i., 17.
[4] *Ibid.*, i., 37.

both a real presence and a miraculous working in the sacrament; but both the presence and the working are spiritual, not material. Christ is present in His divinity, not in His humanity[1]; He is really absent in body, for that is in heaven, but He is really present in spirit; "Christ is with us spiritually present, is eaten and drunken of us, and dwelleth within us, although corporally he be departed out of this world, and is ascended up into heaven"[2]; "He is neither corporally in the bread and wine, nor in or under the forms and figures of them, but is corporally in heaven, and spiritually in his lively members, which be his temple where he inhabiteth."[3] So, too, "the miraculous working is not in the bread, but in them that duly eat the bread, and drink that drink . . . For he is effectually present and effectually worketh, not in the bread and wine, but in the godly receivers of them."[4] "And the true eating and drinking of the said body and blood of Christ is with a constant and lively faith to believe that Christ gave his body and shed his blood upon the cross for us, and that he doth so join and incorporate himself to us that he is our head, and we his members, and flesh of his flesh, bone of his bone, having him dwelling in us and we in him. And herein standeth the whole effect and strength of this sacrament. And this faith God worketh inwardly in our hearts by his holy Spirit."[5] The best summing up of Cranmer's views may also be given in his own words; "figuratively he is the bread and wine, and

[1] *Works*, i., 49.
[2] *Ibid.*, i., 12; *cf.* p. 52.
[3] *Ibid.*, i., 53-54.
[4] *Ibid.*, i., 34.
[5] *Ibid.*, i., 43.

spiritually he is in them that worthily eat and drink the bread and wine; but really, carnally, and corporally he is only in heaven, from whence he shall come to judge the quick and the dead."[1]

These words represent Cranmer's mature opinion,[2] from which he only varied during some six weeks in 1556; and when that moment of weakness had passed he returned to the position here indicated, and in his last hour declared that he believed as he had taught in his book against the Bishop of Winchester. His view of the Sacrament has been denounced as a "low" one; but the only ground for the charge is the fact that Cranmer's doctrine reduces the importance of the priest as an intercessor between God and man, and emphasises the direct as against the indirect relationship. The Sacrament still remains a miracle, but it is a miracle wrought by God and not by priests, a miracle feeding the souls of men, and not transforming material bread

[1] *Works*, i., 139.

[2] Gardiner again replied to this book of Cranmer's in 1552, and the Archbishop was engaged on a further rejoinder when death cut short his work under Queen Mary; *see* below, p. 357. Another controversial work attributed to Cranmer is *A Confutation of Unwritten Verities*, which was published by an English exile, E. P., in 1558, and professed to be a translation from a Latin original by Cranmer; but the only part that Cranmer appears to have had in the work was that it is based on a collection of passages from the Scriptures and the Fathers compiled by the Archbishop and preserved among his commonplace-books in the British Museum (*Royal MS.*, 7, B. xi., xii.). It has been admitted into the various editions of Cranmer's *Works*, but Jenkyns is very doubtful as to its claim to be his, and remarks that "it cannot be safely quoted as evidence of Cranmer's tenets."

and wine, a miracle relating not to the things seen which are temporal, but to the unseen things which are eternal.

The denial of this material miracle wrought by the hands of priests struck at the root of the mediæval Church system, and it is for this reason that the religious controversies of the sixteenth century centred round the doctrine of the Mass. The sacerdotal claim had always been that the grace of God flows only through priestly channels, and that none could be saved except by resort to the priestly monopoly. Hence came clerical privilege and clerical rule; "shall the hands that have made God," asked indignant churchmen in the time of Henry II., "be bound like those of a common malefactor?" Cranmer denied that the hands of the priest could "make God"; and therefore the whole superstructure fell to the ground. But this denial was the only means of its overthrow.

"What availeth it," he asked in his preface, "to take away beads, pardons, pilgrimages, and such like popery, so long as the two chief roots remain unpulled up? Whereof, so long as they remain, will spring again all former impediments of the Lord's harvest, and corruption of his flock. The rest is but branches and leaves, the cutting away whereof is but like topping and lopping of a tree, or cutting down of weeds, leaving the body standing and the roots in the ground; but the very body of the tree, or rather the roots of the weeds, is the popish doctrine of transubstantiation, of the real presence of Christ's flesh and blood in the sacrament of the altar (as they call it), and of the sacrifice and oblation of Christ made by the priest for the salvation of the quick and the dead; which roots, if they be suffered to grow in the Lord's vineyard, they will overspread all the ground again with the old errors and superstitions."

CHAPTER IX

CRANMER AND THE SECOND BOOK OF COMMON PRAYER

THERE is no greater mistake, and none more common, than to assume that the whole reign of Edward VI. is one period, marked throughout by the same characteristics, methods, and aims. In reality it is as misleading to identify the policy of Somerset with that of his successor, Northumberland, as it would be to confuse Girondins with Jacobins in the history of the French Revolution. The year 1549, when Somerset fell, saw a change not merely in the *personnel* of the Government, but in every sphere of its activity, in its attitude towards civil and religious liberty, in its treatment of social questions, in its view of the relations between Church and State, and in its management of foreign affairs.[1] The one element of continuity was that Cranmer remained Archbishop of Canterbury under Northumberland's *régime* as he had been under that of Protector Somerset. But Cranmer had never been in a position to dictate the ecclesiastical policy

[1] For a detailed proof of this statement see the present writer's *England under Protector Somerset*, chap. x.

of the Government, and his continuance in the Primacy no more proves that the Second Book of Common Prayer was the natural and inevitable outcome of the First than it proves that the Six were the natural and inevitable outcome of the Ten Articles. It was this revolution of 1549 and its consequences which provoked and embittered reaction and brought the chief actors in it, and others less guilty, like Cranmer, to a violent and untimely end.

The First Act of Uniformity, and the First Book of Common Prayer represented the maximum of religious reform which the nation, as a whole, was prepared in 1549 to accept.[1] This Act of Uniformity was the mildest ever passed by the English Parliament; it imposed no penalties for recusancy on the laity, and those imposed on the clergy were lighter than in any succeeding Act. It was a strenuous attempt to effect reform with as little offence as possible. Like all compromises it was received with derision at both ends of the religious scale. But while the Protestants contented themselves with denouncing what they considered the puerilities and absurdities of the new service-book, the Catholics in the west broke out in revolt. It is not, however, clear that the various risings of 1549 had any close connexion with the Book of Common Prayer. There had been many disturbances in the previous year due to the enclosure of common lands and

[1] The only other Act of ecclesiastical importance passed in 1548–49 was one which granted a grudging legality to the marriage of priests.

conversion of tillage to pasture, a movement which threw numbers out of work and was at the bottom of most of the rebellions in the sixteenth century. But popular discontent was turned to account by priests of the old persuasion, and even by emissaries from France then on the eve of war with England.[1] Hence the statement of grievances, which were no doubt drawn up by priests, laid more emphasis upon religious matters than the mass of insurgents would naturally have done themselves. The men of Cornwall had, however, a tangible reason for disliking the new service-book, because many of them understood no English. They comprehended the old Latin no better; but they were accustomed to its sound, and men tolerate the incomprehensible more readily than the unfamiliar.

To Cranmer fell the task of replying to the articles[2] drawn up by the insurgent leaders, and it was a matter of no great difficulty to prove their want of reason and logic. The first article demanded the observance of the decrees of all the General Councils and Popes; but, as Cranmer pointed out, these were full of contradictions. Moreover, one decree de-

[1] A defence of the insurgents written in French but not printed until 1550 is summarised by Pocock (*Troubles*, etc., Camden Society, pp. 18–20). Pocock thinks this is a translation from an English original, which is lost. It is more probably an original emanating from the French ambassador or one of his agents. Henri II. had previously attempted to use Lord Seymour's conspiracy as a means of embroiling England in civil war (see *Hatfield MSS.*, vol. i., no. 268).

[2] These articles are printed with Cranmer's reply in Cranmer's *Works*, ii., 163–188, and also with Nicholas Udall's reply by Pocock in *Troubles*, etc., pp. 141–193.

clared that whosoever did not acknowledge himself to be under the obedience of the Bishop of Rome was a heretic; but such an acknowledgment would be treason by English law. Another said that all princes' laws against papal decrees were void; that would invalidate not merely the legislation of Henry VIII. but the statutes of *Præmunire* and Provisors, the taxation of the clergy, and all the anti-ecclesiastical legislation of the Middle Ages. A third forbade men to reprove the Pope even though his conduct might be imperilling thousands of souls. The second demand of the insurgents required the restoration of the statute of Six Articles, though this Act was, as Cranmer showed, inconsistent with several decrees of General Councils. The third insisted upon the revival of the Latin mass with no communicants except the priest; the fourth demanded compulsory worship of the sacrament and the execution of all recusants as heretics—a ferocious requisition which deprived its authors of all title to mercy. The fifth would have the sacrament distributed but once a year—at Easter—and then in one kind only; this was a curious illustration of the working of the conservative spirit, for the rebels wished to stereotype a custom which, as Tunstall explained, had grown up "by coldness of devotion."[1] To the sixth article, requiring the administration of baptism on week-days as well as on holy days, the Archbishop replied that there was nothing to prevent it. The seventh and eighth asked for the restoration of candles, ashes, palms, and holy water, and repudiated

[1] Burnet, v., 201.

the new service because it was "but like a Christmas game," and the Cornishmen understood no English. The ninth and tenth required prayers for souls in purgatory and the suppression of the English Scriptures because otherwise the clergy would not be able to confound the heretics.[1] The eleventh and twelfth articles demanded the release of two divines in prison, the pardon of Cardinal Pole, and his promotion to the Council. The thirteenth proposal was that no gentleman should keep more than one servant unless he possessed lands worth more than a hundred marks a year; and the fourteenth demanded the restitution of some of the suppressed abbeys and chantries.

These last, and perhaps the seventh and eighth, were the only articles which can be supposed to represent a really popular sentiment; and the inner mind of the authors of this document is best revealed in the reason given for the proposed suppression of the English Bible; illiterate priests wanted protection from the results of their own illiteracy, while their dangerous temper is illustrated by the demand for the execution of all who refused to worship the sacrament. Hard words are used, and not without justice, of the zealots who imperilled the cause of the Reformation by their arrogance; but the fanaticism was not all on one side, and a demand like this enforced by armed rebellion would have driven the most liberal Government into acts of

[1] This was a very natural demand on the part of the clergy when not half of their number in the diocese of Gloucester could repeat the Ten Commandments.

PROTECTOR SOMERSET.

AFTER THE PORTRAIT, DATED 1548, IN THE POSSESSION OF SIR EDMUND VERNEY, AND NOW IN HIS HOUSE AT RHIANVA. REPRODUCED BY THE OWNER'S PERMISSION.

repressive severity. Cranmer took the truest and the most charitable view, when he wrote that the rebels as a body did not know the meaning of that for which they were made to ask.

He was, moreover, to some extent in sympathy with the social discontent which clerical agitators turned to their own account in the West. In his address to the people at St. Mary's, Oxford, on the day of his death he uttered a solemn warning to the rich, bidding them remember how hard it was for such to enter the kingdom of heaven, and earnestly exhorting them to show compassion to the poor in those days of their penury.[1] The same sympathy impelled Latimer[2] to denounce the covetousness of the landlords in inclosing lands, and reducing the peasant to poverty, and stirred the Protector to undertake that championship of poor men's causes which led to his ruin. The bills for their relief which he promoted in Parliament were thrown out, and the commissions he appointed to check inclosures proved powerless in face of the packing of juries, intimidation of witnesses, and perjury practised by the landed gentry and encouraged by the Protector's own colleagues.[3] Baulked of the hopes

[1] Strype, *Cranmer*, i., 556.

[2] In his famous sermon "Of the Plough" (Latimer, *Sermons*, Parker Soc., pp. 59–78).

[3] For details see *England under Protector Somerset*, chapters viii.–ix. "The people," wrote Hooper to Bullinger, on 25 June, 1549, "are sorely oppressed by the marvellous tyranny of the nobility" (*Original Letters*, i., 66). A good statement of the poor men's complaints will be found in Robert Crowley's *Works* and *Four Supplications*, both published by the Early English Text Society.

of redress, which Somerset's policy held out to them, the peasants rebelled in every direction, and the revolt attained its most serious dimensions in Norfolk, where Robert Kett instituted a poor men's commonwealth.

Nor were these the only difficulties with which the Protector had to deal. The unscrupulous egotism of his brother, the Lord High Admiral, led him into treason and plot; and the Protector's consent to his execution, extorted from him by cunning schemers who hoped to profit by his fall, fatally weakened his own position. The rebellions in the West and the East diverted troops which should have been sent into Scotland and France, and the French king seized the opportunity to declare war and attack the English Pale. Both there and in Scotland the English lost ground. In England Warwick defeated the English rebels, and his victory made him the hero of the gentry, who now looked for revenge upon those who had hoped and dared to impede their career of prosperous pillage. The Protector himself was the head and front of offence, and in September, 1549, the party of Warwick determined upon his ruin.

The Earl of Warwick, better known by his later title of Duke of Northumberland, was one of the ablest and most unprincipled party-leaders who have ever turned to their own advantage the resources and wealth of their country. A brilliant soldier, a skilful diplomatist, and an accomplished man of the world, he was aptly described at the time as a second Alcibiades; and few men have exhibited a greater skill in intrigue, or a smaller regard for principle. For the moment Catholic and Protestant alike were to be his tools in contriving the Protector's destruction. The former disliked the new Prayer Book, so rumours were spread of reaction; the Catholic Southampton was Warwick's chief ally, and hopes were entertained that Gardiner and Bonner would be released from the Tower. Protestant zealots, on the other hand, were annoyed at the Protector's tenderness towards the Princess Mary and mass-priests, and anticipated under Warwick a more earnest prosecution of the Gospel's enemies. The rich men abhorred the patron of Latimer; and the governing classes, with few exceptions, hated the liberty on which Somerset set so much store. All was grist to Warwick's mill.

With this intrigue the Archbishop had nothing to do. He was in attendance with Somerset, Paget, Cecil, and Sir Thomas Smith upon the young King at Hampton Court in September, 1549, while the cabal assembled in London. In the first week of October the storm burst. On the 6th Somerset hurried the King to Windsor, and from there carried on a war of words[1] with the Council in London. But his cause was hopeless; men daily deserted his side, and his efforts to raise the peasants were defeated by Herbert and Russell, the victorious commanders returning from the West. Cranmer and Paget endeavoured to mediate between the two

[1] Most of this correspondence is printed in Tytler's *Edward VI. and Mary*, i., 203–247, and in Pocock, *Troubles* (Camden Soc.); see also *England under Protector Somerset*, chap. ix.

parties, and obtained from the Council a promise that the Protector should not suffer in lands, in goods, or in honour. Somerset then submitted, and Cranmer and Paget removed his servants.[1] But the Council failed to observe its promises; the Protector was sent to the Tower, his adherents were driven from office, and the Government fell under the exclusive control of Warwick and his friends.

What was to be their policy—reaction or reform? For months the balance trembled. "Those cruel beasts, the Romanists," as one Reformer called them, "were now beginning to triumph" over the downfall of the Duke, the overthrow of the Gospel, and the "restoration of their darling the Mass."[2] "The papists," echoed Hooper on 7 November, "are hoping and earnestly struggling for their kingdom"; and if Bonner were restored to his see, Hooper counted on being "restored to my country and my Father which is in heaven."[3] At Basel it was reported that Bucer and other reformers had been arrested with the Protector,[4] and that Somerset's fall would bring the Reformation to ruin. Bonner's appeal against his deprivation by Cranmer in September was under consideration; Gardiner had petitioned for release from the Tower; and Southampton, who was by

[1] Tytler accuses Cranmer of treachery in this action, but the charge is scarcely justified. By Somerset's submission the Government had passed to the Council, and in removing the Protector's servants from about the King, the Archbishop was only carrying out a natural and necessary measure.

[2] *Original Letters*, ii., 464.

[3] *Ibid.*, i., 70.

[4] *Ibid.*, i., 353.

some credited with the chief share in the successful plot, had re-established Catholic influence in the Council.

It was a critical moment in English history, but there is insufficient evidence to show clearly the forces and circumstances which determined the result. Parliament met, as usual, early in November, and whatever doubt might exist as to its religious attitude there was none about the spirit in which it proceeded to deal with social questions. The landlords were resolved to have their revenge on the peasants. Acts were passed enabling them to inclose as much land as they liked, and imposing the severest penalties upon all who ventured on opposition[1]; and it was actually declared a felony for poor people to meet with the object of reducing rents or prices.[2] Treason-laws were restored and strengthened, and the Protector's guarantees against their abuse were abolished. The penalty of treason was extended to offences against Privy Councillors, and even to all assemblies for the "altering of the laws."[3] Never did Henry VIII., or Charles I., or James II., aim such blows at English liberties as the men who controlled the fate of the Reformation in the latter days of Edward VI.

In spite of the apparent success of militant Protestantism during these years, from 1549–1553, the cause of reform and Cranmer had fallen on evil days. There was naturally little sympathy between Northumberland and the Archbishop, and on many

[1] 3 and 4, Edward VI., c. 3. [2] *Ibid.*, 18. [3] *Ibid.*, 5

questions, political and religious, they came into conflict. Once Northumberland sought to put John Knox into the see of Rochester to serve as a "whetstone to quicken and sharp the Bishop of Canterbury whereof he hath need"[1]; and subsequently Cranmer declared that the Duke had often gone about to effect his destruction.[2] Other leaders of reform were less clear-sighted. Hooper hailed Northumberland as "that most faithful and intrepid soldier of Christ," and declared that England could not do without him, for he was "a most holy and fearless instrument of the Word of God."[3] In the eyes of foreign Protestants he and his dupe, the feeble-minded Dorset (afterwards Duke of Suffolk),[4] were "the two most shining lights of the Church of England."[5] Some likened Northumberland to Joshua, and Bale compared him with Moses. He had, in fact, made Bale an Irish bishop, and Hooper also had cause for gratitude, for he wrote, "unless he had been on my side, in the cause of Christ, it would have been all over with me five months since, when the Duke of Somerset was in such difficulties."[6]

Besides these particular reasons for faith in Warwick, the Reformers ascribed to him the overthrow of the Romanist hopes. It is not, however, likely that Warwick would have espoused their cause un-

[1] *Calendar of Domestic State Papers*, 1547–80, p. 46. *Tytler*, ii., 142.

[2] Cranmer to Queen Mary, *Works*, ii., 444.

[3] *Original Letters*, i., 82, 89.

[4] The father of Lady Jane Grey.

[5] *Original Letters*, p. 399.

[6] *Ibid.*, i., 83.

less he had thought it the winning side, and he was probably led to this conclusion by the ease with which Parliament and especially the Lower House of 1549–50 passed anti-Catholic and anti-ecclesiastical measures. The most important of these was the Act ordering the destruction of all the old service-books except the *Primers* of Henry VIII. Another Act was passed once more enabling the Crown to appoint a commission for the reform of the Canon Law,[1] and a third empowered a commission of six Bishops and six others to draw up an Ordinal.[2] It was, however, evident that the change of Government had widened the breach between Church and State. During Somerset's rule there had always been a large attendance of Bishops in the House of Lords, and he had always secured a majority of episcopal votes for his measures. Only nine Bishops, however, out of twenty-seven were present at this meeting of Parliament, and a much larger proportion of them voted against the Government. Cranmer, Holbeach of Lincoln, Ridley of Rochester, and Ferrar of St. Davids—all staunch Reformers—as well as the accommodating Goodrich of Ely, and Catholics like Tunstall, Thirlby, Heath, and Day, dissented in vain from the second of the above-mentioned Acts; and such a consensus of Church opinion against a bill promoted by Government was a new

[1] Previous Acts to this effect had been passed in 1534, 1536, and 1544.

[2] That is to say, a "form and manner of making and consecrating of archbishops, bishops, priests, deacons, and other ministers of the church."

thing in the history of the Reformation. The Bishops met with a similar rebuff when they complained that their jurisdiction was openly contemned and derided; and their efforts to strengthen their authority by parliamentary legislation met with no success.[1]

The brief period of comparative religious liberty which the nation had enjoyed under Protector Somerset had come to an end, and the expulsion of the remaining Catholics from the Council was soon followed by religious persecution. Early in 1550 Warwick had the Earl of Arundel and Sir Richard Southwell imprisoned, and on the second of February Southampton's name was struck off the list of members.[2] Their offices and those of Somerset's friends were now distributed among the faction of Warwick, who packed the Council, as he afterwards packed the House of Commons with his nominees; and thus was constituted what has gravely been termed the "Reformed Administration."[3] It is

---

[1] The bill which the Bishops introduced was thought to claim too much, and was referred to a committee on which Cranmer served, but even as modified by this committee the bill failed to become law.

[2] Wriothesley, *Chron.*, ii., 33.

[3] By Froude, who arrived at this conclusion by failing to distinguish between the deeds of Somerset and those of Warwick; for instance, he accuses Somerset of gross laxity in pardoning Sir William Sharington, who had been convicted of treason for tampering with the coinage, whereas Sharington was not pardoned until November, 1549, after Somerset's fall. His pardon, indeed, illustrates the charge brought by Bishop Ponet against the new system, viz., that "corrupt officials took council with crafty Alcibiades (*i. e.*, Warwick) how to make non-accompt." (*Treatise of Politicke Power*, 1556). For Sharington, see the present writer in *Dict. Nat. Biogr.*; he had been one of Lord Seymour's accomplices.

probable that no English ministry has been more corrupt. Under its sway, complaints of bribery in the courts of justice grew louder than ever, and the sale of offices was recognised even by Parliament. Somerset had effected a slight improvement in the coinage, but under Warwick it reached a lower depth of debasement than under Henry VIII. Popular discontent led to proposals for Somerset's restoration, and the fear lest Parliament should take up this cry prevented Warwick from calling it together,[1] while the lack of parliamentary supply compelled the Government to look elsewhere for resources. The Church was the readiest mine to plunder, and the Chantry lands, the bulk of which had hitherto been reserved for application to educational purposes, were laid under requisition. Some of this wealth went to relieve public necessities, but much found its way into the pockets of courtiers. These lands, says Fuller, were regarded as the last dish in the last course of the feast provided by the Church, and in July, 1552, a commission was appointed for taking the surrender of all that remained.[2] Cranmer in vain resisted, pleading that these endowments might be kept till the King should come of age.[3] "I have heard," wrote Ridley, "that Cranmer and another whom I will not name were both in high displeasure, the one for shewing his conscience

[1] It met on 4 November, 1549, and then not again until after Somerset's death in January, 1552.

[2] *British Museum Addit. MS.*, 5498, f. 40; *Stowe MS.*, 141, ff., 59–63.

[3] *Narratives of the Reformation*, p. 247.

secretly but plainly and fully in the Duke of Somerset's cause, and both of late, but specially Cranmer, for repugning as they might against the late spoil of Church goods, taken away only by commandment of the higher powers without any law or order of justice."[1] Then greedy eyes were turned on episcopal revenues; the surrender of a manor or two was the general condition imposed on a prelate before his elevation; and Ponet was even made to give up all the endowments of Winchester in return for a stipend of two thousand marks. The bishopric of Westminster was abolished, and a nefarious project of Northumberland's to suppress the great see of Durham was only defeated by his own expulsion from office.[2]

Oppression went hand in hand with corruption, and practically all the cases of religious persecution quoted by Roman Catholic writers date from this period of the reign. The Princess Mary had been allowed by the Protector to have mass celebrated in her household; but this licence was now withdrawn.[3]

---

[1] Ridley, *Works*, Parker Soc., p. 59.

[2] He hoped to gain £2000 a year by this transaction. (*Tytler*, ii., 143.)

[3] Cranmer had little or nothing to do with the ill-treatment of Mary; he was only present at one out of the score or so of meetings of the Council to discuss her case; and when the question of her licence to hear mass was referred to him, Ridley, and Ponet, they replied that it was permissible under pressure to tolerate such an infraction of the law. So, too, his action in Gardiner's case seems to have been purely "official." He was head of the commission to try him, but took no part in the proceedings which led up to the issue of that commission, did not sign it, and was not present at the Council meeting when it was issued.

Bonner, indeed, had been deprived of his bishopric by Cranmer for contumacy on the eve of Somerset's fall, but the sentence was not confirmed until February, 1550, when the Catholics had been driven from the Council; and Gardiner, although confined in the Tower, was not deprived until February, 1551. That same year saw the deprivation of Heath of Worcester, and Day of Chichester, and the resignation of Voysey of Exeter, while Tunstall was sent to the Tower on an absurd charge of treason. Two heads of Oxford colleges, Dr. Cole, of New, and Dr. Morwen, of Corpus Christi, were imprisoned and a similar fate befell two of Gardiner's chaplains; four other Catholics fled from the country — John Boxall, afterwards Queen Mary's secretary, William Rastell, the nephew of Sir Thomas More, Dr. Richard Smith, the Catholic controversialist, and Nicholas Harpsfield.

At the other end of the religious scale, Joan Bocher was burnt in May, 1550, and for her execution the Archbishop has been held primarily responsible. He had protected her during the persecution of the Six Articles in 1541–42, but her opinions grew more and more heterodox, and in May, 1549, she was condemned by Cranmer for heresy. She was then left in Newgate prison for a year "in the hope of conversion," and Cranmer, Ridley, Goodrich, Latimer, Lever, Whitehead, and Hutchinson all tried their hands at persuasion. "I had her," declared Lord Chancellor Rich,[1] "a sevennight in my house after the writ was out for her to be burnt,

[1] Foxe, vii., 631.

where my lord of Canterbury and Bishop Ridley resorted almost daily unto her." The gravamen of the charge against Cranmer rests upon the story of Foxe that the Archbishop had much ado to persuade the young King to sign a warrant for her execution, and that Edward "lay all the charge thereof upon Cranmer before God."[1] The alleged incident was used by Foxe to invest the King with a compassion which he certainly did not possess, and this "importunity for blood"[2] has been objected against the Archbishop by nearly all his critics. But Foxe's story is a work of imagination; the incident is not mentioned by Edward himself in his journal,[3] nor alleged against Cranmer at his trial. As a matter of fact the young King, then only thirteen years of age, could not and did not sign any warrants at all. They were signed by the Council, and upon this authority a writ *de hæretico comburendo* was issued by the Lord Chancellor to the Sheriff of London. Moreover, at the particular meeting of the Council at which the warrant was signed the Archbishop himself was not present and so did not

---

[1] Foxe, v., 699.

[2] Hayward, *Life and Raigne of Edward Sext*, 1630, p. 7; the way in which stories grow may be seen by the reckless fashion in which Hayward has "embellished" Foxe's account; according to him, the Archbishop was "violent both by persuasions and entreaties" and "prevailed with mere importunity," and he winds up with the remark that "not many years passed but this Archbishop also felt the smart of the fire." He treats it, in fact, as a tale to point a moral.

[3] *Literary Remains of Edward VI.*, p. 264; the terms in which he records Joan's execution do not imply much sympathy. "She reviled," says Edward, "the preacher that preached at her death."

sign the warrant.[1] Joan's pitiful story is no evidence against the mildness of Cranmer's character, but it illustrates the narrowness with which most Reformers interpreted the doctrine of private judgment. Liberalism was no part of their creed, and even the martyr John Philpot, when himself on trial for heresy, declared that Joan was a "heretic, well worthy to be burnt, because she stood against the manifest articles of our faith."[2]

Yet the religious persecution of Warwick's administration must not be exaggerated; for, after all, Foxe is justified in the boast that during the whole reign of Edward no one, save Joan Bocher and George van Parris, lost his life for the sake of religion,[3]—a striking record compared with the reign of Mary, whose moderation is held to be proved by the reduction of the number of ascertained victims to something short of three hundred! The severity of Warwick's government was, in fact, directed mainly against his political foes and the poorer classes. Religion to him was really an indifferent matter, and his chief object was to secure

---

[1] *Acts of the Privy Council*, 1550–52, pp. 15, 19; nor, of course, was the King present at meetings of the Council. The warrant is in Brit. Mus., *Harleian MS.*, 6195, No. 10. See also Hutchinson, *Works*, Parker Soc., pp. iii.–v., *Lit. Remains of Edward VI.*, pp. ccvi., ccxi.; and Latimer, *Remains*, p. 114. A year later an Anabaptist, George van Parris, was burnt in the same way.

[2] Foxe, vii., 631.

[3] *Ibid.*, 700. The claim to include those who suffered in the western rebellion among martyrs for religion can scarcely be admitted; for one does not usually include in that category those who fell in Wyatt's rebellion under Queen Mary.

himself in power and to please those on whose support he depended. His rival, the Protector, was ultimately brought by the foulest means to the scaffold,[1] and the violence of his rule so disgusted the nation that as soon as the opportunity arose it declared with one voice against him. That he was able to go on so long unmolested was largely due to a most favourable conjunction of foreign affairs. He made a most ignominious peace with France in March, 1550, which, although it surrendered all that the Tudors had fought for in Scotland, and prepared the way for the dangers which threatened England under Elizabeth, yet gave his government temporary security. Then in 1551–52 war approached between France and the Emperor, and the rising of Germany against Charles V.[2] left Warwick free to pursue his own devices without fear of external alarms.

It was under these circumstances that the Reformation was prosecuted in England during the later years of Edward VI. The new Ordinal, which Parliament had empowered a commission to compile, was published in March, 1550, and it is probable that Cranmer, assisted by Ridley, had the chief share in its composition.[3] The commissioners took no advantage of the liberty allowed by the Act to

[1] See *England under Protector Somerset*, chap. xi: the means included a good deal of perjury and probably forgery.

[2] See the present writer in *Cambridge Modern History*, vol. ii., chap. viii.

[3] The names of the commissioners are not known; the Privy Council Register (1547–50, p. 379) mentions their appointment but not their names.

provide for the ordination of "other ministers"—*i. e.*, ostiaries, lectors, exorcists, acolytes, and subdeacons—below the rank of deacon; and their formulary swept away a vast mass of gorgeous ritual contained in the old Pontificals. It was a long step in the direction of simplicity, "but all that was necessary to convey the clerical character was nevertheless preserved"[1]; and like every other measure that Cranmer took it excited the displeasure of the extremists. Bishop Heath of Worcester was sent to the Fleet prison for refusing to subscribe the book, and on the other hand, Hooper, the favourite of Warwick,[2] and the most popular preacher at this time in London denounced the Ordinal as soon as it was published. In a letter to Bullinger he spoke of the "fraud and artifices by which they promote the kingdom of anti-Christ especially in the form of the oath."[3] For this he was summoned before the Council at Cranmer's instance, and upbraided by the Archbishop, but at length, he says, "the issue was for the glory of God." At Easter Warwick offered him the bishopric of Gloucester.[4] He was appointed by letters patent on the 3rd of July, but objected to taking

[1] Dixon, iii., 194; the most important point was perhaps the retention of the exclusive power of Bishops to ordain.

[2] Dr. Gairdner (p. 177) attributes Hooper's preferment to Somerset's influence; but Hooper ascribed his safety in November, 1549, to Warwick, and to Warwick he must have owed his appointment as Lent preacher in 1550, as Somerset was then in the Tower. Warwick, moreover, was his support in the "vestiarian" controversy, and on Warwick all Hooper's praises were lavished at this time. Against this evidence I do not think the assertions of John ab Ulmis (*Orig. Letters*. ii., 410) and of Froude (v., 210) have much weight.

[3] *Orig. Lett.*, i., 81.

[4] *Ibid.*, i., 87.

the oath by the Saints and using the "Aaronic" vestments required by the Ordinal. After much argument he persuaded the young King to put his pen through this objectionable oath,[1] and to write a letter to Cranmer recommending his consecration in the simpler form. The Archbishop had too much respect for the constitution to obey, and merely referred Hooper to Ridley who endeavoured to remove his scruples. His efforts were vain, and at the end of July Hooper "obtained leave from the King and the Council to be consecrated by the Bishop of London without superstition." Ridley, however, convinced the Council that Hooper was wrong, and the Bishop-elect of Gloucester was confined to his house. Cranmer, meanwhile, appealed to Bucer and Martyr,[2] while Hooper sought the advice of John à Lasco. The two former rebuked Hooper's scruples, but the Pole encouraged resistance. Hooper kept neither his house nor silence; he rushed into print with a confession of faith, and the Council in January, 1551, ordered him into the Archbishop's custody "either there to be reformed or further to be punished as the obstinacy of his case requireth."[3] A fortnight later Cranmer reported that his prisoner could not be brought to

[1] Canon Dixon (iii., 214 n.) appears to disbelieve this story and remarks that Foxe has nothing about it; but it is narrated in a letter from Hooper's confidant, Micronius, to Bullinger on 28 August, 1550. (*Orig. Lett.*, ii., 567.)

[2] This letter of Cranmer is in Brit. Mus. *Add. MS.*, 28571, *f.* 46. It is printed not in the Parker Society's collected *Works* but in Pocock's *Troubles*, p. 130. Bucer's answer is in his *Scripta Anglica*, p. 681, À Lasco's in Dalton's *Lasciana*, Berlin, 1898, p. 329.

[3] *Acts of the Privy Council*, 1550–1552, p. 191.

Copyright Photo., Walker & Cockerell.

KING EDWARD VI.

PAINTED AFTER A DRAWING BY HOLBEIN.

conformity; and he was therefore sent to the Fleet. There, much to the grief of the Zwinglian party, Hooper at length submitted to be made a Bishop in the ordinary way. He draws a veil over his own discomfiture and writes to Bullinger that "as the Lord has put an end to this controversy, I do not think it worth while to violate the sepulchre of this unhappy tragedy."[1]

Cranmer and Ridley had thus vindicated the Church against the "Father of Nonconformity," but Ridley's visitation of his London bishopric in 1550, and conversion of altars into communion-tables, indicated that both prelates had made considerable advances towards the Swiss doctrines, of which Hooper was the most uncompromising champion. The fact that these views were held abroad has often been used to involve them in odium—as if Catholic doctrines were not also accepted by foreigners; as if Christianity itself were not a foreign product; and as if theological truth were a matter to be determined by national prejudices! Cranmer took the more liberal view and thought that truth should be admitted even though it did come from a foreign source, and he entertained the idea of assembling in England a body of divines whose weight should counterbalance that of the Fathers at Trent.[2] The disturbed state of Germany assisted

---

[1] *Original Letters*, ii., 712. Hooper's letter to Cranmer signifying his submission is in Brit. Mus. *Add. MSS.*, 28571, *ff.* 24–26.

[2] This project was always in Cranmer's mind, but he made special efforts to bring it to pass in 1548 and 1549. See Cranmer's *Letters*, Nos. cclxxxvi., cclxxxix., ccxcvi., ccxcvii., and ccxcviii.

his efforts, and many a noted Reformer fled from the vengeance of Charles V., and was entertained by Cranmer at Lambeth.

Among those who arrived in 1547 was Pietro Martire Vermigli,[1] a native of Florence, who was better known as Peter Martyr, and like Luther had been an Augustinian monk. He came from Strassburg, stayed for a time with Cranmer before becoming Regius Professor at Oxford, and was invited by the Archbishop to suggest emendations on the First Book of Common Prayer. From the same city came Tremellius,[2] the Hebraist, a Jew of Ferrara, who found a home and employment at Cambridge; and from Augsburg came Bernardino Ochino,[3] a Franciscan and a native of Siena. These three Italians had been driven from Italy by the failure of the Reformation there, and from Germany by the victory of Charles over the Schmalkaldic League. In 1548 the Pole, John à Lasco,[4] reached Lambeth, and shares with Ridley and Latimer the disputed honour of having sapped Cranmer's belief in the Real Presence; he was accompanied by John

[1] P. M. Vermigli (1500–1562). See *Dict. Nat. Biogr.*, lviii., 253.

[2] John Immanuel Tremellius (1510–1580) studied at Padua, was converted from Judaism by Cardinal Pole, and then became a Protestant; entertained by Cranmer at Lambeth in 1547, made King's reader in Hebrew at Cambridge, 1549, and prebendary of Carlisle, 1552, fled to the Continent in 1553. (*Dict. Nat. Biogr.*, lvii., 186.)

[3] Bernardino Ochino (1487–1564), noted for his eloquent preaching, was made prebendary of Cranmer's cathedral in 1548; he fled to Basel in 1553. His theological works, written in Italian, were translated into English (*D. N. B.*, xli., 350.)

[4] See above, pp. 216, 266,

Utenhove,[1] a native of Ghent. The great Melanchthon himself was invited, but preferred to remain at Wittenberg. The second most famous of living German divines was, however, induced to come in the person of Martin Bucer,[2] who, like his friend Fagius,[3] exchanged Strassburg for Cambridge and died there. Lesser lights among this galaxy of distinguished strangers were Francis Dryander, the Spaniard; Martin Micronius, the friend of Bullinger; Valeran Poullain, the superintendent of the colony of Flemish weavers established by Somerset at Glastonbury; Peter Alexander of Arles, once chaplain to Charles V.'s sister Mary, Regent of the Netherlands, and Jean Véron, a Frenchman, who wrote vigorous tracts denouncing the mass.[4] It is, however, probable that these foreign divines exercised less influence than the Englishmen who had fled from the persecution of Henry VIII., imbibed foreign ideas, and returned under Edward VI. Hooper, for instance, who had sat at Bullinger's feet, was more potent than Bucer; Coverdale, who had lived abroad for fifteen years, may well be

[1] John Utenhove (*d.* 1565) resided in England, 1548–53, helped to plant the Flemish colony at Glastonbury, and in Elizabeth's reign was "first elder" of the Dutch Church, London (*D. N. B.*, lviii., 73.)

[2] Bucer was the most influential of foreign divines in England, see *D. N. B.*, vii., 172, and the more recent life by A. Erichson (Strassburg, 1891).

[3] Paul Fagius (1504–1549), a native of the Palatinate, was made Hebrew reader at Cambridge in 1549, and died there in the same year.

[4] See *D. N. B.*, lviii., 283; he was author of the *Five Abominable Blasphemies Contained in the Mass*, 1548, described by Pocock, who had not traced the author. in *Engl. Hist. Rev.*, x., 419–420,

compared with Martyr; and smaller men, such as Bishop Bale, John Rogers, the "proto-martyr," and Bartholomew Traheron, popularised foreign ideas more effectively than immigrants who knew little English. Yet again it must not be forgotten that the English Church in the sixteenth century assimilated little that had not been taught by the English Wycliffe,[1] and that it involves a distortion of terms to label it at any time Lutheran, Zwinglian, or Calvinistic.[2]

All these forces were, however, thrown into the balance against the compromise which had been embodied in the First Book of Common Prayer, particularly with regard to the Real Presence. Cran-

[1] The extraordinary parallelism between Wycliffe's ideas and the English Reformation is often neglected. Wycliffe called upon the State to reform a corrupt church; that was the basis of the whole Tudor policy. He "habitually treats the papacy in its present form as the most signal manifestation of the spirit of Anti-Christ"; that is precisely Cranmer's position. Wycliffe "denounces the whole principle of monasticism"; Henry VIII. uprooted it. Wycliffe "pleads for the permission of clerical marriages, though he seems to regard celibacy as the higher ideal"; that is exactly the tone of the 1549 Act of Parliament. Wycliffe "strenuously insisted upon the supreme importance of spiritual religion . . . and the comparative unimportance of ceremonies"; here in a nutshell is the motive of Edward VI.'s legislation. Finally he reduced the "Real Presence" in the Eucharist to a spiritual presence. (The above quotations are from Dr. Rashdall's article on Wycliffe in *D. N. B.*, lxiii., 220–1.)

[2] A loose habit has grown up of speaking about Calvinistic influence in England during the reign of Edward VI. The Low Church influence of that time was Zwinglian, not Calvinistic; and Bullinger, not Calvin was then the oracle of the most advanced Reformers. It was not till Elizabeth's reign, after the return of the Marian exiles from Geneva, that Calvin exercised any great influence on the English Church.

mer had given up that doctrine in 1548, and in 1550 during the controversy with Gardiner[1] maintained that it was not really recognised—at least not in the sense in which Gardiner interpreted it—in the Prayer Book. This controversy may have suggested or emphasised to the Reformers the need for revising the First Book of Common Prayer; and the more important changes in the Second seem designed to enforce and establish that interpretation of the First Book which Cranmer upheld against Gardiner[2]; the door was at last to be shut on the Old Learning. But these points often and not unnaturally coincided with those in which Bucer insisted that the First Book needed revision, and to his *Censura*[3] has sometimes been ascribed the determining influence in the matter. It is, in fact, impossible to discriminate precisely the respective shares of these collaborating forces in producing the Second Book of Common Prayer; but, on the whole, the changes in the Second Book went farther than Bucer recommended. Bucer represented a compromise between Luther and Zwingli; the First Book was more Lutheran, the Second more Zwinglian

---

[1] See above, pp. 237–241.

[2] "Everything in the First Prayer Book upon which Gardiner had fixed as evidence that the new liturgy did not reject the old belief, was in the revision carefully swept away and altered."—Gasquet and Bishop, p. 289.

[3] This *Censura* is printed in Bucer's *Scripta Anglicana* (Basel, 1577, fol.). It was addressed, not, as has often been assumed, to Cranmer, but to Bucer's diocesan, Bishop Goodrich of Ely. Laurence in his *Bampton Lectures* (pp. 246–7) minimises Bucer's influence.

than he liked. His advice was taken when he urged the adoption of Zwinglian forms, rejected when he pleaded for the retention of the semi-Lutheran phrases of 1549. At his request words in the Communion Office which might be construed as implying the "permanence of the body and blood of Christ under the species of bread and wine," and as justifying adoration of the Sacrament, were deleted.[1] On the other hand, his exhortations were neglected when he argued against the excision of certain phrases, the absence of which would, he thought "cast a doubt on the reality of the Act of Communion."[2]

Besides Bucer, Peter Martyr also submitted the Book of 1549 to an examination; but his work was not done with the same care and learning as Bucer's, and it had little influence on the Book of 1552. Even Bucer's opinion prevailed only so far as it coincided with those of Cranmer and Ridley, to whom was due the chief share in the compilation of the Second Book of Common Prayer. The principal changes were made in the Communion Office, and the motive for them was doubtless the fact that, the sequence of the 1549 Office being substantially that of the old mass, Catholic priests were able by mumbling the words and repeating the old manual acts to make the new form appear almost indistinguishable from the old "idolatrous Mass." In the 1552 Office no room was left for this representation or misrepresentation. The service was so arranged as to exclude the ideas of sacrifice and corporal

[1] Gasquet and Bishop, p. 295, note.

[2] *Ibid.*, p. 293.

presence which had interpenetrated every word and action in the Mass.[1] The word "altar" was expunged; the *Kyrie Eleison* instead of being an invocation of the presence of the Lord was changed into an ordinary prayer for grace to keep the Ten Commandments; the *Gloria in Excelsis*, instead of being placed at the beginning of the Office and heralding the presence of God, was placed at the end; and the words, "Blessed is He that cometh in the name of the Lord," were omitted as implying the same conception. The *Agnus Dei* was also left out, ordinary instead of unleavened bread was to be used, the wearing of the alb, chasuble, and cope were expressly prohibited, and the minister was ordered to stand at the north side of the "communion-table," which henceforth was to be placed in the body of the church and not at the east end.[2] Scarcely less drastic were the changes effected in the Orders for Baptism, and Confirmation, and in the revision of the Ordinal published in 1550.

With the exception of several points, the importance

[1] The alterations can best be appreciated by consulting Parker's *First Book of Common Prayer*, where the offices are printed side by side; they are summarised and elucidated in Gasquet and Bishop, pp. 289–297.

[2] Several of these changes were annulled in the Prayer Book of 1559, which revived some of the usages of 1549; with regard to ornaments the controversy is whether the rubric relating to them enjoins the ornaments of the 1549 Prayer Book or those in use before that Prayer Book; the rubric says those "in use by the authority of Parliament in the second year of Edward VI." The First Prayer Book did not receive the royal assent till the third year of Edward VI., but it is not certain that the rubric did not mean the ornaments of the First Prayer Book, although the phrase is inaccurate.

of which is variously estimated by different schools of High and Low churchmen, the Prayer Book of 1552 is substantially the same as that of the present day. It has been criticised in recent years as approaching too nearly to continental Protestantism and particularly to the views of Zwingli's successor Bullinger. But that would seem no ground for objection to Cranmer; the insularity and isolation which is now the pride and the boast of the average Englishman had not then laid so firm a hold upon him, and Cranmer thought that to differ in religion from the rest of the world implied a presumption of error rather than truth. He had no wish to make the Anglican Church national in doctrine or ritual, but only in jurisdiction and government. It was to remain in communion with the Catholic Church purified of papal corruptions. The changes effected between 1549 and 1552 were designed to facilitate an accommodation with the Reformed Churches abroad; and this purified Catholic Church was by means of a Reformed General Council to bring the whole of Christendom into a new and scriptural unity. No one can describe that ideal as ignoble, and Cranmer cannot be condemned for failing to see that the unity of the visible Church was shattered for ever. To the clearest vision of the sixteenth century it remained hidden that the national and secularising forces which came to birth in that age would go on ever increasing in strength and ever widening the breach between the modern world and that world in which one Church universal was possible and that Church could rival the State.

CHAPTER X

THE DOWNFALL OF ENGLISH PROTESTANTISM

THE Second Book of Common Prayer was ushered into the world amid signs and portents which boded ill for its long life and prosperity. It was imposed on the nation by a new Act of Uniformity which for the first time threatened penalties against the "great number of people in divers parts of the realm" who did "wilfully and damnably refuse to come to their parish churches"[1]; and the reluctance of the nation to accept moderate reforms was to be cured by passing more radical measures and increasing the rigour with which they were to be enforced. The remains of the liberal system which Somerset had established were to be swept away; the Protector himself was sent to the block,[2] and the Council

[1] If they neglected to attend Common Prayer on Sundays and holy days they were to be punished with ecclesiastical censures and excommunication; if they attended any but the authorised form of worship they were liable to six months' imprisonment for the first offence, a year's imprisonment for the second, and lifelong imprisonment for the third.

[2] 22 January, 1552.

began to pack the House of Commons.[1] Even so, it proved too independent for Northumberland's purpose. It rejected a treason bill designed to replace the expiring act of 1549, and passed another which re-enacted in a limited form some of the precautions against injustice which the Protector had introduced in 1547.[2] It also threw out a bill of attainder against Tunstall, Bishop of Durham; but Northumberland would not be baulked of the bishopric, and so Tunstall, who had been confined to the Tower on a bogus charge of treason, was deprived by a civil commission—a novel extension of secular jurisdiction.

Dimly the nation was beginning to feel that its ruler was bent on reckless and selfish aggrandisement. As early as October, 1551, tales were told of a new coinage to be minted at Dudley Castle bearing on its face the bear and ragged staff, Northumberland's badge[3]; and in 1552 behind closed doors men freely ascribed to him the design of aiming at the crown[4]; while a few may perhaps have perceived that the chief motive in his zeal for religion was to make the Romanist Mary an impossible candidate for the throne of a Protestant kingdom, and thus to pave the way for his own advancement.

[1] At first this method was only applied to filling up vacancies caused by the death of members (see *Acts P. C.*, 1550–2, pp. 400, 457, 459, 470).

[2] The best-known of these was the clause requiring two witnesses in cases of treason.

[3] *Acts P. C.*, 1550–52, p. 377; *Lit. Remains of Edward VI.*, pp. clxvi., 374; *Greyfriars' Chron.*, p. 73.

[4] *Harleian MS.*, 353, *ff.* 120–121.

The most sincere Reformers began to think it was time to slacken the pace.

"Your Sacred Majesty," wrote Bucer to Edward VI.,[1] "has already found by experience how grave are the evils which ensued on taking away by force false worship from your people, without sufficient preliminary instruction. The instruments of impiety have been snatched from them by proclamations, and the observance of true religion has been imposed by royal command. Some have on this account made horrible sedition, others have raised perilous dissensions in the State, and to this very day wherever they can they either cause new trouble or increase what has already been excited. . . . The example of our Lord and of all pious princes shows that it is first of all necessary to explain to men the mysteries of the kingdom and by holy persuasion to exhort them to take up the yoke of Christ. Your Sacred Majesty will perceive that to this end all your thoughts and care must be directed, and that those are not to be listened to who will that the religion of Christ be thrust upon men only by proclamations and by laws, and who say that it is enough if the sacred services of Christ are said to the people it matters not how. It is greatly to be feared that the enemy actuates men of this mind, who strive to hand the government of the religion of Christ to men who are both unfit for it and who do not suffer themselves to be advised, and who thus make way for the greed of men to seize the wealth of the Church, and little by little to do away altogether with Christ's religion. For those led by this spirit hope that when once the church property is confiscated there

[1] Bucer, *De Regno Christi*, lib. ii., cap v., pp. 60–61; Gasquet and Bishop, pp. 299–301.

will be none found voluntarily to consecrate themselves to her ministry."

Bucer's words were written at the end of 1550, and within two years Cranmer was driven into a similarly hostile attitude. His opposition to the confiscation of the chantry lands profoundly irritated Northumberland, who now regarded John Knox as the godliest of divines. Knox did not prove compliant enough to suit as Bishop of Rochester and whetstone for Cranmer; but it was owing to Knox's exhortations that Cranmer and the Council came into conflict over the yet unpublished Second Book of Common Prayer. Knox had apparently been appointed one of the six royal chaplains,[1] four of whom were to be always employed on evangelical circuits; and before setting out for his sphere on the Scottish borders he was commanded to preach before the King. He took the opportunity to denounce the practice of kneeling at the sacrament, and so impressed the Council that the printing of the new Prayer Book, in which that posture was enjoined, was stopped. Cranmer was hastily ordered to consult with Ridley and Peter Martyr as

[1] Canon Dixon (iii., 478–479 note) denies that Knox was ever royal chaplain and disputes the arguments of Lorimer and Perry; but the references in the *Privy Council Register* and Edward VI.'s *Journal* show that two royal chaplains were to preach in 1552 on the Scottish borders; that Knox was employed in this work, receiving £40 as a reward at the end of his year's service on 27 October, 1552, and being officially commended for his zeal; he and the five other chaplains also revised Cranmer's articles for subscription by candidates for ordination. (*Lit. Remains of Edward VI.*, pp. 377–378 notes, 464; *Acts of the Privy Council*, 1552–54, pp. 148, 154, 190.)

to whether it would not be better to omit the rubric. The Archbishop was ready enough to take advice, but protested earnestly against the change. Kneeling had commended itself to the Bishops and other learned men who had deliberated on the Book, and it had been prescribed by the authority of Parliament. Was it wise, he asked, for the Council to reverse a decision of Parliament at the bidding of turbulent spirits who would find fault with the Book were it altered every year? Kneeling, they say, is not commanded by Scripture; neither is standing, nor sitting, he replied.[1] Cranmer's firmness saved the custom of kneeling, but he could not prevent the Council from inserting on their own and the King's authority what is known as the Black Rubric in such copies of the Second Book of Common Prayer as had not already issued from the press. This declaration explained that, although the gesture of kneeling was retained, there was no superstitious adoration of the sacrament implied in such an attitude.[2]

Another project at which Cranmer had long and

[1] This letter is not in any edition of Cranmer's *Works*; it is extant dated 7 October, 1552, among the *Domestic State Papers* in the Record Office (Ed. VI., vol. xv., No. 15; see Calendar, 1547–80, p. 45), and is printed by Perry (*Declaration on Kneeling*, p. 77), and by Lorimer (*Knox in England*, p. 103). See also Canon Dixon, iii., 477, note.

[2] "A runagate Scot," said Dr. Weston to Latimer in 1554, "did take away the adoration of worshipping of Christ in the sacrament, by whose procurement that heresy was put into the last Communion Book; so much prevailed that one man's authority at that time" (Foxe, ed. Townsend, vi., 510.) Townsend and others refer this to Alexander Aless, but undoubtedly Knox is meant.

anxiously laboured was brought to naught by the opposition of Northumberland and the tendencies of the time, and that was the reformation of the laws of the church. The mediæval canon law was an elaborate edifice, with the Papacy as the key-stone of the arch.[1] When the Papal jurisdiction in England was abolished Canon Law fell into ruin, from which it has never recovered. Its decrepit state and the absence of any substitute introduced the greatest confusion into the legal and moral codes; the marriage laws,[2] for instance, were subject to the wildest interpretations, of which Henry VIII. had not been slow to avail himself. The confusion of the Canonists was viewed with ill-concealed satisfaction by civilians, by common lawyers, and by a large section of the community which had no desire to see ecclesiastical discipline re-established on a firm and lasting basis. But such a state of things could scarcely commend itself to churchmen, and least of all to the Archbishop, who was, under the King, the highest authority in the law of the Church.

The various Acts passed, empowering the King to appoint a commission for the reform of the Canon Law, had hitherto borne no fruit[3]; but Cranmer

---

[1] See Professor F. W. Maitland's *Roman Canon Law in England*, 1899.

[2] Every variety of opinion was held at this time on the subject of divorce, and Henry VIII.'s matrimonial adventures were by no means peculiar to himself, except in so far as he was in a unique position for getting rid of his encumbrances.

[3] The Act of 1533 declared that such canons as were not "contrarient to the laws, customs and statutes of this realm, nor to the damage and hurt of the King's prerogative royal," should remain in

had not been idle. As early as 1544 he had made a collection of passages from the Canon Law[1]; but these were of little constructive use, as they were mainly passages asserting the supremacy of the Pope over temporal sovereigns and the immunity of the clergy from lay tribunals. In October, 1551, however, a selection of thirty-two commissioners was actually made, and in the following month a committee of eight was nominated "to rough hew the Canon Law, the rest to conclude it afterwards."[2] Even then the commission was not formally made out, and it was not till February, 1552, that Cranmer and his colleagues received authority to proceed with the work. As usual, the chief burden fell upon the Archbishop, and his principal advisers were Peter Martyr, Walter Haddon, the Latin scholar, and Sir John Cheke, Edward VI.'s tutor. Their labours were not completed when the three-years' term, imposed by the Act of 1549, expired, and the bill introduced in 1552 to renew the commission failed to become law, largely owing to Northumberland's opposition.[3]

force; but the "customs" were sometimes too strange, and the "King's prerogative royal" capable of too liberal an interpretation to make this proviso very definite.

[1] This collection is extant in Lambeth MS., 1107, and Corpus Christi Coll., Cambridge, MS. cccxl., and is printed in Burnet, iv., 520, and in Cranmer's *Works*, i., 68–75; several of the passages were used by Cranmer in his answer to the Devonshire rebels in 1549.

[2] Edward VI.'s *Journal*, p. 398.

[3] The greatest confusion exists with regard to the history of this matter, from which even Canon Dixon and that most accurate of writers, Dr. Gairdner, are not free. Canon Dixon states that the bill introduced in 1552 became law, but it is not on the Statute

Yet the *Reformatio Legum Ecclesiasticarum*, as the work of the commissioners was called, is an important illustration of Cranmer's ideas, and its contents explain why it never received official sanction. Both its good and its bad points were repugnant to the spirit of the age, and it is doubtful which of the two qualities contributed the more to its unpopularity. It began with an exposition of the Catholic faith, and enacted the punishment of forfeiture and death against those who denied or blasphemed the Christian religion; for the Church was claimed the exclusive right of jurisdiction in such matters, the action of the civil magistrate being limited, as in the Middle Ages, to the execution of its decrees; and excommunication was said to deprive sinners of the protection of God and to consign them to everlasting damnation. The Church of England aspired to hurl those thunderbolts which

Book; and Dr. Gairdner (*History of the Church*, p. 300) concludes his account by saying that after all, on 6 October, 1552, the whole thirty-two commissioners were appointed and divided into four companies; but this appointment is really of 6 October, 1551 (*Acts P. C.;* 1551–52, p. 382). Both mistakes are derived from Strype's *Cranmer* (i., 388–389). The most accurate statement of the affair is in Nichols's *Literary Remains of Edward VI.*, pp. 397–399. The commission was thus abortive, and, although a remarkable document entitled *Reformatio Legum Ecclesiasticarum* was compiled, and although Edward in his will urged the completion of the project, the accession of Mary put an end to it and the document remained in MS. until 1571, when, having been edited by Foxe, the Martyrologist, it was at length printed; but it never received any legal authorisation either by Parliament or Convocation. It was edited in 1850 by Dr. Edward Cardwell. One of the MS. drafts (*Harleian MS.* 426) contains numerous corrections in Cranmer's hand.

Popes had so often launched in vain.[1] Reformers commonly work in the spirit of the abuses they seek to remove, and few churches have willingly abandoned the weapons of persecution; but such a pretension ran counter to the spirit of Tudor times, not because sixteenth-century statesmen[2] were averse to persecution, but because they wanted it done by the State and not by the Church.

In other respects the code was both too liberal and too drastic for that or the present time. To restore and invigorate the action of the Church, which had suffered so much from the encroachments of the State in Henry's reign, Cranmer proposed to revive the diocesan synods from which he would not have excluded the laity. Divorce was allowed to both parties not only on the ground of adultery but of desertion, long absence, and cruel treatment; the innocent party was permitted to marry again; and confirmed incompatibility of temper justified separation but not divorce. Marriage was thus made less rigid, but its sanctity, so long as it lasted, was guarded by stringent penalties. Adultery was to be punished with imprisonment or transportation for life; if the wife be the offender she forfeits her jointure; if the husband, he restores his wife's dower and adds to it half his own fortune. The clergy as

---

[1] *Ref. Legum Eccl.*, ed. Cardwell, pp. 167–188.

[2] Edward VI. himself objected to the bishops, being entrusted with these powers of persecution not, as Froude implies (v., 197), because a bishop is naturally incapable of justice, but because the bishops of that day were some papists, some ignorant, some too old, some of bad repute, etc. (*Lit. Remains*, pp. 478–479).

guardians of morality were threatened with special severity: if a married cleric committed adultery he forfeited his benefice and surrendered his whole estate for the support of his wife and children; if unmarried he gave all up to his bishop for charitable uses. So that if Cranmer claimed for his order great powers, he saddled it also with burdens.[1]

The other great scheme with which Cranmer was busily occupied during these last years of his power did not prove abortive. He had endowed the Church with a Bible in English, with her own English liturgy, and had sought to establish her jurisdiction; he now brought forth a confession of faith which she and none other professed. As early as 1549 he had drawn up a series of articles which he compelled applicants for licence to lecture and preach to subscribe[2]; and in 1551 he submitted these or another list to his fellow-bishops for their opinion. On 2 May, 1552, the Council ordered him to produce these articles and to show whether they had been "set forth by any public authority or no."[3] This was, no doubt, a rebuke

[1] See Dixon, iii., 352–382; Cranmer's scheme was based upon the Roman Canon Law, and interwoven with the "agitated formularies of the sixteenth century." The attempt to pour new wine into old bottles was not successful, though Canon Dixon thinks that if the *Reformatio* had been carried out "the activity and vigour of the Church of England would have been raised to a height which it has never reached," and "the modern history of the Church of England would have been altogether different."

[2] *Orig. Letters*, i., 71, 76; Nichols (*Lit. Rem. of Edward VI.*, p. 377) doubts whether these articles were the same as the later Forty-two. There is no certainty about the matter, but they were probably the germ.

[3] *Acts P. C.*, 1552–54, p. 32.

such as Northumberland liked to administer to the Archbishop for presumption in acting without his permission. The articles were returned to Cranmer for revision, a task which he completed by the middle of September. He then sent them to Cheke and also requested Cecil to consider them well.[1] A month later the Council directed six divines—Harley, Bill, Horne, Grindal, Perne, and John Knox to re-examine them.[2] On 20 November they were returned with amendments to Cranmer,[3] who four days later sent them back with the request that they might now be authorised by the King, and submitted to all the clergy for subscription. "And then I trust that such a concord and quietness in religion shall shortly follow thereof, as else is not to be looked for many years."[4]

So wrote Cranmer in the incurable optimism of his soul; but he was not more deceived when he hoped to rebuild the jurisdiction of the Church than when he thought to bring peace by a creed.

[1] Cranmer, *Works*, ii., 439.

[2] *Acts P. C.*, 1552–54, p. 148. All these divines were men of eminence whose lives are recorded in the *D. N. B.* Harley became Bishop of Hereford, Bill, Dean of Westminster, Horne, Bishop of Winchester, Grindal, Archbishop of Canterbury, and Perne, Dean of Ely, while Knox was greater than most bishops or deans. The Scottish Reformer had before this denounced the rubric on Kneeling in the Book of Common Prayer, and now took exception to the Thirty-eighth Article, which declared the ritual of the Book to be agreeable to the liberty of the Gospel.

[3] *Ibid.*, p. 173, where, curiously enough, the Editor inserts a marginal note, "changes in the Prayer Book"; the articles were, of course, not yet a part of the Prayer Book.

[4] Cranmer, *Works*, ii., 141.

At the first attempt to enforce the Articles, in May, 1553, there were many resisters[1]; and from that day to this the roll of dissidents has swelled. That the Forty-two Articles of Religion or something like them should have been evolved was perhaps inevitable, for every Church like every party must have its platform; nor need the Articles have been a root of bitterness and the seed of strife but for the attempt to make them a perpetual bond to shackle the minds of men for ever. For, however irksome a yoke they may appear, they were not in 1552 an illiberal interpretation of the English faith; and there is this at least to be said for Cranmer and his colleagues, that the Forty-two Articles were more comprehensive and less dogmatic than any subsequent edition of them.

"The broad soft touch of Cranmer," says Canon Dixon, "lay upon them when they came from the furnace; a touch which was not retained wholly in the recension which reduced them afterwards to Thirty-Nine. Nearly half of them are such as are common to all Christians; but even in these the brevity of statement and the avoidance of controversy is to be admired."[2]

The first controversial article came not first but fifth in place. Freedom of the Will was explicitly asserted, and Justification by Faith only was affirmed in brief and moderate terms, while the much-contested

[1] *Greyfriars' Chron.*, p. 77.

[2] iii., 520. The literature of the Forty-two and Thirty-nine Articles, is of course, enormous. See Dixon, iii., 520–527, and his references.

Good Works were undefined. It was admitted that General Councils might err, but contention was not provoked by specifying the errors of other Churches. With regard to the sacraments there was less circumspection, and here the Articles seem to be directed against the decrees of the Council of Trent.[1] It was no ordinance of Christ that the Eucharist should be reserved, carried about, elevated, or adored; "sacrifices of masses" are pronounced "figments and dangerous impostures"; and five of the mediæval sacraments are not maintained as such. On the other hand, it is affirmed that the sacraments are not merely marks of profession but effectual signs of grace, and there was no article requiring communion in both kinds.

For the crooked and disingenuous way in which the Articles were presented to the nation the Archbishop was not responsible. Their title-page bore a legend to the effect that they had been "agreed upon by the bishops and other learned and godly men in the last Convocation at London"—a statement which was inaccurate in itself and can only have been designed to create a false impression.[2]

[1] These decrees were published at various times during the prolonged existence of the Council, some as early as 1547, much to the disgust of Charles V. who was endeavouring to pacify the Lutherans in Germany. See *Cambridge Modern History*, vol. ii., cp. viii.

[2] A long array of writers from Heylyn (1661) to Hardwicke (1851) have sought to invest these articles with some sort of synodical authority, but until fresh evidence is produced, the arguments of Canon Dixon (iii., 514 *et sqq.*) against this view must be regarded as conclusive. They were published with Bishop Ponet's *Catechism*, and at the same time there were in existence Fifty-four Articles designed to

They had not as a matter of fact been submitted to Convocation, and Cranmer, who had not been consulted in the matter of this title, rebelled against its dishonest implication. He complained to the Council, and was told that all the title meant was that the Articles were set forth *in the time* of Convocation,[1] —an assertion which seems to have been no more true than the other. They were, in fact, published by the sole authority of the King; and although that was perhaps legally sufficient, it was more than ever necessary to pretend an ecclesiastical sanction when Northumberland's government was most obnoxious to the great majority of the nation and the Church, and when the crisis of his fortunes was obviously at hand. For the Articles did not receive the royal signature until 12 June, 1553, and within a month the King was dead.

It needed more than sleight of hand to carry Northumberland through the storm which he himself had raised. His overbearing temper, unscrupulous ambition, and unprincipled government had alienated the nation, the Parliament, the Church, and even the Duke's own favourite preachers. Knox afterwards spoke of him as "ruling the roost by stout courage and proudness of stomach," and claimed to have rebuked him to his face.[2] Dear

enforce unity of ritual, as the Forty-two were to enforce unity of doctrine; these Fifty-four have entirely disappeared, leaving scarcely a trace behind them.

[1] Foxe, vi., 468.

[2] Knox's *Faithful Admonition*, 1554, p. 53. "Was David, said I, and Hezekiah abused by crafty counsellors and dissembling hypocrites? What wonder is it that a young and innocent king be

Horne wrote that he could not tell whether Northumberland was or was not a dissembler in religion[1]· and

> "as for Latimer, Lever, Bradford, and Knox," wrote Ridley, "their tongues were so sharp they ripped in so deep in their galled backs to have purged them no doubt of that filthy matter that was festered in their hearts of insatiable covetousness, of filthy carnality and voluptuousness, of intolerable ambition and pride, of ungodly loathsomeness to hear poor men's causes and to hear God's words; that these men of all others, these magistrates then could never abide. Others there were, very godly men, and well learned, that went about by the wholesome plasters of God's Word, howbeit after a more soft manner of handling the matter; but, alas! all sped alike."[2]

Of these latter, no doubt, was Cranmer. In December, 1551, he was suggested as a possible Keeper of the Great Seal during the sickness which Lord Chancellor Rich feigned in order to

---

deceived by crafty, covetous, wicked, and ungodly councillors? I am greatly afraid that Ahithophel is councillor and that Judas bears the purse and that Shebna is scribe, controller, and treasurer." There is probably imagination as well as recollection here.

[1] Froude (v., 136) erroneously attributes this saying to Knox; it is recorded in Northumberland's letter to Cecil, 7 December, 1552 (Tytler, ii., 148), when the Duke protests that he had "for twenty years stood to one kind of religion, in the same which I do now profess"; less than a year later he explained that he had always been a Catholic at heart.

[2] Ridley, *Works*, p. 59; Foxe, vii., 573.

escape liability for the Duke's illegal acts[1]; but the appointment was given to the more pliant Bishop Goodrich, of Ely. In March, 1552, the Archbishop provoked Northumberland's wrath by opposing almost alone in the House of Lords an unconstitutional bill for the deprivation of Tunstall[2]; and a year later, in the last Parliament of Edward VI., he again came into collision with the Duke when he endeavoured to obtain the sanction of the legislature for his *Reformatio Legum Ecclesiasticarum.* Northumberland, with his usual arrogance, bade Cranmer mind his own business, and threatened the Bishops with dire consequences unless they stopped the presumption of preachers who had dared in their sermons to reflect upon the deeds of their superiors.

So strong was the popular discontent that Northumberland feared to meet a freely elected Parliament, and the House of Commons which gathered in March, 1553, was little more than an assembly of the Duke's nominees. To it he thought he might safely address language such as Henry VIII. had never employed. A year earlier he had threatened to confiscate the liberties of the City of London, because he thought prices too high; and now he proposed to hector the members of Parliament in

[1] *Cal. of Hatfield MSS.*, i., 94; cf. *England under Protector Somerset*, p. 290; the measure to which Rich particularly objected was a resolution of the Council that the King's signature alone was sufficient to give documents validity; Edward was only just fourteen, and completely under Northumberland's influence.

[2] Lord Stourton was the only peer who supported Cranmer in this act of justice and independence, although there were fourteen bishops present—another curious instance of Cranmer's "servility."

much the same tone. "We need not seem," he wrote to the Lord Chamberlain,[1] "to make account to the Commons of His Majesty's liberality and bountifulness, in augmenting of his nobles or his benevolence shewed to any of his good servants, lest you might thereby make them wanton." He had excellent reasons for concealing the extent to which he and his friends had helped themselves from the royal domain; and with characteristic meanness he attributed the financial deficit to the administration of his rival, Somerset, who had been dead twelve months and had fallen from power three and a half years before.[2] Few of the bills which he hoped to pass became law, and Parliament was dismissed within a month of its meeting.

A subsidy was, indeed, granted after much debate,[3] but it was only to be paid in two years, and meanwhile the Duke attempted to fill the exchequer by seizing what church plate he could find. The excuse was that much of it had been rendered useless by the greater simplicity of ritual now pervading religion, and on 15 February, 1553, an order was issued for the appointment of commissioners to seize church goods in every shire.[4] In April and May they went forth on their labour of pillage.

[1] Northumberland to Darcy (not to Northampton, as Froude says, v., 127), on 14 January, 1553, *Domestic State Papers*, Edward VI., vol. xvi., No. 6; Tytler, ii., 161.

[2] The preamble to the Act for a subsidy, drawn up by Northumberland, conveniently expatiates on the dead man's misdeeds to cover those of the living.

[3] See *Commons' Journals*, 7 and 11 March, 1553.

[4] *Acts P. C.*, 1552–54, p. 265.

"All such goods," says a contemporary chronicler,[1] "were taken away to the King's use; that is to say, all the jewels of gold and silver, as crosses, candlesticks, censers, chalices, and all other gold and silver, and ready money . . . . and all copes and vestments of cloth of gold, cloth of tissue, and cloth of silver." Cranmer had sought to prevent this spoliation, for a previous commission had been issued in July, 1552,[2] and in the following November he had been charged with neglecting the King's business, because he made no haste in the matter. Now a more potent safeguard intervened. On 6 July, 1553, Edward VI. died at Greenwich, and the triumph of Mary checked a campaign which had been designed to provide the sinews of war for her overthrow.

That Northumberland had long foreseen this event scarcely admits of doubt. Years before Edward came to the throne men had spoken of him as not likely to live long: an attack of measles and small-pox in April, 1552, further weakened an originally sickly and consumptive frame: and in March, 1553, he was too ill to go down to Westminster Palace to open Parliament. The worse the health of Edward grew, the wider spread the rumour that Northumberland had designs on the crown for himself and his family: for the most secretive of governments cannot long keep its schemes completely hidden, and in May and June the Tower of London was gradually filling with prisoners accused of seditious language against the Duke. His first nibble at royalty appears to have

---

[1] Wriothesley, *Chron.*, ii., 83; *Greyfriars' Chron.*, p. 77.

[2] *Acts P. C.*, 1552–54, p. 219; Cranmer, *Works*, ii., 440.

been a proposal that his only unmarried son, Guilford Dudley, should wed Lady Margaret Clifford, a granddaughter of Henry VIII.'s sister Mary, but she was too distant in the line of succession [1] and was passed over to the Duke's brother, Andrew. Guilford Dudley was reserved for Lady Jane Grey, of the elder branch of the Suffolk line, for which Henry VIII. had destined the crown if all his children died without issue: Lady Jane's sister was at the same time betrothed to Lord Herbert, son of Northumberland's ally, the Earl of Pembroke: and the Duke's daughter was married to Lord Hastings, who might also have claims on the throne as a descendant of Edward IV.'s brother Clarence. Northumberland's design was to unite all interests and all claims against those of Mary and Elizabeth who were to be excluded from the throne on the ground of their illegitimate birth.

Lady Jane, he determined, should be the new Queen, and his son, her husband, should have the crown matrimonial, while he himself remained the power behind the throne before which all men

[1]
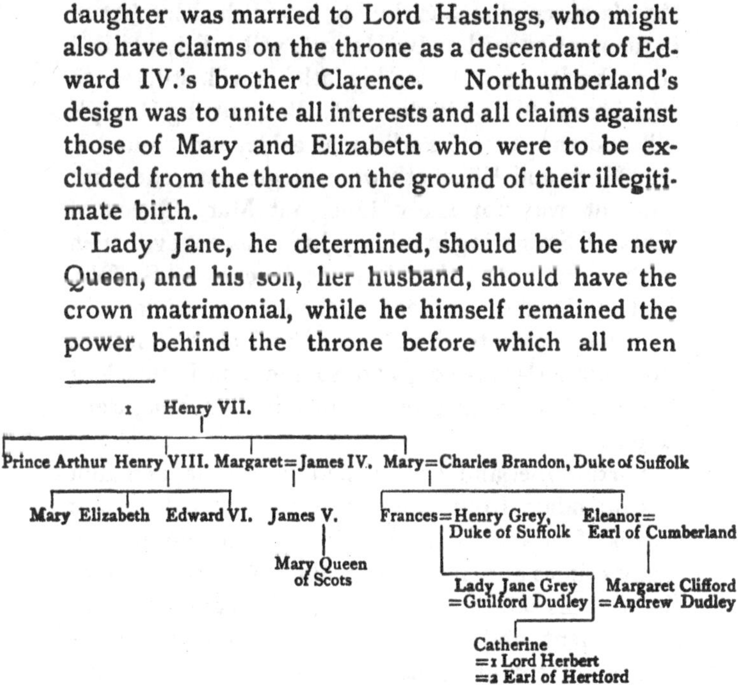

should bow. Never did ambition o'erleap itself in so hopelessly illogical, illegal, and unconstitutional a fashion. Edward VI., he said, might bequeath the crown by will as well as Henry VIII.; but Henry had been expressly given this power by Act of Parliament, whereas Edward VI. had not. Moreover, the succession of Mary and Elizabeth did not depend only on Henry's will; for another Act of Parliament had provided that unless Henry willed otherwise, Mary and Elizabeth should succeed, if Edward had no issue. Henry did not will otherwise, and therefore Mary's succession was doubly established by Act of Parliament as well as by Henry's will. Edward had no authority to set aside his father's will, still less to override an Act of Parliament. But, putting Henry's will and the Act of Parliament aside, and assuming that Mary and Elizabeth were illegitimate, the next claimant was not Lady Jane, but Mary Queen of Scots. Eliminating her, Lady Jane was not even then the heir, but her mother, Frances, Duchess of Suffolk. Had the Duchess succeeded, the crown matrimonial must have gone to the Duke of Suffolk, and not to Northumberland's son, and so she was induced or compelled to waive her claims in her daughter's favour.

Northumberland's career had, indeed, landed him in a quandary from which there was only a desperate means of escape. His ambition had led him into so many crimes and had made him so many enemies that he was safe only so long as he controlled the government and prevented the administration of justice. He could expect no mercy when once his foes were in a position to bring him to book; and the prospect drove him to make one last frantic bid for life and for power. There were other temptations which led him to stake his all on a single throw. No immediate interference need be feared from abroad. The Emperor had too much on his hands with war in France and Germany to come to the help of his cousin Mary in England. France would welcome the success of Northumberland's plot, for Mary's accession would mean an alliance between England and Spain, and possibly a repetition of the disasters of 1521–25, when the same combination had produced the rout of Pavia; and Scotland was now little more than a province of France. No woman, moreover, had yet reigned over England, and the popular impression was that none could—at least unless she married and shared the throne with a man. Lady Jane was, indeed, as much a woman as Mary; but Mary would marry a foreigner, and reduce England to dependence like that of the Netherlands on Spain, or Hungary on Austria; whereas Lady Jane had married an Englishman.

These were not the arguments with which the Duke won Edward's consent. "Consider also," he said to the Council, "that God's cause, which is the preferment of His word, and fear of Papists' entrance hath been (as ye have here before always known) laid the original ground, whereupon ye, even at the first motion, granted your good wills and consents thereunto."[1] These were the motives which appealed to the King. To him the Duke painted the

[1] *Chronicle of Queen Jane*, pp. 6–7. Holinshed, iii., 1068.

horrors of a Romanist reaction, the undoing of the glorious work of the Reformation on which Edward VI. prided himself more than any one else in the kingdom. Should they rebuild the altars of Baal and restore the idolatrous mass? Should the elect be handed over to the minions of Antichrist? The dying King would not bequeath such woes to his kingdom, and without any resistance he concurred in Northumberland's scheme. The majority of the Council, consisting as it did mainly of the Duke's nominees, and ruled, as Chief-Justice Montague[1] said, by the Duke as he pleased, had no doubt already consented; and the judges and lawyers were now called in to give Edward's "devise" a legal form. On the 12th of June they were brought into the young King's presence at Greenwich. They declared the attempt to be treason. Northumberland, on hearing of their decision, burst into the Council-chamber trembling with rage and fury; he called the Chief-Justice a traitor to his face, and said he would fight in his shirt with any man in that quarrel. The lawyers departed in fear of their lives. On the 14th they were again summoned before the King. With sharp words and angry countenance he demanded the reason for their disobedience to his commands; and as he upbraided them, the lords of the Council muttered "Traitors" in their ears.

Terrorised by threats, the judges and lawyers snatched at the excuse offered by the King's promise

[1] Montague's narrative is the authority for the following description; it was first printed in Fuller's *Church History*, Bk. VIII., section 2.

to call a Parliament to ratify whatever they did. Edward, they considered, would not punish them for a crime committed at his behest; and no such offence was known to the law as treason to a future sovereign. Parliament would, if it met before Edward died, enact their indemnity, while if they refused it might attaint them of treason. They preferred the devil to the deep sea, and sorrowfully did as Northumberland wished, receiving a formal commission and pardon for their proceedings. On the 21st the "devise" was completed; it was signed by the judges and lawyers who drew it up, by the greater part of the Council, and eventually by a hundred and one prominent personages.

Cranmer's name stands first on the list, but he was the last of the Council to sign.[1] To no one was Northumberland less likely to confide his secrets;

[1] Many pitfalls await even those students who use original documents, and one of them consists in attaching too much value to signatures. Documents were not signed in the order in which the signatures read, but spaces were left for the signatures which might be added later but would in order of precedence stand first. Thus Somerset's original signature appears to acts of the Privy Council passed in London during his absence in Scotland, the explanation being that a space was left for his name, and he signed up these acts on his return; this happened in Cranmer's case above. There is even an instance in which signatures were added to a document two years after the document was drawn up,—two years after Gardiner's committal to the Tower (30 June, 1548) St. John and Russell were required to sign the order of committal. In the meantime they had been created Earls of Wiltshire and Bedford, and they began to sign under those styles; then, recollecting that such were not their legal signatures in 1548, they crossed them out, and signed as St. John and Russell (see the present writer in *English Hist. Rev.*, xviii. 567–568).

"his heart," wrote Cranmer, "was not such toward me (seeking long time my destruction) that he would either trust me in such matter, or think that I would be persuaded by him."[1] Cranmer had never taken a very keen interest in politics, and, since the fall of Somerset, had gradually withdrawn more and more from secular affairs. He does not appear to have attended the Council after the 8th of June, 1553, and he knew nothing of the Duke's intrigues. He was, however, the first subject of the Crown, and his signature was regarded as necessary. So, "when the whole council and chief judges had set their hands to the King's will, last of all they sent for the Archbishop, requiring him also to subscribe the will, as they had done."[2] Cranmer refused: such a deed would be perjury, for he had sworn to Mary's succession. They, replied the Council, had consciences as well as he; yet they had subscribed the will, although they were sworn to Mary; he must not be more particular. Cranmer held out and demanded leave to speak with the King in private. This was denied him: the Councillors feared he might turn the King from his purpose, and Northampton and Darcy

[1] *Works*, ii., 444.

[2] *Narratives of the Ref.*, p. 225. For a refutation of Cecil's claim to have signed last, and for an exposure of the methods in which he shifted responsibility from himself to his brother-in-law and other intimates, see Tytler, ii., 202–206. The original authorities for this extraordinary plot are for the most part printed in Tytler, in John Gough Nichols's *Literary Remains of Edward VI.*, pp 561-576, and in *Chronicle of Queen Jane and Queen Mary* (Camden Soc.). Some additional light is shown by the transcripts in the Record Office, occasional fragments of which are printed in Froude.

were sent to counteract his arguments. To their presence Cranmer ascribed his failure; and his attempt to dissuade Edward again brought down the wrath of the Duke; before the whole Council, Northumberland declared that it became not the Archbishop to speak to the King as he did.

The scene between King and Archbishop was painful to both. Cranmer was not told of the judges' scruples, but no doubt he used much the same arguments. He made no impression; Edward had all the Tudor obstinacy. He informed the Archbishop that the judges and his learned counsel were of opinion that the Act of his father entailing the crown could not be prejudicial to him, but that he being in possession of the crown could leave it by will. "This seemed very strange unto me," writes Cranmer, "but being the sentence of the judges and other learned counsel in the laws of the realm (as both he and his counsel informed me) methought it became not me, being unlearned in the law, to stand against my prince therein." Still he demurred till the King appealed to him not to "be more repugnant to his will than the rest of the Council were." This reflection on his loyalty in the mouth of a dying King grieved Cranmer sore, and then at last he yielded.

The die was now cast, and the Council set to work to secure the Tower, raise troops to overawe London, and man the fleet. On the 2nd of July, Dr. Hodgkin, suffragan Bishop of Bedford, preaching at St. Paul's, omitted to pray for the ladies Mary and Elizabeth; and on the following Sunday, Ridley, to the disgust of his audience, pronounced them bastards. The death of Edward on the 6th was concealed in the hope of securing the person of Mary, by inveigling her to London. She came as far as Hoddesdon in Hertfordshire, when on the 7th she received secret news of her brother's death. Instantly she mounted on horseback and rode full speed for Kenninghall in Norfolk, whence she wrote to the Council, indignantly asking why they had not proclaimed her Queen. The stratagem had failed; there was no longer need for concealment, and on the 10th the heralds announced the accession of Queen Jane. To Mary the Council wrote a letter, which they all, including Cranmer, signed, declaring that she was illegitimate and requiring her submission to her lawful sovereign.

For nine days and no more that ill-fated Queen was to reign, and she never ruled. Scarcely had the Council replied to Mary's letter when tidings arrived that she had been joined by the Earls of Bath and of Sussex and proclaimed Queen amid universal rejoicings in various parts of the kingdom. On the 12th Northumberland took the field against her, amid the blackest of omens; "the people press to see us," he said to a comrade as he rode through Shoreditch, "but not one saith 'God speed.'" Northumberland out of the way, the Council began to turn with the tide. While the Duke advanced to Bury St. Edmunds, and then, finding that no succours reached him, while Mary's forces had swollen to thirty thousand men, fell back upon Cambridge, his friends and victims in London perceived that the game was up.

LADY JANE GREY.

FROM THE PICTURE NOW IN THE POSSESSION OF EARL SPENCER AT ALTHORPE. BY PERMISSION OF LORD SPENCER.

On the 19th they proclaimed Queen Mary. "Great was the triumph here in London," writes an eye-witness; "for my time I never saw the like, and by the report of others the like was never seen. The number of caps that were thrown up at the proclamation were not to be told. . . . I myself saw money was thrown out at windows for joy. The bonfires were without number, and what with shouting and crying of the people, and ringing of the bells, there could no one almost hear what another said, besides banquetings and singing in the street for joy."

Yet this was Protestant London, where three weeks later an attempt to say mass caused a riot; and of the thirty thousand who flocked to Mary's standard in Norfolk, most came from East Anglia, next to London the most Protestant part of the kingdom. The Catholic parts of the realm had no time to make their voice heard; it was Protestants who declared against Jane and bore Mary in triumph to her throne, and one of them, strange to say, thought the Gospel would be plucked away unless Queen Mary succeeded! Indeed it was no question between the new and the old religion; it was not for the mass nor the Pope that men threw up their caps and lost their ears in the pillory. The sentiment of legality, and affection for the Tudor family contributed to the result; but neither stirred the people to the depths. The passion that moved them was detestation of the Duke; no ruler of England has been more bitterly or more deservedly hated. The "great devil," "a cruel Pharaoh," "that false Duke," "the ragged bear most rank," "with whom is neither mercy, pity, nor compassion," are some of the epithets hurled at him in a Protestant tract printed in London on 13th of July when his triumph was still quite possible. His own daughter-in-law, Lady Jane Grey, avowed that he was "hated and evil spoken of by the commons," and that "his life was odious to all men." If he succeeded, they said, he will "pull and poll us, spoil us, and utterly destroy us, and bring us in great calamities and miseries." His failure, writes another contemporary, was due "partly to the right of Queen Mary's title, and partly to the malice that the people bore him, as well for the death of the Duke of Somerset and other cruelty by him used." And in more measured terms the French ambassador ascribed Mary's victory less to love for her than to the great hatred which people felt for the Duke who had sought to rule by a reign of terror. That the cause of the Reformation in England was once linked with his fate was perhaps the greatest misfortune that ever attended its history, for that association was a stain which could only be cleansed in the blood of the Marian martyrs.

CHAPTER XI

CRANMER'S CHARACTER AND PRIVATE LIFE

THE first Lord Houghton, who took a dilettante interest in the Tractarian movement and a reflected interest in the Anglican Reformation, has described Cranmer as " the most mysterious personage," and, next to Henry VIII., " the most influential factor" in the history of that convulsion.[1] Cranmer's influence on the Reformation is an obvious fact, but the mystery of his character disappears before a closer study of his environment. In reality his was one of the simplest of characters, and the ambiguities which obscure his career arise not from the complexity of his mind but from the contrasts and contradictions of the age in which he lived. It was the age of the Renaissance as well as of the Reformation, of the New Monarchy and State-despotism as well as of revolt against established forms of belief. New forces in literature, commerce, art, religion, and politics jostled one another and produced many strange and startling combinations; Calvinists and Jesuits might join in preaching tyrannicide while other

[1] Prefatory note to *Bishop Cranmer's Recantacyons*. London 1885.

papists and Protestants proclaimed the sanctity of kings. There were many cross-currents in that turbulent stream, and it was not possible for man to steer a straight and unvarying course. Yet Cranmer, although like a swimmer he was carried hither and thither and buffeted by the waves, consistently set his face in the same direction. The stream in the main was with him, but when caught in the eddies he struggled against them ; and if during one brief space of a month or more his courage gave way, he did no worse than the stubborn Queen Mary herself, who in similar time of stress subscribed to terms at least as humiliating[1] as any contained in Cranmer's recantations.

Apart from his recantations, the charges against him relate to his conduct as Archbishop, in which capacity he did many things, it is said, at variance with his private convictions. He continued to say mass for instance, under Henry VIII., long after he had ceased to believe in the doctrine of Transubstantiation.[2] The fact does not admit of doubt, and

[1] In 1536 when she acknowledged that the marriage between Henry VIII. and her mother was "by God's law and man's law incestuous and unlawful," and "utterly refused the Bishop of Rome's pretended authority." Like Cranmer's recantations, these phrases, were of course, dictated to Mary and reflect more discredit upon the dictator than upon the subscriber.

[2] Pocock in *Troubles Connected with the Prayer-Book* (Pref., p. v.) after some other contemptuous remarks about the Archbishop, says "for those who want to form an estimate of his character, without the trouble of wading through the history of the Reformation, it will be sufficient to give a reference to Lord Macaulay's account of him in his review of Hallam's *Constitutional History of England* or to an article in the *Saturday Review* for July 25, 1868." It is curious

the offence was perhaps not less than that of reciting the Athanasian creed or subscribing the Thirty-nine Articles after one's faith has outgrown the bounds of these formularies. But Cranmer's official position and the constitutional views of his age afford a justification which cannot be pleaded to-day by private persons. Voluntary resignation of an office on the ground that the holder's conscience could not put up with its duties was then a thing unknown. Men believed with a fervour never since equalled that next to the service of God they were created to serve the State, while the claims of individual conscience were as dust in the balance. Unless the King desired to relieve a minister of office, that minister was bound to retain it; he had little voice in the matter himself. Ministers then, like civil servants of to-day, had to carry out the orders of Government without any regard to their own predilections. They were no more allowed to relinquish an office of State or a

---

to find a High Churchman appealing to Macaulay's verdict on a churchman. His prejudices, his "hectoring sentences and his rough pistolling ways," as Mr. John Morley calls them, render his account of Cranmer the veriest travesty, and admirably illustrate Mr. Morley's saying that "what we find in Macaulay is that quality which the French call brutal" (Morley, *Critical Miscellanies*, i., 280, 287). Macaulay's attacks delighted the extreme Tractarians; "Why," wrote Hurrell Froude in 1835, "do you praise Ridley? Do you know sufficient good about him to counterbalance the fact that he was the associate of Cranmer, Peter Martyr, and Bucer? N. B. How beautifully the *Edinburgh Review* has shown up Luther, Melanchthon, and Co.! What good genius has possessed them to do our dirty work?" (*Remains of R. H. Froude*, pp. 393–394). A few days before he had written, "I hate the Reformation and the Reformers more and more" (*Ib.*, p. 389).

seat in the House of Commons[1] than a man would to-day be permitted to resign his duty to serve on a jury or his obligation to pay rates and taxes. Hence we find the same men in office under Henry VIII. and Edward VI., under Mary and Elizabeth. Even so upright a man as Sir Thomas More remained Lord Chancellor while Henry was pushing his divorce from Catherine of Aragon—a measure which More abhorred. The principle was likewise applied to the Church when the King became its Supreme Head; Bishops, whether Catholic or Protestant, give effect to legislation whatever its character. Heath, afterwards Mary's Chancellor, Tunstall, Day, Thirlby, and other Catholics administered the First Act of Uniformity; they might be deprived or forced to resign, but to resign of their own free will would have been considered a dereliction of duty to themselves and to their King. Their action involved at least as great a sacrifice of conscience as Cranmer was required to make under Henry VIII., and he held higher views than they did of the duty of subjects to their King.

Even from modern ideas it does not follow that Cranmer was wrong. For to maintain that a public man is to take immediate action on every conviction

[1] As is so often the case, the form of this obligation has survived, though its spirit has departed. Members of Parliament can only "resign" by applying for a nominal office of profit under the Crown, the grant of which *ipso facto* makes their seat void. If the Government declined to grant this office no member could retire. In the sixteenth century even a peer could not absent himself from Parliament without royal licence; then a seat in the House of Lords involved duties as well as privileges.

is to set up a standard which would make all rule impossible. Every Government and especially a reforming government, whether it be an individual or a committee, must perforce wear a mask in public behind which it gradually forms its own convictions; and it must wear this mask not merely until such convictions are formed but until the time has come for attempting to carry them out. This wearing a mask may seem hypocrisy in religion, but it is a necessary part of the price which a Church has to pay for connection with the State; and even in the freest of Churches it cannot be completely discarded. Moreover, if Cranmer could have resigned, the step would have made things worse for the cause of Reform; and he chose the better part when he remained at his post and successfully laboured to change a system of which he disapproved. The argument against him is an instance of that bondage to logic and abstract ideas which often unfits men of the pen to deal with public affairs.

A similar failure to realise the difficulties of practical administration has led to another misconception in treating Cranmer's career and that of his associates. It has been truly remarked that the knowledge of after events has spoiled the writing of history. To the man in the study, with a few recorded facts before him, things seem vastly plainer and simpler than they do to the ruler who has to estimate the weight of a number of forces with nothing but his own insight and very imperfect knowledge to guide him. It is easier to condemn a statesman for trusting a force that failed than to foretell its failure beforehand; and the man of books is apt to forget that to every man of affairs the future is a blank and horrible darkness, and that, however much he looks before he leaps, he peers into the night. He goes farthest, said Oliver Cromwell, who knows not whither he goes; and the great Napoleon warned his subordinates against taking fancy pictures and plans as guides in a country that was really unknown. Never can the future have seemed more dim and uncertain than it did to the men who guided the Reformation, for they were travelling in a country unknown and unlike any that man had traversed before; and to assume that they had a clear and definite goal before their eyes and a straight and easy path at their feet is to sterilise all the teaching of history. Yet this is the way in which Cranmer has sometimes been treated; he is represented as having under Henry VIII. not merely the First Book of Common Prayer in his mind's eye, but the Second, and even a third, of which time forbade the production; and then he is accused of dissembling, because he did not resign or secure the immediate adoption of reforms which had not yet entered his head. In truth it would be as reasonable to accuse the Americans of dissimulation in 1765 because they had not published the Declaration of Independence before they resisted the Stamp Act. Nations and statesmen do not as a rule jump to conclusions, but reach them under the slow and painful pressure of circumstances. Convictions thus obtained are lasting; and the fact that Cranmer's work has stood the test of time almost unchanged is astonishing evidence of the fidelity with which he reflected the deepest feelings of the English people. Unless he had struck real chords in English hearts, his Prayer Book would not be in the mouths of millions to-day.

This quality, of course, had its defects, and Cranmer represented some of the worse as well as the better views of the age. He had not abandoned the theory that heresy was an offence to be purged in the fire. He took an official part in the condemnation of heretics, and in his *Reformatio Legum Ecclesiasticarum* prescribed for the offence all the penalties known in the Middle Ages. At the same time no one was more loath to draw the sword than Cranmer. The "importunity for blood" with which he is charged in the case of John Bocher, has been disproved; and the gentleness of his nature made him a hater of rigour and cruelty. His lenience towards the Romanists was often criticised by his friends. "What," he answered, "will ye have a man do to him that is not yet come to the knowledge of the truth of the Gospel, nor peradventure as yet called, and whose vocation is to me uncertain? Shall we perhaps, in his journey coming towards us, by severity and cruel behaviour overthrow him, and as it were in his voyage stop him? I take not this way to allure men to embrace the doctrine of the Gospel."[1] On another occasion Edward Underhill, the "Hot Gospeller" and servant of Edward VI., brought before him the Catholic Vicar of Stepney "for that he disturbed the preachers in his church, causing the bells to be rung when they were at the sermon, and sometimes began to sing in

[1] *Narratives*, p. 246.

the choir before the sermon was half done, and sometimes challenged the preacher in the pulpit." Cranmer, he says, was "too full of lenity; a little he rebuked him and bade him do no more so. 'My Lord,' said I, 'methinks you are too gentle unto so stout a papist.' 'Well,' said he, 'we have no law to punish them by.' 'We have, my Lord,' said I, 'if I had your authority I would be so bold to unvicar him or minister some sharp punishment unto him and such others. If ever it come to their turn, they will show you no such favour.' 'Well,' said he, 'if God so provide, we must abide it.' 'Surely,' said I, 'God will never con you thanks for this, but rather take the sword from such as will not use it upon His enemies.'"[1]

More characteristic of the age and more repugnant to modern ideas was the respect which Cranmer paid to the State and the King. "This is mine opinion and sentence at this present," he once wrote to Henry VIII., "which nevertheless I do not temerariously define, but do remit the judgement thereof wholly unto your Majesty."[2] That Cranmer should have expressed such a sentiment is now pronounced to be strange and almost incredible; but it is only strange to those who have failed to read the signs of that time, and Cranmer, as usual, only

[1] *Narratives*, p. 157.

[2] Burnet, iv., 494; Jenkyns, ii., 103. Bonner's answer, which of course has been suppressed, is quite as submissive as Cranmer's; "ita mihi pro hoc tempore dicendum videtur *salvo judicio melius sententis, cui me prompte et humiliter subjicio.*" Gardiner was abroad at the time; but he complied with all Henry's humours and only resisted the comparatively weak government of Edward VI.

blurted out a thought which possessed all minds and admitted a practice which all pursued. His attitude towards the State was not an idiosyncrasy, but a common feature, nor was it merely due to the weak man's fear of the strong; it had in his case a logical and conscientious basis, which can scarcely be alleged for a similar compliance on the part of Bonner and Gardiner. The Renaissance was a many-sided movement, some of the aspects of which have been unduly neglected. It not only turned men's attention back to the literature and art and religion of classical times, but to the political theory of the primitive Church; and of that political theory Cranmer's views were an exact reproduction. To St. Paul the "powers that be" were of divine ordination, and disobedience was not so much a political offence against man as it was a sin against God. St. Peter proclaimed the Christian's duty of submission "to every ordinance of man," and even in the seventh century Gregory the Great described himself as "dust and a worm" before the Cæsar at Constantinople.[1] These views were the natural outcome of the political conditions of imperial Rome[2]; they disappeared before

[1] Dunning, *Political Theories*, 1902, p. 159.

[2] *Cf.* A. J. Carlyle, *Mediæval Political Theory in the West*, 1903, i., 210. "In some of the Fathers this conception is developed into a theory that the person and the authority of the ruler is so sacred that disobedience to him or resistance of his commands is equivalent to disobedience and resistance of God Himself. By some of the Fathers the divine authority of the State is transferred whole and entire to the particular ruler." These phrases accurately describe the political theory of the Anglican and Lutheran Reformers of the sixteenth century.

the growing influence of the Church and before the onslaughts of the barbarians who made as great inroads upon Roman political theory as they did upon Roman territory. There was little room for such views in polities governed by Teutonic common law or feudal principles; and the increasing power of the Church imposed another check upon the despotism of the State. But after the Renaissance, when men's eyes had been opened to the scientific precision of Roman law, to the beauty of classical literature, and to the primitive purity of the Church, Teutonic common law and feudal theory seemed as barbarous as scholastic theology and mediæval Latinity; and the decadence of the Church weakened the only possible rival of the "New Monarchy." The jurisdiction of the Pope was regarded as a "usurped" authority,[1] and the State stood forth as the one great divine institution. Hence the profound veneration paid to its behests, and hence in comparison the view which Cranmer took of the Church appears to be low. It was not so much that he took a low view of the Church as that he took a high view of the State; not so much that he wanted

[1] The acceptance of the theory of divine institution for the "powers that be" led to controversial dilemmas; for on that theory an authority once legitimate must be always legitimate, and it could never be abolished on such grounds as that it had ceased to perform its proper functions. Hence when Reformers wished to abolish an authority they were driven to maintain that it had always been a "usurped" authority; and this, of course, is always the reason put forward for the abolition of the Roman jurisdiction, and not the real and historical reasons. Yet the primacy of Rome was as legitimate and natural a development as the Royal Supremacy; the one was no more usurped than the other.

to make the Church secular as to make the State religious. Papal theorists had been apt to regard the State as the work and sphere of the Devil, and the Church as the only institution and temple of God. Cranmer saw God in the State as well as in the Church, and thought that He manifested Himself in every good work of man and not merely in religious observances. He would have agreed with Burke's words, that the State "is not a partnership in things subservient only to the gross animal existence of a temporary and perishable nature," but "a partnership in all science, a partnership in all art, a partnership in every virtue, and in all perfection." He would have added "a partnership in all religion and in all godliness."

That ideal, impressive though it was, commands to-day less sympathy than other of Cranmer's mental traits. If his humility, when exhibited in relation to the King, can be interpreted as subserviency, it can hardly be regarded as anything but a Christian virtue when made a rule of life by an Archbishop of the sixteenth century. It was by example as well as by precept, in conduct as well as in doctrine, that Cranmer enjoined a return to the greater simplicity of the age of the Fathers. He alone of Henry's Court stood aloof from the scramble for wealth and the struggle for power, and after Wolsey it was well to show that a prelate could eschew pride, ambition, and vainglory. Wolsey exacted[1] a

[1] See, for example, *Venetian Calendar*, 1527, p. 84, where it is related how Wolsey's attendants had to wait on him on their knees as he sat at table, while the King of France "dispensed with such exaggerated ceremonies."

deference beyond that accustomed to princes; he was believed by Campeggio in 1528 to stand between the Church and her ruin,[1] but it may be doubted whether the Church would not have been wiser to rely on examples like Cranmer's. He has been reproached with officiating in St. Paul's "with no vestment, nor mitre, nor cross,"[2] and these things were indeed indifferent to him.

"For," he wrote, "I pray God never to be merciful to me at the general judgment, if I perceive in my heart that I set more by any title, name, or style that I write than I do by the paring of an apple, farther than it be for the setting forth of God's word and will. . . . Even at the beginning first of Christ's profession, Diotrephes desired *gerere primatum in ecclesia*, as saith Saint John in his last epistle; and since, he hath had more successors than all the apostles had, of whom have come all these glorious titles, styles, and pomps into the Church. But I would that I, and all my brethren the Bishops, would leave all our styles, and write the style of our offices, calling ourselves *apostolos Jesu Christi;* so that we took not upon us the name vainly, but were so even indeed, so that we might order our dioceses in such sort, that neither paper, parchment, lead nor wax, but the very Christian conversation of the people might be the letters and seals of our offices, as the Corinthians were unto Paul, to whom he saith: *Literæ nostræ et signa apostolatus nostri vos estis.*"[3]

To this profession Cranmer strove to be faithful throughout; and the simplicity of his life was the

[1] *L. and P.*, iv., 4898. [2] Dixon, iii., 492, n. [3] *Works*, ii., 305.

outward sign of the simplicity of his character. He amassed no wealth and received no grants from the King except one which Dr. Butts solicited for him without the Archbishop's knowledge; and in 1552 he told Cecil he had more trouble to live as Archbishop than he had when a scholar at Cambridge; he feared "stark beggary" more than the temptations of wealth.[1] Greedy courtiers, anxious to see episcopal lands go the way of monastic endowments, accused him of avarice; they earned for their pains a stinging rebuke from Henry VIII.,[2] and were only pardoned through the intercession which Cranmer was always happy to make on behalf of his personal enemies. On one occasion Cromwell had up a priest from the country for slandering Cranmer as an ignorant ostler. The Archbishop refused to have him punished; the priest, he told Cromwell, was not the first by five hundred who had called him such, and he gently brought the man to a better mind by showing him his own ignorance, and then sent him home in peace.[3] There was no trace of rancour in Cranmer; his friends spoke of his "incredible sweetness of manners," his enemies commended his courtesy,[4] and his forgiving disposition became a proverb. "Do my Lord of Canterbury a shrewd (*i.e.*, an evil)

[1] *Works*, ii., 437.

[2] The story is told in *Narratives*, pp. 260–263. Henry's declaration on this occasion is said by Morice to have prevented the introduction into Parliament of several bills for the confiscation of bishoprics which had been prepared. It is a mistake to suppose that all Church spoliation was due to the King.

[3] *Narratives*, pp. 270–272.

[4] *Bishop Cranmer's Recantacyons*, p. 3.

turn," writes Shakespeare, "and he is your friend for ever."[1] "My Lord," said Heath to the Archbishop one day, "I now know how to win all things at your hand well enough." "How so?" asked Cranmer. "Marry," replied Heath, "I perceive that I must first attempt to do unto you some notable displeasure, and then by a little relenting obtain of you what I can desire." Cranmer was a little nettled at this dissection of his character. "You may be deceived," he said to Heath, "yet I may not alter my mind and accustomed condition, as some would have me do."[2]

Therein at least Cranmer read himself aright; he was utterly incapable of assuming that sphinx-like impenetrability which Henry VIII. and Elizabeth, not to speak of later statesmen, found so valuable an asset. He did not exactly wear his heart on his sleeve, for Morice tells us that he could put on a cheerful countenance when really sick at heart; but this reserve broke down in intimate circles, and few were misled. In him there was no guile; his variations were not calculated, but the faithful reflex

[1] Shakespeare's *Henry VIII.*, Act V., Scene ii. The King says:

> "The common voice, I see, is verified
> Of thee, which says thus, 'Do my Lord of Canterbury
> A shrewd turn, and he is your friend for ever.'"

[2] *Narratives*, pp. 245–246: "This singular freedom from every particle of rancour, and literal fulfilment of the precept to forget and forgive seemed so incredible to Macaulay, who was a Scotchman by descent and a critic by profession, that he has distorted Cranmer's placable disposition into a reproach."—Chester Waters, *Chesters of Chicheley*, p. 386.

of developing convictions. He was never a victim of that infirmity which leads men to pretend that they have always held the same inflexible principles. "This I confess of myself," he wrote in his published answer to Dr. Richard Smith, "that . . . I was in that error of the real presence, as I was many years past in divers other errors, as that of transubstantiation, of the sacrifice propitiatory of the priests in the mass, of pilgrimages, purgatory, and many other superstitions and errors that came from Rome. . . . For the which, and other mine offences in youth I do daily pray unto God for mercy and pardon, saying *Delicta juventutis meæ et ignorantias meas ne memineris, Domine.* Good Lord, remember not mine ignorances and offences of my youth."[1]

Assuredly Cranmer spared no pains to remedy the "ignorances" of his youth. "Commonly," says Morice, "if he had not business of the Prince's or special urgent causes before him, he spent three parts of the day in study as effectually as if he had been at Cambridge."[2] He was one of the most learned theologians of his age; and when it was hinted to Ridley that he and not Cranmer was really the author of the answer to Gardiner on the Eucharist, Ridley replied that it was beyond his capacity to write such a book and that Cranmer "passed him no less than the learned master his young scholar."[3] His theological learning was one of his titles to Henry's favour. "For at all times when the King's Majesty would be resolved in any doubt or question he would but send word to my Lord overnight, and

[1] *Works*, i., 374. [2] *Narratives*, p. 250. [3] Foxe, vi., 436.

by the next day the King should have in writing brief notes of the doctors' minds, as well divines as lawyers, both ancient, old and new, with a conclusion of his own mind; which he could never get in such a readiness of none, no, not of all his chaplains and clergy about him, in so short a time. For being thoroughly seen in all kinds of expositors, he could incontinently lay open thirty, forty, sixty or more somewhiles of authors, and so, reducing the notes of them altogether, would advise the King more in one day than all his learned men could do in a month."[1]

Indisputable evidence of Cranmer's theological attainments is afforded not merely by the testimony of friends and foes, but by the extent of his library, his writings and his commonplace books.[2] His collec-

---

[1] *Narratives*, p. 249.

[2] These commonplace books are now among the Royal MSS. in the British Museum (7 B., xi. and xii.); they are mostly in Morice's hand, with marginal notes, etc., in Cranmer's. These volumes seem to have been secured by Dr. Stephen Nevinson, Parker's commissary (Canon Mason styles him "a certain Dr. Nevison"; he was first cousin to Cranmer's commissary, Dr. Christopher Nevinson, who died in 1551, cf. *D. N. B.*, xl., 308, and *L. and P.*, 1543, ii., p. 330). From him Cecil vainly attempted to obtain them in 1563 (see *Parker Correspondence*, pp. 180–195, 319); they belonged in 1659 to Mr. John Theyer of Cooper's Hill, and in the reign of Queen Anne were purchased for the royal collection by Bishop Beveridge for £50 (Casley, *Cat. of Royal MSS.*, p. 125). Six or seven other volumes were discovered in 1563 in the possession of John Herd, Prebendary of Lincoln (Le Neve, *Fasti*, ii., 162; Cooper, *Athenæ Cantab.*, ii., 40); these seem to have been lost, as do others, for nothing is known of the volumes "about the serious affairs of the Prince and the realm committed unto Bishop Cranmer by Henry VIII. and Edward VI.," which Morice says he was painfully occupied in writing for twenty years (*Lansdowne MS.*, cviii.,

tion of books was broken up at his death, but no fewer than three hundred and fifty printed books and a hundred manuscripts have been traced; his library was more extensive and vastly more valuable and select than that of Cambridge University when Cranmer was there as an undergraduate. Roger Ascham says he found among Cranmer's books "many authors which the two universities could not furnish"[1]; and they were no mere ornaments or furniture of his rooms, but furniture of his mind. There were two Hebrew Bibles, and one of them is interleaved with a Latin translation made by Cranmer with his own hand. There was an almost complete set of the Greek and Latin Fathers and the best of the mediæval schoolmen. With modern writers such as Erasmus he was, as a matter of course, familiar; "I have seen," he writes in 1537, "almost everything that has been written and published either by Œcolampadius or by Zwinglius,"[2] and with the writings of Luther and Melanchthon he was yet more conversant. His commonplace books in the British Museum Library also contain extracts from Calvin, Bucer, Bullinger, Brenz,

---

8). The bulk of Cranmer's library was secured by Lord Arundel, Queen Mary's Steward of the Household; he bequeathed the volumes to his son-in-law, Lord Lumley, on whose death in 1609 they were bought by Prince Henry, the eldest son of James I. Several of them bear the signatures *Tho. Cantuariensis*, *Arundel*, *Lumley*. Most of the volumes which have been traced are now in the British Museum, a few are at Oxford and at Cambridge, and others are in private hands. (See Ed. Burbidge, *Liturgies and Offices of the Church*, 1885, Pref., pp. xvii.-xxxii., where a list is given.)

[1] Todd, *Cranmer*, ii., 525.

[2] *Works*, ii., 344.

Eck, and Pirckheimer—divines of all shades of opinion, ancient and modern, Latin and Greek. Latin, of course, he spoke and wrote with ease; Hebrew we know that he read, from his translation of the Hebrew Bible; Greek he may have acquired after he left Cambridge, and the discovery that εἴδωλον, whence came idolatry, meant the same as *imago*, made a great impression on his mind. When Robert Estienne published his great Greek Testament at Paris in 1550,[1] Cranmer made haste to acquire this *Editio regia*, as it was called, and used it with effect against Gardiner in his work on the Eucharist, published in 1551.[2] Besides these three ancient tongues, all indispensable to a Reformer whose one test of truth was the Scriptures, Cranmer knew French and Italian. He translated Italian news-letters into English for Henry VIII.'s benefit,[3] and it is scarcely possible that he could have wooed Osiander's German niece without some knowledge of the German tongue.

A lover of learning himself, Cranmer was a patron of learning in others. He continued Warham's beneficence to Erasmus, and procured a living and a canonry for John Leland, one of the greatest of English antiquaries. Erasmus repaid him with a letter and Leland with one of his well-known encomiums in verse, in which he styles the Archbishop *eximium decus piorum*.[4] Through him John Sleidan,

[1] Cf. *Cambridge Modern History*, i., 604.

[2] *Works*, i., 24.

[3] *Ibid.*, ii., 332.

[4] It is printed in Strype, *Cranmer*, i., 599; cf. *Dict. Nat. Biogr.*, xxxiii., 14 (the canonry at Oxford, for which no date is there given, was conferred on Leland on 26 March, 1543).

the German historian,[1] was granted a pension by Edward VI.; and Tremellius, the Hebraist, described Lambeth under Cranmer's rule, as "a house of public entertainment to all people of learning and piety."[2] No foreign divine of note came to England in Edward VI.'s reign without being lodged under Cranmer's roof until established elsewhere.

Nor was his patronage and zeal for education limited to eminent scholars; he would extend the benefits of education to every child of ability, whether he were a ploughman's son or a peer's. When the Cathedral school at Canterbury was being refounded, some of his fellow commissioners[3] maintained that none but gentlemen's sons should be admitted. Cranmer denounced the idea; "for," said he, "poor men's children are many times indued with more singular gifts of nature, which are also the gifts of God, as with eloquence, memory, apt pronunciation, sobriety, with such like, and also commonly more given to apply their study than is the gentleman's son, delicately educated." The ploughman's son, it was argued, should follow the plough; only gentlemen's sons were meet to "have the knowledge of government and rule in the commonwealth": there was as much need of ploughmen as of other classes, "and all sorts of men may not go to school." "I grant,"

---

[1] His real name was Johann Philipson; *cf.* Baumgarten *Ueber Sleidan's Leben*, Strassburg, 1878, and *Sleidan's Briefwechsel*, Strassburg, 1881.

[2] Todd, *Cranmer*, ii., 207; Cooper, *Athenæ*, i., 425.

[3] The chief of them was Sir Richard Rich who, when he founded Felsted School in Essex, perhaps remembered Cranmer's words.

replied Cranmer, "much of your meaning herein, as needful to a commonwealth; but yet utterly to exclude the ploughman's son and the poor man's son from the benefit of learning, as though they were unworthy to have the gifts of the Holy Ghost bestowed upon them as well as upon others, is as much as to say that Almighty God should not be at liberty to bestow his great gifts of grace upon any person, nor nowhere else but as we and other men shall appoint them to be employed according to our fancy and not according to his most godly will and pleasure; who giveth his gifts both of learning and other perfections in all sciences unto all kinds and states of people indifferently; even so doeth he many times withdraw from them and their posterity again those beneficial gifts if they be not thankful. If we should shut up into a strait corner the bountiful grace of the Holy Ghost, and thereupon attempt to build our fancies, we should make as perfect a work thereof as those that took upon them to build the tower of Babylon; for God would so provide that the offspring of our best born children should peradventure become most unapt to learn and very dolts, as I myself have seen no small number of them very dull and without all manner of capacity. . . . To conclude, the poor man's son by painstaking for the most part will be learned when the gentleman's son will not take the pains to get it. . . . Wherefore if the gentleman's son be apt to learning, let him be admitted; if not apt, let the poor man's child apt enter his room."[1] Cranmer

[1] *Narratives*, pp. 274–275.

carried his point with regard to Canterbury school, but the views he contested still flourish among the backward classes in England. And another theory has not disappeared against which Cranmer protested when he sought to save the schoolmaster of Ludlow from being deprived of his school on abandoning holy orders; "the man's priesthood," he said, "was no furtherance but rather an impediment to him in the applying of his scholars." [1]

The same generosity of disposition appears in Cranmer's relations with his dependents and friends. "There never was," says Morice, "such a master amongst men, both feared and entirely beloved; for, as he was a man of most gentle nature, void of all crabbed and churlish conditions, so he could abide no such qualities in any of his servants." [2] He always retained a grateful recollection of the kindness shown him by his old college at Cambridge, and endeavoured to repay it in after years when his influence was useful to the society and to its individual members. [3] When Welbeck Abbey was dissolved, the Archbishop purchased its tithes of Aslacton and Whatton and gave them to his nephew, Thomas, who had inherited the family estates; and he has been accused of nepotism in promoting his brother Edmund to the Archdeaconry of Canterbury. But therein he was only following his predecessors,

---

[1] *Works*, ii., 380; for Ludlow School see Leach's *English Schools*, 1896, i., 45-46, 49; ii., 185, 322.

[2] *Narratives*, p. 268.

[3] Cf. *Works*, ii., 247, 303.

Chicheley, Bourchier, and Warham,[1] and his conduct compares favourably with that of Warham and Wolsey. For Warham bestowed the preferment on a nephew who was not in priest's orders and therefore required a papal dispensation from the canonical prohibition to enable him to hold the office; and Wolsey endeavoured to obtain the rich Bishopric of Durham for his illegitimate son while he was yet a minor; he failed in this, but secured for the youth in his teens a deanery, four archdeaconries, five prebends, and a chancellorship.[2] Beside this flagrant example Cranmer's conferment of one archdeaconry on a brother who fulfilled all the canonical requirements seems harmless enough, and it is the only charge of the kind that was ever laid at his door.

A different accusation was that he wasted the lands of his see by granting them away on easy leases, but Morice has successfully vindicated his master's conduct. It was really designed to preserve the cathedral endowments, for unless he had turned the edge of the lay appetite for ecclesiastical property,

---

[1] Chester Waters's account of Edmund Cranmer in *Chester of Chicheley;* Edmund fled on Mary's accession and died abroad in 1571; his descendants were numerous; see the pedigree.

[2] The deanery was Wells, 1526: the archdeaconries were Norfolk, 1523, Suffolk, 1526, York, 1523, and Richmond, 1523; the chancellorship was of Salisbury, 1523; and the prebends were two in York, 1523, two in Southwell, and one in Lincoln, 1522; see Le Neve, *Fasti*, ed. Hardy, i., 153; ii., 187, 484, 489, 651; iii., 134, 141, 188, 216, 438, 441; for each of these preferments a complaisant Pope had to grant two dispensations, one on account of the youth's illegitimacy, the other on account of his minority.

courtiers would probably have secured permanent grants instead of temporary leases. He did, indeed, yield to Henry's demand for the manor of Otford by way of exchange; but to resist in such a case was clearly out of the question. "For," writes Morice, "as touching his exchanges, men ought to consider with whom he had to do, especially with such a prince as would not be bridled, nor be against-said in any of his requests." [1]

With respect to his family life, we have but the scantiest details. There is no doubt that his relations with his domestic circle were as happy as external conditions would permit. Scandal was busy with one of Cranmer's sisters[2]; but it never touched the Archbishop himself, except in so far as to tell that his affection for his wife drove him to curious expedients to retain her company during the dark days of the Six Articles.[3] It has been thought

---

[1] *Narratives*, p. 266. Miss J. M. Stone (*Queen Mary*, p. 385) quotes this sentence, omitting "as touching his exchanges," connects it with Cranmer's phrase about "not temerariously defining, etc.," and distorts it into an acknowledgment that Cranmer surrendered all his *principles!* "Morice," she says, "unconsciously deprived him of every vestige of fidelity to *principle.*"

[2] See above pp. 6, 148.

[3] The story was that Cranmer carried her about in a chest with holes bored into it to admit the air; on one occasion, when the chest was placed upside down, the lady had to make her presence known by screams. The story first occurs in Nicholas Harpsfield's *Treatise of the Pretended Divorce of Catherine of Aragon*, which was written after Cranmer's death; the other early reference to it occurs in *Bishop Cranmer's Recantacyons* (see below, pp. 361–2), which may also have been written by Harpsfield. Neither work was published till the nineteenth century, the *Divorce* by Pocock in 1878, and the

strange that nothing is heard of her during Cranmer's troubles under Queen Mary, and that the only efforts on his behalf appear to have been made by his sister; but the reason is that his wife was far away in Germany. The Archbishop had warned

Recantacyons by Dr. Gairdner in 1885; but copies of the former were circulated in MS. and the story got abroad; it was published in Nicholas Sanders's *De Origine Schismatis Angliæ* in 1585. It was contradicted by Sir John Harington on the authority of Mrs. Cranmer's daughter-in-law, who was related to Lady Harington. (Harington, *Nugæ Antiquæ*, ed. 1804, iii., 16; Harington was himself grandson of Cranmer's "loving friend," Sir John Markham; see Cranmer, *Works*, ii., 358, and *D. N. B.*, xxiv., 385; Catherine [Rogers], the wife of the Archbishop's only son, was cousin of Sir Edward Rogers, Queen Elizabeth's Controller of the Household, and Sir Edward's granddaughter was Harington's wife.) Subsequently, Parsons, the famous Jesuit, repeated the story in his *Treatise of the Three Conversions of England*, 1603, saying that this same daughter-in-law of the Archbishop told it to her friends from one of whom he heard it. This evidence is not so good as Harington's, and the story thus rests upon Harpsfield's statement, which was contradicted by persons in a better position to know than Harpsfield himself. Absolute proof or disproof is not forthcoming. At the same time I cannot find any original authority for the universally accepted story that Cranmer sent his wife back to Germany after the enactment of the Six Articles. There is no allusion to it in the proceedings at Cranmer's trial; there he was accused of having kept his wife secretly during Henry's reign and brought her out in Edward VI.'s,—charges which Cranmer admitted (see *Works*, ii., 219, 550); and the language used does not suggest that she left England in the interval.

By his first wife, Joan, Cranmer had one child who died at birth; by his second he had two daughters and one son. The son, Thomas, disgraced his father's name by loose living in Elizabeth's reign, dissipated what property he had, and died without issue in November, 1598, being buried on the 14th of that month in St. Andrew's, Holborn. His widow, Catherine [Rogers], had three husbands; the first was Hugh Vaughan (*d.* 1576), the second was Thomas Cranmer, and the third was one Randall; she eventually his friends to flee early in the reign, and his natural affection would ensure that his wife and children should be the first to be placed out of the reach of danger. His wife was a heretic like himself and might well have been joined to the army of feminine martyrs who were sent to the stake by Queen Mary.

---

sank into poverty and distress, five shillings and eleven pence being collected for her benefit in St. Olave's, Old Jewry, in 1607. Of the Archbishop's two daughters, one, Anne, died young and unmarried; the other, Margaret, married Thomas Norton (1532–84), a well-known lawyer and politician, but more famous as the joint author of *Gorboduc*, the earliest-known tragedy in English blank verse (see *Dict. Nat. Biogr.*, xli., 221–225). On his wife's death, Norton married her cousin Alice, daughter of Archdeacon Edmund Cranmer; he had no issue, so that the Archbishop's line died out with his children, and the various claims since put forward to descent from him are all baseless. (The pedigree of the Cranmers of Mitcham, Surrey, printed in Manning and Bray's *Surrey*, vol. iii., Appendix, and tracing their descent from the Archbishop, has been conclusively proved to be a fabrication by Mr. Chester Waters.)

The Archbishop's widow married in Germany, perhaps in 1556, as her second husband, Edward Whitchurch, the Protestant printer of Cranmer's Bible and the First Book of Common Prayer, who had fled probably to Germany on the accession of Queen Mary (see *Dict. Nat. Biogr.*, lxi., 30). He died in 1561, and in 1564 she took a third husband, Bartholomew Scott, a justice of the peace for Surrey. She died about 1571; she does not appear to have had any issue by any but her first husband.

With regard to the Archbishop's personal appearance we have his portraits and Foxe's description (viii., 43): "he was of stature mean i. e., medium), of complexion he was pure and somewhat sanguine, having no hair upon his head at the time of his death [it had been shaved by a barber at his degradation, a month before]; but a long beard, white and thick [which he had let grow since Henry VIII.'s death]. He was of the age of sixty-six when he was burnt; and yet (although) being a man sore broken in studies, in all his time never used spectacles." The "purblind" or short sight, of which Morice speaks, was as usual more lasting than long sight.

That the Archbishop himself stood his ground is one among many proofs of deliberate courage. He used to tell Morice that the brutality of his early schoolmaster had destroyed the "audacity" with which he had been by nature endowed, and that he had never been able to repair the loss. The explanation is not convincing. Cranmer was undoubtedly of that shrinking, sensitive nature which usually acts like a red rag on bullies, but every now and then touches a finer chord in the strong man's heart, as it did in that of Henry VIII. But he was no coward; he had, indeed, none of the hardihood which ignorance breeds, nor the courage which springs from an incapacity to realise danger and suffering. Sensitive nerves, imagination, and a somewhat slow and hesitating mind gave Cranmer at times the appearance and feeling of weakness; but when once his mind was made up his courage was not found lacking. He alone, so far as we know, tried to save the monks of Sion from the block; he alone interceded for Fisher and More, for Anne Boleyn and for the Princess Mary, for Thomas Cromwell and Bishop Tunstall. He told Henry VIII. that he had offended God, and Cromwell that the Court was setting an evil example. He maintained almost unaided a stubborn fight against the Act of Six Articles and resisted longer than any one else the Duke of Northumberland's plot. He refused to fly before danger at Mary's accession; and for two and a half years withstood without flinching the pressure of a sixteenth-century prison. If then for a month he wavered between his duty to the

State and that to his conscience; if finally, he tried to concede that impossible change of belief which his inquisitors required, he redeemed his fall by a heroism in the hour of death to which history can find few parallels.

CHAPTER XII

IN TIME OF TROUBLE

QUEEN Mary was borne to the throne on the flood-tide of reaction against a tyrannous government, and the first acts of her reign did not utterly belie the hopes which the nation had conceived. The first words of the first Act of her first Parliament declared that "the state of every king, ruler, and governor of any realm, dominion, or commonalty standeth and consisteth more assured by the love and favour of the subjects towards their sovereign ruler and governor than in the dread and fear of laws made with rigorous pains and extreme punishment." It recalled the fact that many "honourable and noble persons . . . had of late (for words only, without other opinion, fact, or deed) suffered shameful death;" and echoing the words and sentiments of Somerset's repeal of the treason laws, it proceeded to abolish those which Northumberland had re-enacted after the Protector's fall. Another echo of the "good Duke's" days was heard when Mary announced that she graciously meant "not to compel or constrain other men's consciences otherwise than God shall put in their hearts."[1]

[1] *Acts of the Privy Council*, 1552–54, p. 317.

There were some to whom no clemency could extend, and Northumberland, with his intimate abettors, was promptly sent to the scaffold. The Duke did almost as much harm to the Reformation by his death as he had done during his life. This "most intrepid soldier of Christ," one of "the two most shining lights of the Church of England," confessed that he had been an evil liver and had done wickedly all the days of his life, that for sixteen years he had been no Christian, and that all the woes which the realm had endured of late had been due to the Reformation[1]; "there were," says a letter of the time, "a great number turned with his words." A dramatic touch is given to the story of his death by the thrice-repeated statement of an eye-witness that the Duke of Somerset's sons stood by[2]; and according to the Spanish ambassador Northumberland asked their forgiveness for having wrongfully and falsely procured their father's death.[3] But the real tragedy consisted in the fact that Northumberland's fall dragged down better men than he.

Since the 20th of July, when he had attended the Council and signed its letter acknowledging Mary as Queen, Cranmer had remained undisturbed at

[1] The fullest report of Northumberland's confession is in Brit. Mus., *Harleian MS.*, 284, f. 127 (printed in Tytler, ii., 230-232); two others are printed from *Harleian MS.* 353, in the *Chron. of Queen Jane*, p. 21; a fourth and fifth are in *Cotton MS.*, Titus, B. ii., and *Royal MS.*, 12 A., xxvi.

[2] *Chron. Queen Jane*, pp. 19, 20, 21.

[3] Renard, quoted in Froude, v., 36; Northumberland's tool, Sir Thomas Palmer, also confessed, that he had sworn to evidence against Somerset which Northumberland had fabricated.

Lambeth. On the 8th of August he officiated at the obsequies of Edward VI., who was buried according to the rites of his Second Book of Common Prayer.[1] He was not blind to the perils in which he stood; and he, like Ridley, warned his friends to fly from the plague and get them hence, for the time of tribulation was at hand, and the abomination spoken of by Daniel the Prophet was set up in the Holy Place.[2] Many took heed; four bishops, five deans, four archdeacons, and scores of doctors and preachers escaped from the wrath to come.[3] With them went numbers of foreign divines; Peter Martyr, John à Lasco, the Dutch Protestants in London, and the Flemish weavers at Glastonbury struck their tents and sought safety abroad,[4] but Cranmer, Latimer, and Ridley stood by their posts. Cranmer was still Archbishop, and it would ill become him, he said, to fly; he would shew that he was not afraid to own all the changes that were made by his means in religion during the reign of Edward VI.[5]

"Therefore," wrote Ridley a little later, "if thou, O man of God, do purpose to abide in this realm,

[1] *Greyfriars' Chron.*, pp. 82–83.

[2] See Ridley's *Piteous Lamentation* (Parker Soc.), pp. 62–63, and Cranmer's *Works*, ii., 441–442, 444–445.

[3] See list in Strype's *Cranmer*, i., 449–450.

[4] Peter Martyr and others of these foreigners obtained passports, but it seems rather far-fetched to adduce this as a proof that Mary "had no desire to persecute" (Gairdner, p. 321). Peter Martyr had only come by official invitation, and it would have been a flagrant violation of public decency to persecute him; moreover, most of these men were not Mary's subjects, and proceedings against them might have involved awkward disputes with other powers.

[5] Strype, *Cranmer*, i., 449.

prepare and arm thyself to die; for both by Antichrist's accustomable laws and these prophecies, there is no appearance of any other thing except thou wilt deny thy master Christ."[1] Cranmer was soon put to the test. His silence, which was due to respect for the Queen, was interpreted as acquiescence in the restoration of the mass, and men thought he would follow in Northumberland's footsteps. Stories were told that the Archbishop had set up the mass in Canterbury Cathedral, had offered to say it at Edward's burial, and again before the Queen in St. Paul's. They came to Cranmer's ears, and moved him, meek as he was, to a wrathful denial. He drew up a manifesto which he intended to fix on the doors of St. Paul's and other churches in London.[2] "As the Devil," he began, "Christ's ancient adversary, is a liar and the father of lying . . . now goeth he about by lying to overthrow the Lord's holy supper again, and to restore his Latin satisfactoryness, a thing of his own invention and device." Then, recounting the rumours about himself, he proceeds:

"And although I have been well exercised these twenty years in suffering and bearing evil bruits, reports and lies, and have not been much grieved thereat, but have borne all things quietly, yet when untrue reports and lies tend to the hinderance of God's truth, then are they in no wise tolerate or to be suffered. Wherefore

[1] *Works*, p. 62.

[2] See Strype's *Cranmer*, i., 436; *Original Letters*, i., 371. This declaration is printed in Cranmer's *Works*, i., 428–429, from the MS. at Emanuel College, Cambridge; another MS. is at Corpus Christi College, Cambridge.

this is to signify to the world that it was not that I did set up the mass in Canterbury, but it was a false, flattering, and lying monk. . . . And as for offering myself to say mass before the Queen's Highness at St. Paul's, or in any other place, I never did it, as her Grace well knoweth. But if her Grace will give me leave, I will and by the might of God shall be ready at all times to prove against all that would say the contrary, that all that is said in the holy communion set forth by the most innocent and godly prince, King Edward VI., in his court of Parliament, is conformable to that order that Our Saviour Christ did both observe and command to be observed; which also his apostles and primitive church used many years; whereas the mass in many things not only hath no foundation of Christ's apostles nor the primitive church, but also is manifestly contrary to the same, and containeth in it many horrible abuses."[1]

Then he offered to prove in public disputation that "not only the common prayers of the church, the ministration of the sacraments, and other rites and ceremonies, but also that all the doctrine and

[1] It is often argued that neither the Second Book of Common Prayer nor the First was intended to be final; and Bullinger stated in 1555 that "Cranmer had drawn up a book of prayers an hundred times more perfect than that which was then in being, but the same could not take place, for that he was matched with such a wicked clergy and convocation." (Strype, *Cranmer*, p. 382.) This story agrees ill with Cranmer's statement in the text; and is on other grounds improbable. The Second Book of Common Prayer represented the furthest limit of Cranmer's advance towards continental Protestantism. Bullinger's assertion probably embodies a hazy recollection of the perfectly accurate account which his correspondents had given him of the First Prayer Book, where Cranmer's draft was toned down by the hostility of the bishops and others.

religion set forth by our sovereign lord King Edward VI. is more pure and according to God's word than any other that hath been used in England these thousand years."

This challenge was bold to the verge of foolhardiness, and it was the immediate occasion of the beginning of Cranmer's tribulations.[1] The manifesto was not then printed, but the Archbishop gave a copy to Bishop Scory, who indiscreetly communicated it to others; and on the 5th of September the document was read aloud in Cheapside. Next day "every scrivener's shop almost was occupied in writing and copying out the same."[2] It was a counterblast to Northumberland's apostasy which rejoiced the heart of every true Reformer; and copies, says Renard, multiplied as fast in manuscript as the printing-press could have turned them out. A day or two later the Council sent for Cranmer; he appeared before it on the 13th of September. It was busy with the case of Latimer, who on that day was sent to the Tower, and the Archbishop was ordered to attend the following day at the Star Chamber.[3]

His offence, we are told in the Council's register, was long and seriously debated by the whole board; and indeed their lordships' arguments must have been full of unconscious irony. They could, no doubt,

[1] Froude (v., 255) not unjustly remarks, "Considering the position of the writer, and the circumstances under which it was issued, I regard the publication of this letter as one of the bravest actions ever deliberately ventured by man."

[2] Foxe, viii., 38.

[3] *Acts P. C.*, 1552–54, pp. 346–347; *Chron. Queen Jane*, p. 27: *Greyfriars' Chron.*, p. 84; *Wriothesley's Chron.*, ii., 103.

inveigh with a clear conscience against "the spreading about seditious bills moving tumults to the disquietness of the present state," though Cranmer had had little enough to do with the publication of his protest. But the main charge pretended against him was "treason against the Queen's Majesty"—treason in which not a few of them had taken a far less innocent part than Cranmer. Northumberland had objected that many of the peers who condemned him for treason had been partakers in the self-same offence; and Cranmer with more justice might have urged that it scarcely became Councillors to send him to the Tower for a crime which they had committed. That, however, was the result of this long and serious Star Chamber debate. Cranmer went out from the Council's presence and was conveyed forthwith to the Tower; and as the gates clanged behind him they closed on the days of his freedom. Probably by design he was lodged in the cell whence Northumberland had passed to the scaffold.[1]

Two months later, on the 13th of November, Cranmer was put on his trial for treason at the Guildhall in London, and with him were associated Lady Jane Grey, her husband, and two other sons of Northumberland.[2] Their technical guilt was much the same, and so was their moral innocence. All had acted under compulsion; but that was a plea of

[1] "Over the gate against the water-gate, where the Duke of Northumberland lay before his death."—*Chron. Queen Jane.*

[2] See documents relating to the trial in the *Baga de Secretis*, calendared in Appendix II. to the Fourth Report of the Deputy Keeper of Records.

which only courts of equity could take cognisance, and equitable considerations did not count in trials for treason. Cranmer at first pleaded not guilty, but then withdrew that plea and confessed to the charges. All the prisoners were condemned to death, but on Cranmer alone was there any design to carry out the sentence. The Archbishop, wrote Renard, who knew all the secrets of Mary's government, on the 17th of November, "will be executed."[1] But Mary or her ecclesiastical advisers soon discovered a scruple. Such an execution would be a violation of the laws of the Church, which were soon to be revived. By them no cleric could suffer at secular hands until he had been degraded and had lost the inviolability with which ordination invested the churchman. And so, although an Act of Parliament confirmed the attainder, Cranmer's life was spared for the moment.

That he was put on his trial for treason at all was, indeed, an act of revenge, and no sophistry can make it anything else. Treason was not his crime, but his sentence of divorce against the Queen's mother.[2] Winchester and Arundel, Bedford and

[1] Froude, v., 295. Archbishop Heath is reported as saying that the Queen's determination was that Cranmer should only be deprived of his bishopric and given a sufficient living on condition that he kept his house and did not meddle with religion. (Foxe, viii., 38.) These may have been Heath's own merciful sentiments, but they were soon overruled.

[2] Mary's anger was natural enough, but she might have been satisfied with the triumph which established the validity of that marriage and seated her on the throne. She forgave Gardiner, who had been eagerly pushing on the divorce long before Cranmer had expressed an opinion on it,

Shrewsbury, Pembroke and Rich, Paget and Petre, Cheyney and Mason, had all committed worse treason than he, yet all were now sitting in Mary's Council, enjoying her confidence. Suffolk, Lady Jane's father, Northampton, and Cecil, three of Northumberland's strongest supporters, had all been pardoned; but nothing could extort from Mary a pardon for him who had more than once interceded for her[1]; and the whilom friends of the Archbishop, who now basked in the sunshine of Mary's favour, took care not to risk its loss on behalf of the prisoner in the Tower.

"Having no person," he wrote to the Queen, "that I know to be a mediator for me, and knowing your pitiful ears ready to hear all pitiful complaints, and seeing so many before to have felt your abundant clemency in like case, I am now constrained most lamentably and with most penitent and sorrowful heart to ask mercy and pardon for my heinous folly and offence in consenting and following the testament and last will of our late sovereign; which will, God he knoweth, I never liked; nor never anything grieved me so much that your Grace's brother did. And if by any means it had been in me to have letted the making of that will, I would have done it."[2]

Then, after describing his fruitless efforts to prevent that madness, and the compulsion put upon him to sign the will, he admitted that when he subscribed he did it *unfeignedly and without dissimu-*

[1] See above, p. 161.

[2] Cranmer, *Works*, ii., 443–444.

lation. Nowhere does Cranmer's simple, transparent honesty come out so clearly; had he possessed one iota of the dissembling craft with which he has sometimes been charged,[1] he would never have written a sentence like that to Mary. It was not in him to sign a document with mental reservations; when he subscribed the will, he did so with the full intention of keeping his promise, and he blurts out the truth like a child. Another eminent man signed the will, and has left an apology for his conduct; it affords a useful contrast with Cranmer's. Twenty years later the wily Cecil put into the mouth of a servant his version of the affair. He falsely stated that he signed last of all, and then only signed as a "witness"—as if all the others could not have pretended the same excuse![2]

Having made his petition for life, Cranmer next desired leave to quiet his conscience, and incidentally he stated with much precision and clearness his position on a subject's duty when he differed from his sovereign in religion. "I will never, God willing,

[1] "From first to last," says one zealous writer, "he had proved himself so base a dissembler that no confidence could possibly have been placed in the sincerity of his recantations. That he had lied therein also, he admitted by his final recantation of them all."—J. M. Stone, *History of Queen Mary*, 1901, p. 389.

[2] Tytler, ii., 171, 202; Strype, *Annals*, iv., 349. It need scarcely be said that there is no difference between Cecil's signature and those of the other Councillors. Cecil, in fact, was peculiarly responsible, as he had been Northumberland's most trusted secretary of state. No doubt he disliked and distrusted the scheme; but if all who felt the same had acted with courage it would never have passed its initial stages. Cranmer's opposition was useless because the whole weight of Government was already cast in the other balance.

be author of sedition to move subjects from the obedience of their heads and rulers, which is an offence most detestable." Yet conscience required him, considering the place he had held as chief spiritual adviser to his sovereign, to "shew your Majesty my mind in things pertaining unto God." When once he had done that, his conscience would be discharged. "For it lieth not in me, but in your Grace only to see the reformation of things that be amiss. To private subjects it appertaineth not to reform things, but quietly to suffer that they cannot amend." Even this statement of his mind he would not make without the Queen's permission; and, needless to say, he awaited that grace in vain.

Cranmer was now in a very anomalous position. He was a prisoner in the Tower and a condemned traitor; that condemnation deprived him, according to the laws as they stood, of his Archbishopric, and in obedience to those laws he now signed himself merely T. Cranmer.[1] But by the canon law his ecclesiastical character remained still intact; he could only be deprived by spiritual authority after condemnation by a spiritual court for a spiritual offence. Mary, as an orthodox Roman Catholic and devoted Papist, wished to have Cranmer deprived by the Pope's authority and burnt as a heretic; but the laws *de hæretico comburendo* had not yet been revived nor those against the papal jurisdiction abolished.[2] Hence

[1] *E. g.*, in his letter to Mrs. Wilkinson, *Works*, ii., 445.

[2] These legislative changes were not ventured upon until 1554, when Wyatt's rebellion had failed, the marriage with Philip had been completed, the Emperor's support secured, and the sheriffs (not

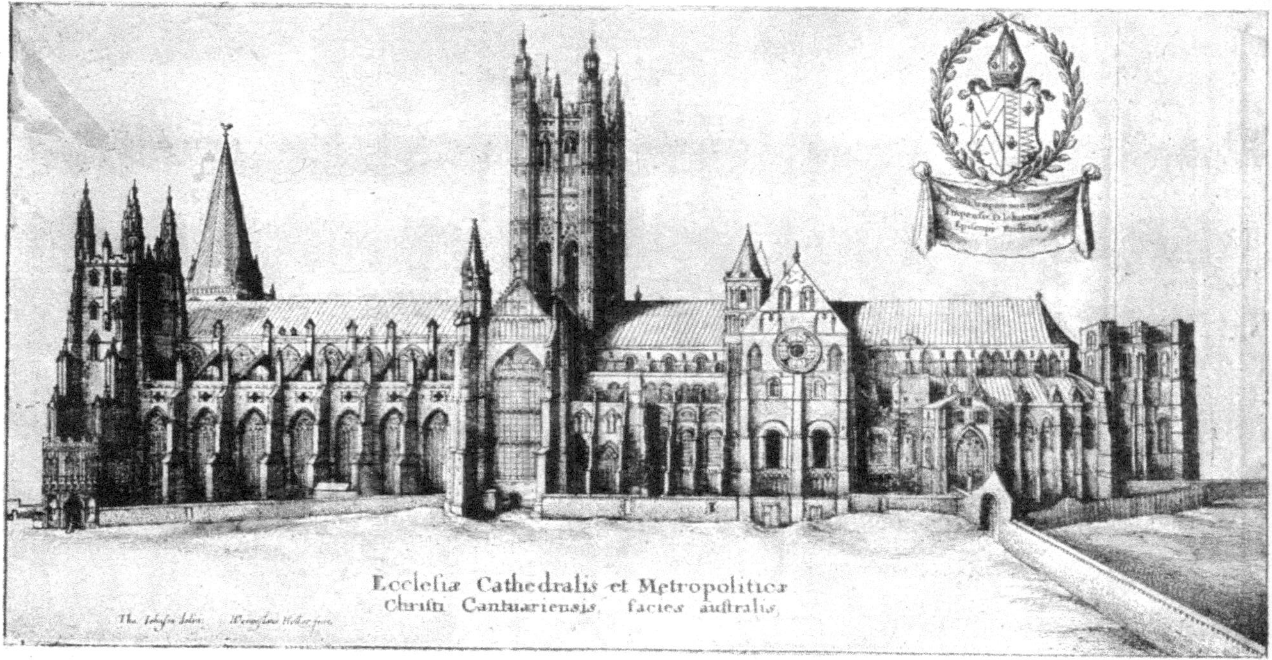

CANTERBURY CATHEDRAL

FROM AN OLD COPPER PRINT.

Cranmer's reprieve; meanwhile he was only sequestered from his Archbishopric, and it was not till after his death that Cardinal Pole stepped into his place. He was even allowed to walk in the Tower gardens, and a greater appearance of clemency was shown if, as is said, he received a pardon for treason.[1] Had this been true, the boon would have resembled that accorded to Somerset, when he was acquitted of treason but condemned to death for felony[2]; and the mercy extended to Cranmer

the constituencies) had been ordered to choose knights, citizens, and burgesses of "the wise, grave, and Catholic sort." This curious situation has created confusion in the minds of historians. Burnet says Cranmer was still considered archbishop. Wharton (*Specimen of Errors*) disputed this statement, showing that commissioners were appointed to exercise the jurisdiction of the see during its vacancy, and that a special register was kept for the period. Yet Cranmer was still archbishop by Roman canon law. The deprivation of Tunstall by the civil power has been considered one of the most illegal acts of Edward's reign, and if Cranmer's deprivation had been complete there would have been no explanation of the sentence of deprivation subsequently pronounced at Rome nor of the delay in filling up the see. It was a question of conflict between the municipal laws of England and the universal law of the Church. By the one, Cranmer ceased to be archbishop on his attainder in November, 1553; by the other, he remained archbishop till judgment was pronounced against him at Rome two years later.

[1] Foxe, viii., 38; Strype, i., 460; but neither gives any date or authority. If he had been pardoned he should have been released, as he had not yet been condemned for heresy. All the evidence is against the story. On 3 May, 1554, the Council, considering what to do with Cranmer, remarked that he had been judged a heretic by both universities, and was besides "already attainted." In September, 1555, Bishop Brooks told him he was a dead man in the eye of the English law, being attainted of treason, and in 1563 an Act of Parliament was required for the restitution of his children.

[2] *England under Protector Somerset*, p. 305.

would have consisted in substituting for death on the scaffold the more long-drawn torture at the stake. As a matter of fact, no pardon was ever granted.

For a few months Queen Mary had enough to do to keep her throne without troubling about Cranmer's or any one else's heresy. The rebellion of Wyatt came nearer to success than any other revolt in Tudor times, but that very circumstance hardened her heart the more, and enabled her Government to maintain that heresy and treason were both the same thing. She had no more loyal subject than Cranmer, and he could not be even an innocent cause of dynastic plots as Lady Jane Grey was. Nevertheless, he was not to escape; on 8 March, 1554, the Lieutenant of the Tower was ordered to deliver Cranmer, Ridley, and Latimer to Sir John Williams to be conveyed to Oxford.[1] The order was not at once carried out; and, the Tower being crowded with prisoners, the three Reformers were placed in one room, where they read and discussed the New Testament. Early in April they were removed to Oxford and lodged in Bocardo[2] prison, opposite St. Michael's Church in the Corn Market. They were to partake in a scholastic disputation on the mass, and on the 14th of April the contest began in the University Church of St. Mary.

[1] *Acts P. C.*, 1552-54, p. 406.

[2] The prison is said to have been so named because it was as impossible to escape from it as from the logical figure known by that name; it really formed part of the northern gate of the city. The door of Cranmer's prison is now in St. Mary Magdalene Church, which is close by the Martyrs' Memorial, and must be distinguished from the University church (St. Mary the Virgin).

Commissioners from Cambridge joined forces with those from Oxford for the debate, and the same men who argued with Cranmer were also to judge whether his or their arguments had prevailed.[1] Nor were Ridley and Latimer permitted to hear his contentions, for each was to dispute alone. By this means they might be led to contradict one another, and the whole weight of all the Catholic disputants might be brought to bear on them singly.

Cranmer was first selected[2]; the Prolocutor began by censuring in detail his past life. He then showed Cranmer the Articles round which the debate was to centre. Cranmer, declaring them to be contrary to God's Word, was required to commit his reasons to paper, and to be ready to maintain them in disputation on the following Monday, the 16th of April. At eight in the morning Weston opened the debate by declaring that their object was not to call Catholic doctrine into dispute, but to confound the heretics; what they wanted, in fact, was not justice but judgment. In that case, replied Cranmer, the disputation was useless. It was, indeed, only designed to register a foregone conclusion and to provide grounds for his condemnation. He was not permitted to read the exposition of his views on the Sacrament, which Canon Dixon terms "learned,

---

[1] Heylyn, ed. 1849, ii., 155, "Commissionated to dispute, and authorized to sit as judges"; but several of the disputants were set apart as "*censores*."

[2] See Foxe, vi., 439–468 for a full report of this disputation; Jenkyns, iv., 4–66; Cranmer, *Works* (Parker Soc.), i., 389–423; and Strype's *Cranmer*, chap. x.

moderate, and noble,"[1] nor was he allowed to cross-examine his numerous adversaries.

"I never," he complained[2] to the Council, "knew nor heard of a more confused disputation in all my life. For albeit there was one appointed to dispute against me, yet every man spake his mind, and brought forth what him liked without order. And such haste was made that no answer could be suffered to be given fully to any argument before another brought a new argument. . . . But why they would not answer us, what other cause can there be but that either they feared the matter, that they were not able to answer us, or else (as by their haste might well appear) they came, not to speak the truth, but to condemn us in post haste, before the truth might be thoroughly tried and heard?"

Chedsey[3] was Cranmer's chief antagonist, but the Prolocutor,[4] the Vice-Chancellor, and half a dozen other divines frequently interposed. In spite of this unmannerly treatment Cranmer bore himself throughout the ordeal with unruffled temper and courtesy. His demeanour towards the court was, if anything, too submissive; but his points were none the less effective, and when, after six hours' controversy, the Prolocutor summed up against him and bade the audience cry "*Vicit veritas*," even his opponents do not appear to have been quite satisfied with

---

[1] Dixon, iv., 189.

[2] *Works*, ii., 445–446.

[3] William Chedsey (1510?–74?) had been chaplain to Bonner, and prebendary of St. Paul's in the previous reign.

[4] *I. e.*, Hugh Weston (1505?–68), Dean of Westminster and Windsor; see the present writer in *Dict. Nat. Biogr.*, lx., 361.

the verdict. At any rate, he was asked to argue again on the following Thursday, when John Harpsfield,[1] Bonner's archdeacon, was to dispute for his degree of D.D.; and on this occasion Weston was moved to commend, not his arguments, but his conduct. "Your wonderful gentle behaviour and modesty," he said, "is worthy much commendation; and that I may not deprive you of your right and just deserving, I give you most hearty thanks in mine own name, and in the name of all my brethren." At which saying "all the doctors gently put off their caps." This tribute was not to affect the sentence pronounced on all the three Reformers on the following day. They were said to have been overcome in the disputations, which Cranmer denied; to be no members of the Church; and were asked whether they would turn or no. With one accord they refused, and were condemned as heretics. "From this your judgement and sentence," said Cranmer, "I appeal to the just judgement of God Almighty."

These proceedings were purely academic; for, as Hooper said, there was yet no law by which they could be condemned; and Gardiner's efforts[2] to carry through Parliament the renewal of the heresy laws was even then meeting with successful

[1] John Harpsfield (1516–78) must not be confused with his better-known though younger brother, Nicholas (1519?–75); both are in the *D. N. B.*

[2] S. R. Maitland and others have defended Gardiner from the charge of persecution on the ground that his actions were only "official," and that he was bound to carry out the law; but the fact is neglected that he did his best to pass laws which should make persecution a part of his ordinary duties.

resistance. Some of the hotter heads were for burning them out of hand, despite the laws and in virtue merely of the commission by which they had been tried. And these unconstitutional views appear to have been expressed even in the Privy Council. It was sorely perplexed what to do; to dispose of the heretics somehow or other was obviously its desire, and on the 3rd of May

> "it was resolved by their Lordships that the judges and the Queen's Highness' learned counsel should be called together and their opinions demanded what they think in law her Highness may do touching the cases of the said Cranmer, Ridley, and Latimer, being already by both the Universities of Oxford and Cambridge judged to be obstinate heretics; which matter is the rather to be consulted upon for that the said Cranmer is already attainted." [1]

The animus behind these words is clear; but the judges and other lawyers no doubt brushed aside the idea that the judgment of a few academics was a warrant for putting any one to death, even though a royal commission had invested their views with a fictitious importance. So Cranmer was sent back to Bocardo, Ridley to the charge of the sheriff, and Latimer to that of the bailiff of Oxford. For a year and a half they languished in prison until the law could be altered so as to secure their execution.

The Romanist flood of reaction meanwhile surged higher and was lashed into greater violence; in

---

[1] *Acts P. C.*, 1554-56, p. 17.

Mary's first Parliament it submerged most of the work of Edward VI.; in her third it now covered the remnant and that of Henry VIII. The Queen herself was its stormy petrel; before the law had sanctioned the death of a single Reformer, she was arranging how they were to be burnt with decency and order.[1] But a suitable Parliament alone could give full effect to her wishes, and of the moderate House of Commons which rejected the heresy bills of May, 1554, not a sixth found seats in that which met in November.[2] Convocation petitioned for the renewal of the statutes *de hæretico comburendo*[3]; in the Commons there was little resistance, and the only fight for mercy was made in the House of Lords. In January, 1555, the great act of persecution became the law of the land. The realm was reconciled with the Pope, and the Church recovered its power of dealing with heretics. The Dudleys who had been condemned with Cranmer for treason could now be released, for Cranmer was safe in the fiercer grip of the heresy laws.

The engine which Parliament had at last let loose did not long remain idle. Six days after the session ended, the heretics in the Tower were arraigned before Gardiner; and a fortnight later John Rogers "valiantly broke the ice" at Smithfield. Then began

[1] Collier, *Eccl. Hist.*, ii., 371; Dixon, iv., 236.

[2] Compare the lists in the *Official Return of Members of Parliament*, 1878; this was the Parliament for which the Queen ordered the election of members "of a wise, grave, and Catholic sort" (see her letter in Burnet, vi., 313–314).

[3] This fact rather goes against Canon Dixon's theory that the clergy were ever backward in persecution.

the bloodiest persecution that England has ever known; and before six months had passed, some fifty Protestant martyrs had suffered at the stake. Among these early victims were Bishops Hooper and Ferrar, and eminent divines such as Rowland Taylor, Cardmaker, and Bradford. Yet this is the period during which Philip II. is said to have exercised a restraining influence over his wife! There is, however, something to be said for the wretched Queen. The idea that she was, in slaying her fellow-creatures, making a burnt-offering acceptable to God[1] may have been due to physical as well as to mental derangement. When she was cherishing for six months the delusion that she was about to become a mother and went so far as to appoint special envoys to announce the happy event to foreign courts with commissions all written out and nothing to fill in except the date of the birth and the sex of the child, it was natural enough that other illusions should darken her mind. And it must also be remembered in extenuation that if she had burnt every one of the thousands of heretics in her kingdom, she would only have been logically giving effect to the tenets of the faith she professed. But the result was that she did more than Henry VIII., more than Edward VI., and even more than Elizabeth to make the victory of the Reformation in England certain.

The delay in dealing with Cranmer was not due to

[1] The origin of the idea that evil spirits possessed men, which could only be purged by burning, lies hidden in primitive mythology, and still survives, in a few savage tribes; it filtered into Christianity like other pagan superstitions during the dark ages.

the mercifulness of Philip II., but to a desire to comply with all the punctilios of Roman canon law. One who had been an archbishop, consecrated with all the rites and ceremonies, clothed in the pallium sent from Rome, and proclaimed in the papal consistory, could, it was thought, only be decently dealt with by papal authority. To the Pope Cranmer was still Thomas, Archbishop of Canterbury, and as such he was cited before the papal commissioners. The academic resolution of April, 1554, was, of course, no condemnation by English law, and it was worth even less at Rome; for the English Church was still barren and dead in a schism until the following year, when the reconciliation with Rome restored it to life and made fruit possible. So Cranmer, Ridley, and Latimer were all to be tried again; and the two latter were judged by three bishops acting on a commission granted by Pole as papal legate. They were sentenced to death on the first of October, 1555, and on the 16th, from the roof of his Bocardo prison, Cranmer watched the flames devour his friends below in the ditch outside Balliol College; he may have heard stout-hearted Latimer bid Ridley be of good cheer, for by God's grace they would light in England that day a candle that never should be put out.

For Cranmer himself a longer trial was in preparation. In their abasement at the feet of papal majesty, the sovereigns of England appeared as parties in a suit against a subject of their own before a foreign tribunal. They "denounced" him to the Holy Father, and the Holy Father deputed the

Prefect[1] of his Holy Inquisition to act in the matter. The Prefect further delegated the conduct of the trial to Bishop Brooks[2] of Gloucester, to the Dean of St. Paul's, and to the Archdeacon of Canterbury. Early in September Brooks arrived in Oxford, and cited Cranmer to appear at Rome in person or by proxy within the space of eighty days to answer such charges as should be laid against him by Philip and Mary. This was merely a formal pretence, for there was no intention of allowing Cranmer to plead in Rome, and on the 12th the subdelegate's court was opened in the Church of St. Mary.[3] Cranmer bowed to Drs. Martin and Story,[4] the proctors of Philip and Mary, but refused to recognise Brooks as the representative of a jurisdiction which he, like his opponents, had once forsworn. Brooks, after remarking that he came neither to judge nor to dispute, but to examine him in certain matters and to make relation thereof to him that had power to judge, exhorted him to repent of his errors and return to the bosom of the Catholic Church. Cranmer, protesting that he made answer not to the Papal subdelegate, but to Martin and Story as King's and Queen's proc-

[1] Cardinal de Puteo (of the Pit, as Cranmer translated it), or Du Puy.

[2] James Brooks, 1512–60, had been master of Balliol College, and succeeded Hooper as Bishop of Gloucester.

[3] For Cranmer's trial see Foxe, viii., 45–63 ; Jenkyns, iv., 79–117.

[4] Dr. John Story had an adventurous career; see the present writer in *Dict. Nat. Biogr.*, liv., 427. He lamented Queen Mary's mildness, wished to put the Princess Elizabeth to death, instigated Alva to establish the Inquisition at Antwerp in 1565, was executed for treason in 1570 and canonised in 1886.

tors, then delivered a strong defence of the Royal Supremacy, of his writings on the Sacrament, and an attack upon the Papacy. "The Bishop of Rome," he declared, "treadeth under foot God's laws and the King's"; "yet I speak not this for hatred I bear to him that now supplieth the room, for I know him not. I pray God give him grace not to follow his ancestors." The warmest dispute arose over the perjury with which Cranmer was charged in breaking his oath to the Pope. He retorted that Brooks had abjured the oath he swore to King Henry. Both accusations were true, and although Cranmer had saved his real consistency by his preliminary protestation that his oath to the Pope was void, that very act laid him open to a further technical charge of perjury. Brooks pronounced no sentence, for that was beyond his commission; he merely sent a certified report of the proceedings to Rome, where it awaited the Pope's decision.

Immediately after this trial Cranmer sent a remarkably bold appeal to Mary,[1] vindicating his own and the nation's conduct in repudiating the papal jurisdiction, in adopting their mother tongue for their own devotions, in renouncing Transubstantiation, and in demanding the administration of the Sacrament under both elements. "Alas!" he wrote,

"It cannot but grieve the heart of any natural subject to be accused of the King and Queen of his own realm and specially before an outward judge, or by an authority coming from any person out of this realm;

[1] Cranmer, *Works*, ii., 447-454.

where a King and Queen, as if they were subjects within their own realm, shall complain and require justice at a stranger's hand against their own subject being already condemned to death by their own laws. As though the King and Queen could not do or have justice within their own realms against their own subjects, but they must seek it at a stranger's hands in a strange land, the like whereof, I think, was never seen. I would have wished to have had some meaner adversaries; and I think that death shall not grieve me much more than to have my most dread and most gracious sovereign lord and lady (to whom under God I owe all obedience) to be mine accusers in judgement within their own realm before any stranger and outward power."

Then, quoting from the Roman canon law, he showed how fatal the papal claims, if admitted, were to national independence; how the Queen herself, her judges, and all other executors of her laws stood condemned as heretics, because not a few of her laws were even then repugnant to the canon law of Rome, and Popes had pronounced all such laws invalid and their authors, executors, and observers cursed. These things, he supposed, had not been explained to Parliament, or the Roman jurisdiction would never have been readmitted. The clergy who knew the truth had their own reasons for silence; they maintained the Pope

"to the intent they might have as it were a kingdom and laws within themselves, distinct from the laws of the crown, and wherewith the crown may not meddle; and so being exempt from the laws of the realm, might live in this realm like lords and kings without damage or fear of any man, so that they please their high and supreme head at Rome. . . . Ignorance, I know, may excuse other men; but he that knoweth how prejudicial and injurious the power and authority, which he [the Pope] challengeth everywhere, is to the crown, laws, and customs of this realm, and yet will allow the same, I cannot see in anywise how he can keep his due allegiance, fidelity, and truth to the crown and state of this realm."

This was the centre of Cranmer's position and, indeed, the heart of the Reformation in England; and in the repudiation of the claims of the Pope and the Church to a jurisdiction not merely independent of national systems but superior to them, the Reformation was ultimately triumphant in Catholic as well as in Protestant countries. The State all over the world has deposed the Church from the position it held in the Middle Ages, and the existence of churches, whether Catholic or Protestant, in the various political systems is due not to their own intrinsic authority, but to the toleration or encouragement extended to them by the State. No ecclesiastic has any appeal to that "outward judge," whom Cranmer denounced, from the national laws of the land in which he lives. The pretensions of Popes to dispense with oaths of allegiance, to root out and destroy, to plant and build again principalities and powers, have disappeared so utterly from the face of the earth that it is hard to believe they ever existed. Yet to Cranmer they were a real and terrible menace; and, as if his previous letter had not been bold enough, he wrote again[1] to Mary, lamenting the

[1] *Works*, ii., 454.

oath she had taken to the Pope, "to be obedient to him, to defend his person, to maintain his authority, honour, laws, and privileges." Such an undertaking was, he averred, inconsistent with the other oath she had sworn, to maintain the laws, liberties, and customs of this realm.

In conclusion, he complained that he was kept from the company of learned men, from books, from counsel, from pen and ink, save for the purpose of writing to her. He was, however, willing to answer his summons to Rome.[1] "And I trust that God shall put in my mouth to defend His truth there as well as here." That request, of course, was not granted; and on 20 November, 1555,[2] the Cardinal-delegate brought his case before the Papal Consistory. Five days later Cranmer was pronounced contumacious for not appearing and was solemnly excommunicated by the Pope in person. The occasion, no doubt, was great, and the scene was perhaps impressive—the pastor of all the world cutting off from his flock the once great Primate of England. But in sixteenth-century Rome there was barely a step from the sublime to the infamous; and in the

[1] Dr. Gairdner in his life of Cranmer in the *Dict. Nat. Biogr.* says that "Foxe tells us that he expressed his willingness to go and defend himself at Rome if the Queen would let him. But the statement is scarcely consistent with the position he had already taken up," etc. The passage in Cranmer's letter above cited apparently escaped Dr. Gairdner's eye. With regard to the inconsistency, Cranmer was not prepared to accept the Pope's jurisdiction; he merely contemplated a sort of missionary enterprise of a very bold and hopeless nature.

[2] Carne's letter to Mary in Tytler, ii., 486–487.

same hour that the Vicar of Christ passed sentence upon the arch-enemy of the Catholic faith, the worldly Prince of the Papal States invoked the same terrific anathemas in a squalid dispute with a petty Italian lord![1]

Pole was then appointed to the vacant Archbishopric, and a papal commission was issued for Cranmer's degradation and delivery to the secular arm. His hour at last was come. Hitherto he had endured more than two years' incarceration and had withstood the assaults of his enemies without flinching. He was now to be put to the supreme and final test whether he could sustain in deed the words of his letter to Mary.

"I have not spoken for fear of punishment and to avoid the same, . . . but I have spoken for my most bounden duty to the crown, liberties, laws, and customs of this realm of England; but most specially to discharge my conscience in uttering the truth to God's glory, casting away all fear by the comfort which I have in Christ, who saith, 'Fear not them that kill the body, and cannot kill the soul; but fear him that can cast both body and soul into hell-fire.' He that for fear to lose this life will forsake the truth, shall lose the everlasting life; and he that for the truth's sake will spend his life, shall find everlasting life."

---

[1] *Foreign Calendar*, 1553–58, p. 202.

CHAPTER XIII

IN THE HOUR OF DEATH

WHILE the Pope was pronouncing him contumacious for taking no care to obey his citation[1] and was condemning him to be deprived and degraded as an obstinate heretic, and while he was being burnt in effigy at Rome,[2] Cranmer was engaged in drawing up an appeal to a General Council. The law of nature,[3] he wrote to a legal friend whose assistance he sought, required every man to defend his own life so far as it might be done without offence to God; and lest he should seem rashly and unadvisedly to cast himself away he had resolved to follow Luther's example in appealing from Leo X. He was bound by oath, he said, never to consent to the reception of the Pope's authority in England; from this came all his trouble, so that the quarrel was personal between him and the Pope, and no man could be a lawful and indifferent judge in his own cause; therefore, he had good reason in appealing to a General Council.

[1] "*Comparere non curaret*," says the Pope.

[2] *Recantacyons*, p. 69.

[3] *Works*, ii., 455–456.

Not that he thought his life would thereby be saved; he was well aware that in 1460 Pius II. by his "execrable" Bull[1] had forbidden all such appeals to a General Council, and had thus made absolute his own jurisdiction. "The chiefest cause in very deed (to tell you the truth)," wrote Cranmer, "of this mine appeal is that I might gain time (if it shall so please God) to live until I have finished mine answer against Marcus Antonius Constantine[2] which I now have in hand."

The appeal was a stirring and striking document.[3] Cranmer paid an eloquent tribute therein to Rome's services in early times.

"The Church of Rome, as it were, lady of the world, both was and was also counted worthily the mother of other churches; forasmuch as she then first begat to Christ, nourished them with the food of pure doctrine, did help them with her riches, succoured the oppressed, and was a sanctuary for the miserable; she rejoiced with them that rejoiced and wept with them that wept. Then by the examples of the Bishops of Rome riches were

---

[1] The bull "*Execrabilis*" is dated 1 Jan., 1460: see *Cambridge Mod. Hist.*, i., 632–633.

[2] *I. e.*, Gardiner, who under this pseudonym published a rejoinder in 1552 to Cranmer's books on the Sacrament. Three books of this reply are said to have been completed by Cranmer when his work was cut short; but all trace of them has disappeared. Nor does any copy of Gardiner's book appear to be known. *See* Cranmer, *Works*, vol. ii., Pref., p. x.; and other references s. v. Gardiner in Gough's *Index to Parker Soc. Publications*. Neither of these works is mentioned by the biographers of Cranmer and Gardiner in the *Dict. Nat. Biogr*.

[3] Foxe, viii., 73–76; Jenkyns, iv., 121–129; *Works*, ii., 224–228.

despised, worldly glory and pomp was trodden under foot, pleasures and riot nothing regarded. Then this frail and uncertain life, being full of all miseries was laughed to scorn, whiles through the example of Romish martyrs men did everywhere press forward to the life to come. But afterward the ungraciousness of damnable ambition never satisfied, avarice, and the horrible enormity of vices, had corrupted and taken the see of Rome, there followed everywhere almost the deformities of all churches growing out of kind into the manners of the church, their mother, leaving their former innocency and purity, and slipping into foul and heinous usages. For the foresaid and many other griefs and abuses, since reformation of the above-mentioned abuses is not to be looked for of the Bishop of Rome; neither can I hope by reason of his wicked abuses and usurped authority, to have him an equal judge in his own cause, therefore I do challenge and appeal in these writings from the Pope."

He protested against being condemned in his absence; he could not appear in person, for he was straitly kept in prison; "and though I would never so fain send any proctor, yet by reason of poverty I am not able (for all that ever I had, wherewith I should bear my proctor's costs and charges, is quite taken from me)."

This appeal Cranmer had no means of lodging, and on 13 February, 1556, Bonner and Thirlby went down to Oxford to execute the papal commission for his degradation. The procedure on such occasions was a monument of exquisite cruelty;[1]

[1] The form is given in Foxe, viii., 77–79; cf. *Pontificale Romanum* by J. Catalan (Rome, 1740), iii., 146–164.

nothing that ingenuity could devise was omitted to abase the victim and wound his spirit; and while Bonner gloated over his task, Thirlby must have suffered at least as much as Cranmer. He was a man of humanity and had received promotion, friendship, and other benefits from the Archbishop. "Whether it were a jewel," writes Morice, "plate, instrument, maps, horse, or anything else, Thirlby had but to admire, and Cranmer would give it him."[1] Calling the prisoner before them in the choir of Christ Church Cathedral, the two papal commissioners read their commission. When they came to the statement that his cause had been indifferently (*i. e.* impartially) heard at Rome and that he had lacked nothing necessary for his defence, Cranmer was moved to anger; "God must needs," he exclaimed, "punish this open and shameless lying." Next he was clothed in the vestments of all the seven orders and with the insignia of an archbishop; a staff was put in his hand and a mitre upon his head. Then Bonner mocked him:

"This is the man," he said, "that hath ever despised the Pope's Holiness, and now is to be judged by him; this is the man that hath pulled down so many churches and now is come to be judged in a church; this is the man that contemned the blessed sacrament of the altar, and now is come to be condemned before that blessed sacrament hanging over the altar; this is the man that like

[1] *Harleian MS.*, 416, fol. 183; in Dixon, iv., 500, the number of the MS. is misprinted as 116.

Lucifer sat in the place of Christ upon an altar[1] to judge others, and now is come before an altar to be judged himself."

So pained was Thirlby at this exhibition that more than once he pulled Bonner's sleeve to stop him. After this they began to strip Cranmer of his robes. As they took off his pall he asked, "Which of you hath a pall to take off my pall?" He was an archbishop, they only bishops; they acted, they replied, not as bishops but as papal delegates. They then wrested the crozier staff from his hands, while he drew from his sleeve his appeal to a General Council.[2] Thirlby said they could admit no appeal, and the degrading rite went on. Bonner scraped his fingers and nails to obliterate the effects of an unction administered twenty-three years before. Divested of episcopal rank, Cranmer was then successively degraded from the orders of priest, deacon, subdeacon, acolyte, exorcist, lector, and doorkeeper. Finally a barber shaved his head to deprive him of whatever grace a long disused tonsure may have originally given him. "Now," exclaimed Bonner in brutal triumph, "now are you no lord any more." "All this," said Cranmer, "needed not; I had myself done with this gear long ago."

[1] This was a scandal which Cranmer warmly repudiated. The truth of the incident was that, Cranmer having to sit in commission at St. Paul's, a scaffold was as usual prepared for him by the Bishop (Bonner) and his officials; and it is possible that the scaffold concealed an altar.

[2] In Foxe and in other accounts the crozier is said to have been taken away first, but the regular and natural order was to begin with the highest insignia, the pall.

Clad in "a poor yeoman-beadle's gown, full bare and nearly worn," Cranmer was now as a layman handed over to the secular authorities, whom Bonner, if he followed the usual form, besought not to expose their charge to any danger of death or mutilation! He was taken back to Bocardo, where two days later he made the first of his dated recantations. It stands fourth among *All the Submissions and Recantations of Thomas Cranmer*, officially published after his death; and according to another recently discovered narrative,[1] he had for six weeks or more been listening to the persuasions of two

[1] This other narrative is entitled *Bishop Cranmer's Recantacyons;* it was privately printed in 1885 by the late Lord Houghton under the editorship of Dr. J. Gairdner. The original MS. is in the Bibliothèque Nationale at Paris; it was found among Nicholas Harpsfield's papers and is thought to have been written either by him or by Alan Cope. Canon Mason thinks the tract was written by Harpsfield; but Harpsfield affected to disbelieve the whole incident of Cranmer's burning his right hand (see Dixon, iv., 545), an incident mentioned in the *Recantacyons*. Dr. Gairdner, Canon Dixon, and Canon Mason have based their accounts of Cranmer's last days largely upon it, but its authority is very questionable. It was, as the author admits, "written to order," to counteract the effect of Cranmer's final triumph, to check the Protestant boasting over his courage (see *Recantacyons*, p. 113), and to prove that he was no martyr—a contention which Harpsfield maintained in his *Dialogi Sex*, 1566, p. 743 (it may also be noted that in the *Recantacyons* and in Harpsfield's *Divorce* we have the only contemporary authority for the story of Cranmer's wife). Moreover, it is full of strange stories of attempted rescues, the appearance of comets, etc. We are told that Cranmer's heart remained unburnt, being hardened by the poison of heresy, as Suetonius relates that Germanicus's heart was made proof against cremation by material poison (*Recantacyons*, p. 109). It states that on his way

Spanish Friars, Pedro de Soto and John de Villa Garcia, and of his gaoler, Nicholas Wodson. He is also said to have asked for an interview with his old friend Tunstall, who replied that Cranmer was more likely to shake him than be convinced by him, and with Cardinal Pole, who gathered up all his skirts when there was fear of contact with heretics. It is as a result of these persuasions that Cranmer is supposed to have signed the first three of his recantations; but they are not really recantations at all. In the official version the first two are merely styled "submissions," and the third still more vaguely a "scriptum." They are, in fact, only submissions

to execution Cranmer declared that he would have maintained his recantation if only the Pope had let him live, and repeated the statement at the stake *palam aperteque* (publicly and openly), which is quite incredible, seeing that a few moments before Cranmer had irrevocably renounced the Pope "and all his false doctrine." There is no word of this in the detailed account of the scene written by a Catholic bystander in a letter to a friend immediately afterwards, nor in the account written by the Venetian ambassador in London three days later; and it is inconsistent with Queen Mary's explanation of her action in putting Cranmer to death, viz., that his "iniquity and *obstinacy* against God and the Queen were so great that her clemency and mercy could have no place with him." (*Foreign Cal.*, 1553–58, p. 224; *Venetian Cal.*, 1553–58, Pt. i., p. 386). Such a declaration made *palam aperteque* would have stultified the whole of Cranmer's action on his last day, and would not have remained unknown until 1885. Finally, the author of this tract gives a wrong date for Cranmer's execution. Under these circumstances it cannot be accepted as an historical authority of much value. The Government had no reason to spare Cranmer's reputation; they even published under official sanction as his words the very opposite of what he spoke. If, therefore, they had known of anything worse than the details embodied in their official version, *All the Submissions*, they would certainly have published it.

to authority, such as Cranmer's political principles almost compelled him to make.

It must always be borne in mind that the English Reformers of the sixteenth century as a rule recognised no such thing as the right to individual judgment, and its necessary corollary, religious toleration. Every form of government is based on a compromise between two principles, either of which, when pushed to extremes, is fatal to human society. The idea of private judgment ultimately leads to anarchy, and the doctrine of authority to slavery. In some cases the law must override individual conscience, while on the other hand, unless individual conscience had occasionally defied the law, there would have been no progress; and men who denounce most vigorously resistance to the law are often first to resist when the law touches their own individual conscience. Cranmer was now at the *crux* of the difficulty. The question for him, as for most others, had been between the authority of the Pope and that of the English State represented by the King. He had unreservedly decided for the authority of the State, and he was deeply imbued with the sixteenth-century notions of the wickedness of resistance to the King's authority. He had in 1549 told the rebels of Devon with unnecessary emphasis that if the whole world prayed for them till doomsday it would not avail them unless they repented their disobedience.

This theory involved but slight inconvenience when Henry or Edward was King, and when their laws concurred with Cranmer's conscience in renouncing the Pope and his doctrine. But when Mary was

Queen the trouble began. If the English sovereign, Church, and Parliament had the right to abolish the papal jurisdiction, had they not also the right to restore it? And this authority restored, on what grounds could Cranmer resist? When arguing with Sir Thomas More about the oath of succession in 1534, he had suggested that More's conscience was doubtful about his duty to swear, but there was no doubt about his duty to obey the King.[1] Even More confesses that he was unable at first to rebut the argument; yet he had surer ground than Cranmer in 1556 when the same reasoning was turned against him. For More could say that the voice of the Catholic Church justified him in refusing in this instance obedience to the King; but Cranmer could not plead the authority of the Church. For good or for ill, he had pinned his faith and allegiance to the State; and logically he was driven to obey the State even when it asserted the jurisdiction of Rome. Was there not also Scriptural warrant for yielding under compulsion? Had not Elisha promised pardon to Naaman whenever he bowed the knee in the House of Rimmon?

It was this distressing dilemma which produced Cranmer's first submission; he recognised the papal authority, not because its claims had any intrinsic weight, but because the law of England, which he was bound to obey, had reimposed that authority. "Forasmuch," he wrote,[2] "as the King's and Queen's

[1] *L. and P. of Henry VIII.*, vii., 227.

[2] Jenkyns, iv., 393, who reprints Cawood's official publication, *All the Submissions*.

Majesties, by consent of the Parliament, have received the Pope's authority within this realm, I am content to submit myself to their laws herein." Yet he was not content; his conscience warred with his logic. Whatever the laws might say, his conscience did not admit the papal claims. He had sworn to renounce the Pope, and that oath represented his real convictions. Scarcely had he signed the first submission before he cancelled it, throwing logic to the winds and taking refuge in conscience. But then, what about his oath of allegiance to Mary and her laws? Was not that also a conscientious oath? Undoubtedly it was: his conscience was now divided against itself, while logic counselled submission. Thus divided, his conscience could not stand, and a second submission followed, more complete than the first.

The date of these two submissions cannot be ascertained. Perhaps they preceded his degradation,[1] on 14 February. If so, they were annulled by the appeal he then presented to a General Council, in which he spoke of the heinous and usurped authority of the Bishop of Rome, and by his declaration during the ceremony that he would never again say mass. Either the indignities then suffered renewed his abhorrence of the papal system or the presentation of his appeal gave him fresh confidence;

[1] On the other hand, in his final recantation, Cranmer repudiated all bills signed "since my degradation." He certainly meant to repudiate all his acknowledgments of papal authority; and, unless he made a mistake, his words must imply that no submissions were signed before his degradation.

for when Bonner visited him in Bocardo on 15 and 16 February he could only extort from him submissions much more guarded than before. These are the third and fourth recantations; the third, while expressing readiness to submit to the laws of the King and Queen concerning the Pope's supremacy, promised with regard to his books submission not to the Pope, but only to the judgment of the Catholic Church and of the next General Council. The fourth recantation, dated 15 February, was the first in which Cranmer made any direct reference to questions of doctrine, and he did so "in terms which might have been subscribed by any of the martyrs that had died."[1] He simply declared his belief to be in accord with that of the Catholic Church; that, of course, had all along been his contention; Popery was a corruption of Catholicism.

These documents Bonner took back to London, where it now devolved upon the Government, that is to say, Queen Mary and Cardinal Pole,[2] to decide what was to be done with the degraded Archbishop. There is no reason to suppose that they ever intended to spare his life. They would have thought it presumption to neglect a papal sentence, and indeed those condemned by the Church were as a

[1] Dixon, iv., 505.

[2] Gardiner, the Lord Chancellor, had died on 12 November, 1555; on his death-bed he is reported to have said, "*Negavi cum Petro, exivi cum Petro, sed nondum flevi cum Petro.*" (*Dict. Nat. Biogr.*, xx., 424.) The "negavi" refers to his repudiation of Rome under Henry VIII., the "exivi" to his deprivation under Edward VI.

matter of course in Mary's reign sent to the stake. From their point of view, Cranmer had done evil for which his death would be but a slight atonement; unable to comprehend the state of mind which led men to reject the doctrine of Rome, they and many others since their time attributed the whole Reformation in England to the divorce of Queen Catherine, in which Cranmer had played no small part. That to Mary was naturally a grievous offence, and others who shared the guilt with Cranmer were not sorry that he alone should bear the responsibility. Nor, although the contrary has often been asserted, was it illegal to burn a penitent heretic.[1]

But Mary and Pole had wider objects in view than the satisfaction of a personal animus against Cranmer or the exemplary punishment of the greatest living heretical Englishman. They desired to serve the general cause of Roman Catholicism. It was not enough that Cranmer should die; he must also be made to ruin the Reformation. Northumberland had "turned many" by his speech on the scaffold; if Cranmer would only repeat the performance, the candle lighted by Ridley and Latimer might be snuffed out after all. Cranmer's weakening on the

[1] Froude describes Cranmer's burning as "an act unsanctioned even by their own bloody laws," and Canon Dixon says that if Cranmer was not a martyr he was a murdered man. But in 1498, for instance, at Canterbury a heretic priest was burnt at the stake, even though Henry VII. himself persuaded him to recant and "got great honour" thereby. (*Cotton MS.*, Vitellins A., xvi., f. 172; *Excepta Historica*, p. 117.) It was, no doubt, considered the proper thing to pardon penitent heretics, but it does not appear to have been a legal obligation.

25

point of the papal supremacy had already suggested that he might be used for this purpose, and after Bonner's return to London means were considered for producing a deeper impression on Cranmer's mind. Terror was first employed, and on 24 February the Queen signed a warrant for his committal to the flames. No date was fixed,[1] but Cranmer was given to understand that the writ had been signed.

When a sufficient interval had elapsed for this information to work on the prisoner's mind, his treatment was suddenly changed. The prison doors were thrown open, and Cranmer exchanged his dungeon in Bocardo for the pleasant Deanery of Christ Church.[2] There he was used with every consid-

[1] This warrant is printed in Burnet, v., 452, 453, where it is erroneously styled a writ; a *warrant* was directed by the Queen to the Lord Chancellor, who would thereupon issue out of Chancery a *writ* for the execution. Burnet's error has led Canon Dixon into confusion on the subject; he disputes Lingard's assertion that the day of Cranmer's execution was fixed (Dixon, iv., 207), and says the day was not fixed in the writ. But he is thinking of the warrant, which did not fix a date; and although it prescribed the form of the writ, the writ itself does not appear to be extant. Dr. Gairdner, on the authority of the *Recantacyons*, p. 75, says that Cranmer was told he was to suffer on 7 March, which is possibly true.

[2] The *Recantacyons* and Dr. Gairdner place Cranmer's removal to Christ Church *before* and not *after* his degradation; but not very consistently the *Recantacyons* represents Cranmer as being influenced by the keeper of Bocardo prison at the time that he is supposed to be faring delicately in Christ Church. Foxe definitely says that it was after the degradation; Canon Dixon takes the same view, and some confirmation of it may be found in the fact that the English witness to the fifth recantation was Henry Siddall, Canon of Christ Church.

eration. He walked in the gardens, played bowls on the green, enjoyed the converse of men of learning and wit, and lacked no delicate fare. Bishop Brooks at his trial told him[1] that, "whereas you were Archbishop of Canterbury and Metropolitan of England, it is ten to one (I say) that ye shall be as well still, yea, even better." All these things might be given him if——

Then Cranmer fell. He signed his fifth or real recantation,[2] in which he anathematised the whole heresy of Luther and Zwingli, confessed his belief in one holy and visible Catholic Church, beyond the pale of which there was no salvation, and recognised the Pope as Christ's vicar and supreme head of the Church on earth. The true body and blood of Christ were, he declared, really present under the forms of bread and wine in the sacrament; the bread was translated into the body and the wine into the blood of Christ. He acknowledged the six other sacraments and the existence of Purgatory. This was no mere submission to outward authority, but a professedly complete recantation of inward belief extorted from him by the poignant contrast between the pleasant prospect of life and the vivid horror of an agonising death. He surrendered every point for which he had fought; the "comfort he had in Christ" had not, as he hoped, enabled him "to cast away all fear."

Unfortunately, human frailty has made Cranmer's

[1] Foxe, viii., 48. No definite promises are known to have been made, unless Foxe's authority be accepted, but Cranmer's treatment was suggestive.

[2] Jenkyns, iv., 395.

case a type rather than an exception among religious leaders. But they lived in times far removed from the comfortable immunity which now attends doctrinal vagaries; and it is more charitable and perhaps more fruitful to attempt to understand the psychological problem presented by cases like those of St. Peter, Hus, Jerome of Prague, Savonarola, Cranmer, and Galileo[1] than to make broad our phylacteries and point the finger of scorn at those who succumbed to a test which their critics have never stood. How comes it that an ordinary dervish will face death without flinching when great religious leaders have quailed? No doubt the horrible mode of a heretic's death supplied an additional terror, and courage comes easier on the spur of the moment and in the heat of the battle than after prolonged reflection. But it is also true that the more sensitive the mind is, the greater is the fortitude required to confront danger. It is easy for the dull brain to face death; a dog, could it reason, could never be made to recant, because it would fail to imagine death. But an impressionable imagination like Cranmer's paints the unknown horrors of the stake in the most vivid colours. It was the working of his imaginative and susceptible mind which drove Cranmer to yield when less impressionable men like Hooper, Ridley, and Latimer successfully bore the strain.

[1] For Hus and Jerome, see Creighton, *History of the Papacy*, Bk. II., chap. v; for Savonarola, see Villari's *Life*, and for Galileo see Fahie's *Life*. The scientist is perhaps the least to be excused, for he had means of verifying his conclusions which were not available for the theologians; his certainty was objective, theirs only subjective,

In another respect Cranmer was less fitted than his colleagues to withstand the attack. A man who sees only one side of truth at a time is proof against doubt; but the man of broader intellect, who knows that truth is relative and feels the force of hostile arguments, is inevitably less dogmatic and less absolutely sure of the impregnability of his position. In these days of comparative study it might almost be said that to be positive is to be ignorant; and few there are who would give their bodies to be burnt on the assumption that their opinion was the whole truth and nothing but the truth. Cranmer was much nearer this modern position than his contemporaries; he knew, none better, that on the impregnable rock of Holy Scripture could be based arguments against him as well as for him, and that the voice of the Church had varied in various ages. Even General Councils, he knew, could err; was he, then, unique and infallible? His distressing dilemma between a conscience which bade him renounce the Pope and a conscience which bade him obey his sovereign opened a breach through which doubts rushed in and submerged him.

The date of his fifth recantation is uncertain, but it was in print before 13 March, when the Privy Council summoned the printers before them and ordered all copies to be burnt.[1] An English translation of this document, writes the Venetian ambassador on 24 March,[2]

---

[1] *Acts P. C.*, 1554–6, p. 247.

[2] *Venetian Cal.*, 1553–58, Pt. i., p. 386. This is the nearest contemporary account of the incident; cf. *Original Letters*, i., 173,

"was published in London, and as it was signed by Father Soto and his associate, both Spaniards, . . . the Londoners not only had suspicion of the document, but openly pronounced it a forgery; so the Lords of the Council were obliged to suppress it and to issue another witnessed by Englishmen."

It may have been partly to demolish for ever these suspicions of forgery that Cranmer, who was now—if not before—sent back to Bocardo, was required to make a sixth and still more debasing confession[1]; but the main object seems to

where Sampson writes from Strassburg on 6 April: "A certain absurd recantation, forged by the papists, began to be spread abroad during his life-time, as if he made that recantation; but the authors of it themselves recalled it while he was yet living." Foxe also plainly believes it was forged, and in more recent times Whiston, Todd, and Soames have doubted whether Cranmer recanted at all. There is little ground for this view, which would destroy the significance of Cranmer's action in burning his right hand. With regard to the suppression of the first edition of the fifth recantation various theories have been suggested. Dixon thinks it was suppressed because it was issued by an "obscure" firm merely at the instance of the Oxford theologians, Lingard because it infringed the patent of Cawood, the Queen's printer, and others because it really was forged. Dixon's idea of Copland's being an obscure firm will not stand against the two pages about him in the *Dict. Nat. Biogr.*, and there may be something in Lingard's view, as Cawood undoubtedly had the right to publish official documents. Yet there was probably some truth in the Venetian ambassador's story. Dixon says it is inaccurate because Siddall (not Soto) and Garcia are the witnesses; so they are in the later edition of Cawood; but what the ambassador says is that Soto and Garcia witnessed Copland's first suppressed edition, of which no copy is known. Probably Siddall, as an Englishman, was substituted for Soto; he was one of the most active turncoats in that canting and recanting age. See *Dict. Nat. Biogr.*, lii., 193.

[1] Printed in Jenkyns, iv., 396–397.

have been to cover the whole history of the Reformation with shame and indelible infamy. Hitherto Cranmer had only professed a complete change of mind, without directly accusing his past career. Now he was to depict his misdeeds in the blackest hues, and to attribute to his own sinister influence the whole series of woes which had lately afflicted the realm. "I have sinned" (such were the words put into his mouth)[1] "most grievously, before Heaven and against the realm of England, yea, against the whole Church of Christ; I have persecuted more furiously than Paul; I have blasphemed, persecuted, and maltreated." He was then made to compare himself with the thief on the cross, and to imply that, like the thief, he only repented when his means to do harm had failed. He was most deserving, proceeded the confession, not only of all human and temporal, but of divine and eternal punishment,

"because I did exceeding great wrong to Henry VIII., and especially to his wife, Queen Catherine, when I became the cause and author of their divorce; which crime, indeed, was the seed-plot of all evils and calamities to this realm. Hence came the death of so many good men, hence the schism of the whole realm, hence heresies, hence the confounding of so many minds and bodies. . . . I opened wide the windows to heresies of every sort, of which I myself was the chief doctor and ductor. . . . In this indeed I was not

[1] The real author of this document was probably Cardinal Pole; its style bears a striking resemblance to that affected by Pole; and the view of the origin of the Reformation is that expressed by Pole in a letter to Mary in 1553 (*Cambridge Modern History*, ii., 519).

only worse than Saul and the thief, but most accursed of all whom the earth has ever borne. . . ."[1]

This last shameful confession,—more shameful to those who dictated it than to the heart-broken captive who signed it,—was dated 18th March. It would reach London on the following day. Queen Mary and Pole had now got what they wanted and all they could hope to obtain. Here was a version of recent history even more pleasing to them than that of Northumberland. When the chief prophet of Reform had cursed it in terms like these, who should be found to bless or defend? A signal and final service had Cranmer performed; he could be of no further use except to repeat in public his private confession; he might now be dismissed to the stake. Orders were given at once, which would reach Oxford on the 20th, that Cranmer should be burned on the following day. Dr. Cole, Provost of Eton, was warned to prepare a sermon, and Lord Williams of Thame and other local magnates were directed to summon their forces to maintain order at the coming execution. Cole arrived in Oxford on the 20th, and the lords and their retainers in the early hours next morning.

---

[1] Notwithstanding the outcry about the witnesses to the fifth recantation, this sixth document has no witness at all, and in this respect it resembles all the recantations except the fifth. It was scarcely surprising that the fifth recantation was the only one known to Foxe; if all the documents were unwitnessed they might all be considered equally authentic; but the fact that in the official version one is witnessed and the others are not seems to imply a distinction either in importance or authenticity.

It was probably on the day before his death that Cranmer composed what is called his seventh recantation.[1] It consisted of the address he should make to the people at his execution, and when he wrote it out he must have already known that he was to die on the morrow.[2] His sixth recantation had bent the bow to the uttermost; could a religious system which involved such cruelty be just or true? He was still in the valley of doubts and fears, but the light had begun to glimmer, and the harrowed mind to hope. Although this seventh document asserts the real and substantial presence of Christ in the Eucharist, and repudiates the books he had written against that doctrine since the death of Henry VIII., it contains no such shameful

[1] Jenkyns, iv., 398-400: it is neither signed, witnessed, nor dated; but most of it, at any rate, was Cranmer's composition.

[2] Otherwise how could he have written "I am now come to the last end of my life," etc.? The idea that Cranmer did not know he was to die on the 21st until that same morning originated with Foxe, who was not acquainted with the seventh recantation, a document carefully prepared on the assumption that he was to die. That he *wrote* this and not merely *spoke* it is clear from the fact that this recantation is printed in the official version by Cawood. Cranmer appears to have made more than one copy of this document, and from one of these the Government printed it. Strype, Todd, and Froude accuse Bonner of fraud in printing this account of what Cranmer meant to say, when it was the opposite of what he did say, and also suggest forgery. But Bonner would not have forged so lame and halting a submission, and if he had forged he would also have added a signature, if not witnesses and a date. Moreover, he only professed to print what Cranmer had *written*, not what he *said*. Of course, it was not, even so, a very honourable thing to do; but the object was to counteract the immense effect of Cranmer's spoken words.

language as its predecessor, and not a word of submission to the Pope: apart from the Sacrament it merely professes the creed of the English Reformers. "I believe," he says, "every article of the Catholic faith, every clause, word, and sentence taught by our Saviour Jesus Christ, His Apostles, and Prophets in the New and Old Testament and all articles explicate and set forth in the General Councils."[1] Could it be that Cranmer was going over again in brief the history of his mental development? His previous recantations had carried him back to the state of belief in his youth, but they had not represented any deep change of conviction, and now it seemed that the revulsion had already begun. Gradually he began to recover lost ground, and in this seventh recantation there is nothing inconsistent with his position under Henry VIII. after the breach with Rome.[2]

But the process did not stop here in a half-way house; and a further mental struggle ensued during the night between this recantation and the dawn of

---

[1] These significant limitations in this last recantation have not hitherto been noticed, and it is mainly on them that I base the above view that Cranmer's mind had begun to react earlier than is usually supposed. Canon Mason puts the change as late as the scene in St. Mary's on the 21st, but the alterations of this seventh writing which Cranmer made in his oral address lead so naturally to his conclusion that they can scarcely have been improvised on the moment. I feel sure that they must have been thought out before he left his prison.

[2] It may be worth noting that there is no mention of the *Ave Maria* after the Lord's Prayer in this document, and that the Lord's Prayer was in English, not in Latin.

his dying day.[1] Of that night of agony we have no record, but it needs none to depict the depth of Cranmer's conflicting emotions, his shame and humiliation, his dread of approaching torture and of the yet more dark hereafter, his intense desire to salve his conscience, and his aching to be at peace. The papist tractarian tells us that he sought comfort in the Penitential Psalms, but we may be sure that petitions from his own great Litany sprang no less readily to his lips:

"that it may please Thee to succour, help, and comfort all that be in danger, necessity, and tribulation . . . and to show Thy pity upon all prisoners and captives; . . . that it may please Thee to bring into the way of truth all such as have erred and are deceived . . . that it may please Thee to strengthen such as do stand, and to comfort and help the weak-hearted, and to raise up them that fall, and finally to beat down Satan under our feet."

[1] There are several stories about Cranmer's last night which are mutually destructive and cannot be corroborated. Foxe says he was visited by Garcia early in the morning and induced to sign copies of "articles"; this is almost certainly wrong, for the Government would assuredly have published these "articles" with the other submissions. Neither Foxe nor the author of the *Recantacyons* is to be trusted implicitly (*cf.* Dixon, iv., 525–526). According to the *Recantacyons*, Cranmer supped and talked with companions till a late hour, and then slept peacefully till five o'clock. If that is so, it is difficult to see where he found time to compose his last recantation and speech; and the further statement that he signed fourteen copies of it in the morning of the 21st is incredible, for if such was the case, how was it that the Government could not find a single signed copy to print, but printed one without any signature at all?

The morning broke in a storm of rain, and the crowds which thronged St. Mary's came out to see a reed shaken with the wind. The reed was bent and sorely bruised, but it was not broken yet; even now it might be fashioned into a rod. To St. Mary's Cranmer was led in procession between two friars, and as they approached the doors a significant *Nunc Dimittis* was raised. Inside, Cranmer was placed on a stage opposite the pulpit,[1] from which Dr. Cole was to preach a sermon. Cranmer had given no sign to Cole or the friars who visited him in the morning; but he had told a poor woman, on whom he bestowed some money, that he would sooner have the prayers of a good layman than those of a bad priest. That boded ill for his final profession, and both Romanists and Reformers passed from hope to fear and from fear to hope as they witnessed Cranmer's demeanour. He was made the touchstone of truth, and his foes themselves had determined that his conduct should test the strength of the two forms of faith.

He stood there, "an image of sorrow," while Cole delivered his not unmerciful sermon.[2] With more

---

[1] "The pillar on the north side of the nave of St. Mary's where Cranmer stood has a cut in it, a foot or two from the ground, where it was hewn to receive the wooden stand on which he was placed. Cole's pulpit of stone was exactly opposite, a few inches eastward of the present wooden pulpit on the south side. The front of that pulpit has been preserved and is built into the wall above a door in the church."—Dixon, iv., 527, note.

[2] It was charity itself compared with the terms of Cranmer's sixth recantation; with regard to the Divorce, for instance, Cole admitted that Cranmer acted "not of malice, but by the persuasion and advice of certain learned men."

kindliness than consistency he recalled for Cranmer's comfort the fate of the three faithful children of Israel, who refused to bow before the false god which the King had set up, and passed through the fire unscathed. When he had ended he asked them all to pray for the contrite sinner. Cranmer knelt with the congregation. Then he rose and gave thanks for their prayers, and began to read from a paper he held in his hand.[1] It was his seventh recantation—amended. First came a prayer—"the last and sublimest of his prayers[2]"; then followed four exhortations. He besought his hearers to care less for this world and more for God and the world to come; to obey the King and Queen, not for fear of them only, but much more for the fear of God, for whosoever resisted them resisted God's ordinance; to love one another like brothers and sisters and do good to all men; and finally he reminded the rich how hard it was for them to enter the kingdom of heaven, and moved them to charity; for what was given to the poor was given to God.[3]

[1] Lingard says he had two papers, one a copy of a recantation, the other a retractation of them all; the first was to be used if a pardon came, the second if he was to die. His real intention was to burn the recantation as he did his hand. The Venetian ambassador says he actually did this; the *Recantacyons* says it was taken from him before he was bound to the stake.

[2] Dixon, iv., 534.

[3] The most authoritative account of these final scenes is the British Museum *Harleian MS.*, 422, ff., 48–53; this consists really of two documents; (1) a letter of a Roman Catholic signed J. A., and written to a friend on 23 March, two days after the execution which it describes; (2) a paper headed "Cranmer's Words before his Death,"

"And now," he went on, "forasmuch as I have come to the last end of my life, whereupon hangeth all my life past and all my life to come, either to live with my Saviour Christ for ever in joy, or else to be in pains ever with the wicked devils in hell; and I see before mine eyes presently either heaven ready to receive me, or else hell ready to swallow me up: I shall therefore declare unto you my faith without colour or dissimulation; for now is no time to dissemble whatsoever I have written in time past." [1]

Then Cranmer began the real work of that day. Having recited the Lord's Prayer in English he began the profession of faith contained in the seventh recantation; but now he declared no unlimited belief in General Councils. He had completely re-covered the ground lost in his recantations and re-gained the position of 1552.[2] If his audience perceived the drift of these changes, the tension must have grown almost unbearable. The climax was reached; his trial was over, his triumph began.

written in the same hand and enclosed with the letter; this was apparently copied by J. A. from a still earlier MS., written possibly on the very day of execution. Strype has manipulated these two documents so as to form a continuous narrative (Dixon, iv., 532–533). Another narrative (*Harleian MS.*, 417, ff., 90, *et seq.*) is printed in Nichols's *Narratives of the Reformation*, pp. 218–233. The next in value is that of the Venetian ambassador, written on 24 March.

[1] The last phrase of Cranmer's conveyed no sure indication to others, but it was a significant departure from the seventh recantation he had written in prison the day before; that ran, "whatsoever I have said, preached, or written in time past," and referred to his Reforming activity. By leaving out "said, preached, or" he now indicated his written recantations.

[2] The Forty-two Articles of that year admitted that General Councils might err.

PORTRAIT OF CRANMER DURING THE REIGN OF EDWARD VI.

FROM THE ORIGINAL PICTURE AT LAMBETH PALACE.

"And now I come to the great thing that so troubleth my conscience, more than any other thing that I said or did in my life: and that is my setting abroad of writings contrary to the truth, which here now I renounce and refuse as things written with my hand contrary to the truth which I thought in my heart, and written for fear of death, and to save my life, if it might be; and that is all such bills which I have written or signed with mine own hand since my degradation; wherein I have written many things untrue. And forasmuch as my hand offended in writing contrary to my heart, it shall be first burned. And as for the Pope, I refuse him as Christ's enemy and Antichrist, with all his false doctrine. And as for the Sacrament——"

He got no farther; his foes had been dumb with amazement, but now their pent-up feelings broke loose. "Stop the heretic's mouth!" cried Cole, "take him away!" "Play the Christian man," said Lord Williams; "remember your recantations and do not dissemble." "Alas, my lord," replied Cranmer, "I have been a man that all my life loved plainness, and never dissembled till now against the truth; which I am most sorry for"; and he seized the occasion to add that as for the Sacrament he believed as he had taught in his book against the Bishop of Winchester. The tumult redoubled. Cranmer was dragged from the stage and led out towards the stake.

There was no need of a spur for his lagging steps. His desire was now to be gone. He had done with the quicksands of logic, legal formulas, and constitutional maxims, and had gained a foothold in conscience. The fight had been long and bitter, but he had reached a conclusion at length; he had "professed a good profession before many witnesses." The Reformation would not be shamed in him, and the gates of hell should not prevail against it. Over it, as over his own ashes, he would write the legend *Resurgam*. Eagerly he pressed forward to the scene of his final victory, and the friars could scarcely keep pace. Through Brasenose Lane and out of the gate by St. Michael's they sped to a spot in the present Broad Street in front of Balliol College; there Ridley and Latimer had suffered six months before, and now it is marked by a plain stone cross[1] in the ground.

The friars ceased not to ply him with exhortations; "Die not in desperation," cried one; "Thou wilt drag innumerable souls to hell," said another. But Cranmer was out of their reach; it was not to perdition that he thought those souls would go. Cheerfully he put off his upper garments and stood in his shirt, which reached to the ground. There was no hair on his head, but a long white beard flowed over his breast. He was then bound to the stake with a steel band,[2] and light was set to

[1] The Martyrs' Memorial stands round the corner in St. Giles's; it was erected in 1842 in spite of the opposition of the Tractarians (see Liddon, *Life of Pusey*, ii., 64-76). The spot was then an empty ditch, probably the remains of a moat which ran round the old city walls. Pusey thought it "not respectful that carts, etc., should drive over the place where [the martyrs] yielded up their souls" (*ibid.*, ii., 66). The "carts, etc." are now kept off by an electric-light standard which obstructs the road.

[2] The steel band is still preserved in private hands; see *Gentleman's Magazine*, July, 1857, pp. 61, 75; the account of moneys paid for the faggots and furze used at the execution is printed by Strype.

the hundred and fifty faggots of furze and the hundred faggots of wood which made up his funeral pyre. As the flames leapt up, he[1] stretched out his right hand, saying with a loud voice, "This hand hath offended," and held it steadfastly in the fire until it was burnt to ashes. Thus openly did he proclaim his faith by the gesture in which the mind of posterity paints him. No one could falsify that recantation; it was a sign which none could misread. His body might perish, but his cause was won. He saw the travail of his soul and was satisfied.

"His patience in the torment," writes a hostile eye-witness, "his courage in dying, if it had been taken either for the glory of God, the wealth of his country, or the testimony of truth, as it was for a pernicious error, and subversion of true religion, I could worthily have commended the example, and matched it with the fame of any Father of ancient time."

No cry escaped his lips, no movement betrayed

[1] The Venetian ambassador says: "At the moment that he was taken to the stake he drew from his bosom the identical writing (probably the Fifth Recantation), throwing it in the presence of the multitude with his own hands into the flames, asking pardon of God and of the people for having consented to such an act, which he excused by saying that he did it for the public benefit, as, had his life, which he sought to save, been spared him, he might at some time have still been of use to them, praying them all to persist in the doctrine believed by him, and absolutely denying the Sacrament and the supremacy of the Church. And, finally, stretching forth his arm and right hand, he said: 'This which has sinned, having signed the Writing, must be the first to suffer punishment,' and thus did he place it in the fire and burned it himself."

his pain, save that once with his unburnt hand he wiped his forehead. The flames might scorch and consume his flesh, but his spirit had found repose; for conscience had ceased to torment, and a peace which passed understanding pervaded his soul.

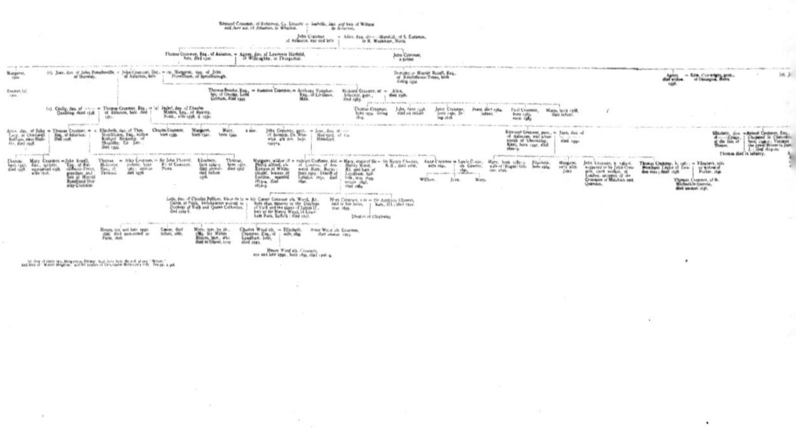

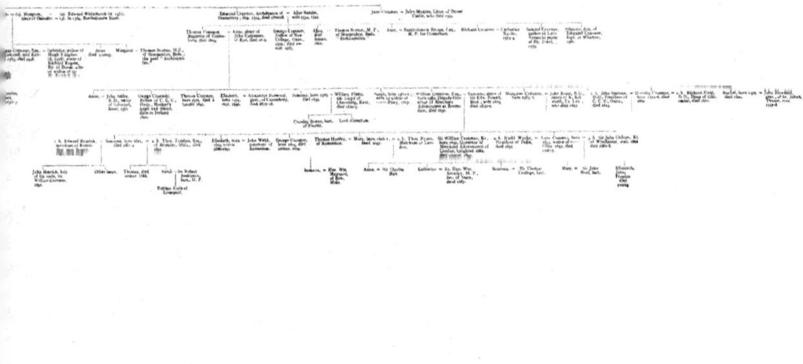

INDEX

C

D

I

Q

R